Red Genesis

SUNY series in Chinese Philosophy and Culture
─────────
Roger T. Ames, editor

Red Genesis

*The Hunan Normal School and the
Creation of Chinese Communism, 1903–1921*

Liyan Liu

Published by State University of New York Press, Albany

© 2012 State University of New York

For information, contact State University of New York Press, Albany, NY
www.sunypress.edu

Production by Eileen Meehan
Marketing by Anne M. Valentine

Library of Congress Cataloging-in-Publication Data

Liu, Liyan.
   Red genesis : the Hunan Normal School and the creation of Chinese communism, 1903–1921 / Liyan Liu.
       p. cm.
   Includes bibliographical references and index.
   ISBN 978-1-4384-4503-8 (hardcover : alk. paper)
   1. Hunan Sheng di yi shi fan xue xiao—History.   2. Communism—China—History.   3. Educational change—China—History—20th century.   I. Title.
II. Title: Hunan Normal School and the creation of Chinese communism, 1903–1921.

   LB2127.C4854L58 2012
   378.51'215—dc23   2012019746

10 9 8 7 6 5 4 3 2 1

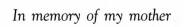

In memory of my mother

Contents

List of Illustrations

Maps

Figure

Table

Illustrations

Acknowledgments

This book is the product of a long journey of intellectual inquiry. During the past fifteen years or more that this book was being conceived, written, and repeatedly revised, many people offered invaluable support. Teachers were the first to encourage my pursuit of this topic in graduate school. At the outset, I express deep gratitude to my previous PhD adviser, Hao Chang, for having directed me to this subject, and for guiding me, encouraging me, and teaching me throughout the research. His preeminent scholarship had a strong influence on me while I was conducting research and in the early stage of writing this book. My sincere gratitude goes to James R. Bartholomew, my co-adviser, for his unfailing support, warm encouragement, and valuable advice. I owe an equal debt of gratitude to Christopher A. Reed for his generous support, academic encouragement, insightful advice, and criticism. I am very grateful to him for reading parts of my work and providing many valuable insights and criticism. I also am grateful to Kirk A. Denton for his strong support and invaluable comments and advice.

I am particularly grateful to Yan-shuan Lao, whose unfailing help and encouragement continued after my graduation and helped me to pursue and accomplish this work. His sinological erudition, especially in the area of classical Chinese, helped me in many valuable and concrete ways. He receives my heartiest thanks.

I am greatly indebted to Charlton M. Lewis who pointed me to the materials of Hunan and guided me through the maze of Chinese documents in the early stage. He also read different versions of parts of this work and gave very valuable comments and advice. Dajiang He and Jingshen Xia helped me interpret some classical Chinese into graceful modern Chinese in the early stage of writing, which made it much easier for me to write in English.

When I was doing research in China in 1997, I benefited tremendously from the help of several scholars and institutions. Foremost among them was Wang Xingguo of Hunan Provincial Social Science Institute to whom I owe a great debt of gratitude for sharing with me his wide-ranging knowledge of Yang Changji and Mao Zedong, and also for guiding me to many valuable sources, including his manuscript about famous people in Hunan. I benefited greatly from many discussions with him and his insights on Yang and Mao while I was writing and revising this book. I would like to thank Sun Hailin, former vice principal of Hunan First Normal School, for helping me to gain access to some fascinating materials on First Normal and for granting permission to reproduce the photos at the school's archives and use my interviews with him in the book. I am grateful to Dai Zuocai of Hunan People's Press for helping me gain access to valuable and relevant materials at archives in Hunan.

In the process of writing and revising this book, many friends and colleagues kindly read and commented on parts or all of the book manuscript at one stage or another. I am grateful to Barry Keenan, Xiaobing Li, Kathryn Bernhardt, the late Stephen C. Averill, George Wei, Robert Culp, Merle Rife, Yi Sun, and Sam Gilbert for their invaluable suggestions and corrections.

Particular gratitude goes to Kristin Stapleton for her strong support and warm encouragement over the years and for her insightful comments and criticism on this work. I owe special thanks for her help and for being a very special friend. Special thanks go to my good friend Xiaoping Cong, who read numerous drafts of parts of the work, offered invaluable criticism and suggestions, and shared with me her resources and expertise. I benefited greatly from our many discussions together. I am grateful to my friend Greg Epp, who read the manuscript and offered valuable comments and helped polish the prose.

Special thanks to my colleagues in the Department of History at Georgetown College. First of all, I am deeply grateful to James Klotter for his unfailing help. He read numerous drafts of the manuscript and offered helpful remarks, suggestions, and edits. He has been an invaluable source of intellectual guidance as well as a reliable friend who was always there whenever I needed his help. I am equally indebted to Lindsey Apple who read several various versions of the manuscript and offered valuable comments, suggestions, and editing. I thank him for his help and for being a very special friend. I also appreciate the inspiration and support that I received in various ways from my colleagues Harold Tallant, Clifford Wargelin, Ellen Emerick, and Lisa Lykins, who have now become my friends. Special appreciation goes to Provost Rosemary Allen for her warm support and assistance, which made the publication of this book occur sooner. I would like to express my gratitude to Georgetown College for the Henlein Junior Faculty Research Fellowship in spring 2006, which greatly facilitated the writing of the manuscript. Finally, a number of people provided other kinds of intellectual and technical assistance or helped with materials. For their help, I thank Pingchao Zhu, Xiaoming Chen, Xiansheng Tian, Wu Yunji, Vince Sizemore, and Grover Hibberd. Thanks also go to Zhu Yumo for letting me use pictures he took of the Hunan First Normal in the book.

Many thanks are due to the staff of the following libraries and archives for their kind assistance in finding many precious documents that have enriched my research: the Ohio State University Library, the Hunan Provincial Archives and Library, the Hunan First Normal School Archives and Library, and the Georgetown College Library. My colleague, Susan Martin at the College Library even helped me get materials from as far as Aberdeen in Scotland. She receives my sincerest appreciation. I also thank the Hunan Provincial Archives and the Hunan First Normal School Archives and Library for granting permission to reproduce the photos and maps in the book. Parts of Chapter 5 appeared as "The Man Who Molded Mao: Yang Changji and the First Generation of Chinese Communists," in *Modern China*, vol. 32 (2006). Chapter 7 is based on a revision of an article, "A Provincial Scholar becomes a Young Radical" published in *Twentieth-Century China*, vol. 32, No. 2 (2007). I am grateful for the permission to quote from those articles. I truly appreciate the support from all of the above colleagues, friends and institutions. Nonetheless, any errors of fact or judgment in this book are my own.

I thank my SUNY Press editors, Nancy Ellegate, for having endorsed this project in the first place and having found knowledgeable readers to review this manuscript; Eileen Meehan for her production skills; Robin B. Weisberg for copyediting; and Anne Valentine for marketing. I am also grateful to the anonymous readers who made critical comments and invaluable suggestions that have made this a better book.

Finally, my deepest gratitude is directed to my family—my husband Xinhe and our son Chris—for their boundless support and love. During the past fifteen years as the dissertation was written and then revised into a manuscript, they have helped me to endure those stressful and hectic times during which I nearly lost sight of the final goal. Their confidence in my work and in me made this book possible.

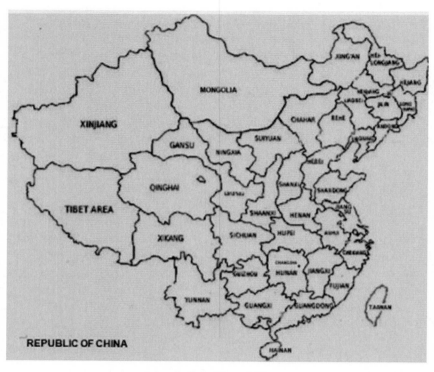

Map 1. Republic of China.

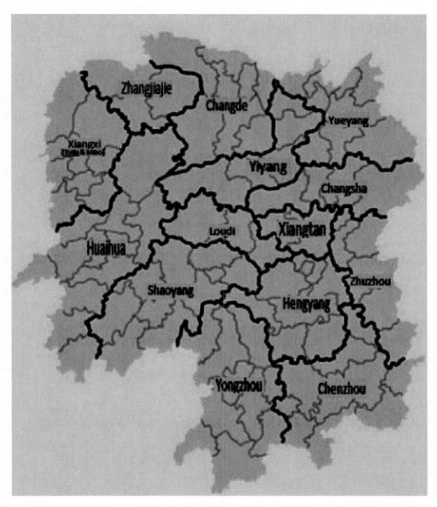

Map 2. Map of Hunan Province.

Introduction

The Exceptional Normal and the Paradox of Hunan

On an early autumn day in 1913, in the capital of Hunan province, a crowd of young adults gathered with trepidation outside the Hunan First Normal School. They scanned the acceptance lists being posted on the wall, with the least qualified names listed first. Each time a new group of names was posted, a mixture of excitement and disappointment swept over the crowd. Finally, the names of all the accepted students had been posted, except the top three.

Reportedly, in a sparsely decorated conference room inside, the faculty heatedly debated the ranking of the top three—and specifically whether Cai Hesen's (1895–1931) essay should be given the top spot. At this time, Yang Changji (1871–1920), a well-known Neo-Confucian scholar specializing in the School of Principle (*Li*) who had recently returned from abroad, came in—with the intention of declining his appointment to the school. However, he was quickly invited to read the essays and add his judgment to the deliberations. After he read Cai's essay, Yang could not contain his enthusiasm for whoever could write such electrifying prose as a candidate to eventually graduate and become a future pillar of the state. Not only was Cai chosen to be the top candidate, but Yang decided to stay and teach at the First Normal School.[1]

Yang also had a joint appointment at the Hunan Fourth Normal School where a similar selection of candidates for admission was also held. Mao Zedong (1893–1976) was chosen to be the top candidate at the Fourth Normal School early that spring. In the following year, the two teacher's colleges merged to become one institution. Thus, far out in the hinterland of China, the lives of two talented students and their impressive teacher converged in a common bond that was to prove historic in China's later history.

1

At the intersection of crisis and innovation, China's early twentieth-century modernizers had created Hunan First Normal School to produce students who would possess the knowledge and skills needed to save the nation. Their education would include the best elements of Chinese, European, and Japanese schooling. The history of Hunan First Normal is a tapestry woven of traditional Chinese and modern Western threads. Chinese tradition formed the character of the school, yet Western ideas and contemporary social, political, and intellectual circumstances strongly shaped its policies and practices. These several ideological strands from a turbulent twentieth century comprised a colorful and intricate fabric of conflicting classes, forces, and social agendas. This study brings into focus the varied patterns of the tapestry by examining the school's curriculum and culture, the teaching staff drawn from an earlier generation of social reformists, and the economic and social backgrounds of the students. The combined moral, intellectual, and institutional features of the community created at the school would have an important influence on subsequent Chinese history.

Students who attended Hunan First Normal School in the second decade of the twentieth century went on to become the founders, principal ideologues, and leading activists of the Chinese Communist Party (CCP). Among them were Mao Zedong, Cai Hesen, He Shuheng (1876–1935), Zhang Kundi (1890–1930), Chen Chang (1894–1930), Xiao San (1896–1983), Li Weihan (1896–1984), and Luo Xuezan (1893–1930). How could this apparently ordinary teacher's college have fostered so many radical intellectuals? What special chemistry was at work? What effect did the members of a new elite—the teachers—have on the intellectual development of their students? What explained the growth of intellectual and political radicalism in the 1910s and 1920s? How were the new schools and the educational reforms intertwined with the rise of radicalism? In short, how did this relatively obscure school become so important in shaping the careers and thoughts of those who became the founding figures of the CCP and later the leaders of China?

Many scholars have examined the emergence of communism in twentieth-century China. In the West, Maurice Meisner and Benjamin Schwartz establish an orthodox narrative with their claims that the Russian Revolution of 1917 sparked the interest of Chinese radicals in Marxism. Arif Dirlik complicates the picture with a study that examines the impact of anarchism on the emergence of Chinese communism. Peter Zarrow traces the source of Chinese communism back to China's rich tradition of political thought, with special attention given to Daoism.

Such scholars have provided much insight into the intellectual movements in the early decades of the twentieth century, but their research
focuses on a small group of elite intellectuals. How were the radical
ideas of this group transformed into a mass movement, and how were
they spread in subsequent decades?[2]

Although scholars in the West—with the exception of Zarrow—
often fail to appreciate fully the relationship between Chinese tradition
and the early Chinese Communist movement, scholars in China such
as Jin Guantao and Peng Dacheng have seen Chinese communism as
a fundamentally Chinese adaptation of Marxism.[3] However, the educational reforms of the first two decades of the twentieth century and the
curriculum and ethos of Hunan First Normal infused in the students a
philosophy and an ethics that wedded Confucian values, such as moral
cultivation and humanity, and Western elements, such as Kantian ethics, T. H. Green's concept of self-realization, J Rousseau's humanistic
and liberal ideas, and Spenserian utilitarianism, with a commitment to
social change. Mao and his classmates emerged from this milieu ready
to set out on the path to reform.

Although many studies have been published on modern education
and educational reforms in China, most scholars have focused on educational and social transformation rather than the political role the new
schools played. The full affect of the new schools on the cultural politics
of the late Qing and early Republic remains relatively unexplored. The
crucial aspect of the educational reform movements in fostering intellectual and political radicalism is even less known. Most scholars see these
two phenomena as quite distinct. Although the late Stephen C. Averill
studied the transition from urban to rural revolution in 1920s Jiangxi,
demonstrating the connections, little further work has emerged. Xiaoping Cong's recent publication, an excellent study of teachers' schools in
Republican China, focuses on the social and political role these teachers'
schools played in the changes sweeping Chinese society. However, her
work is a general study of teachers' schools in 1930s. She neither talks
about the schools in 1910s, nor the Hunan First Normal School.[4]

In tracing the course of educational reform in Hunan, a few studies, such as those of Charlton Lewis and Joseph Esherick, examine the
causes of the 1911 Revolution. Stephen Platt's recent scholarship focuses
on the development of Chinese regionalism from the second half of the
nineteenth century to the first two decades of the twentieth century,
using Hunan as a case study. However, these works have not touched
the subject of the Hunan First Normal School. This work shows how

modern schools helped mediate the transmission of new ideas in early twentieth-century China. They contributed to the rise of radicalism and provided the context and impetus for new political movements among the elite.[5]

In China's modern schools, traditional ideas and newly imported ones clashed and combined, shaping a new generation of students. What specific changes resulted? By studying Shi Cuntong (1899–1970), a man from a traditional family who became a communist, Wen-hsin Yeh shows that modern schools nurtured and spread new ideas.[6] Yeh, in *Provincial Passages*, employs a unique spatial approach to examine the impact of the culture, geography, educational structure, and history of Zhejiang on one group of radicals; her focus is on an early anarchist and a founding member of the CCP who later left the communist mainstream and embraced democratic centrist views. This approach, apparently inspired by G. William Skinner's regional systems theory of Chinese socioeconomic history, Yeh extends into the cultural realm while contending, contra Skinner, that China's traditional rebellions and its modern revolution were not based only in the peripheries and along the regional frontiers. She suggests that the specific historical and intellectual circumstances of Zhejiang facilitated the radicalization of Shi Cuntong and others who joined the May Fourth Movement.[7]

By looking into the rural backgrounds of provincial radicals during and after the May Fourth period, Yeh uncovers a neglected but important part of early Chinese communism. She concludes that its early years were dominated by urban radicalism, but that later, revolutionary communism was an outgrowth of conservative, Confucian-bound, rural China.[8] Yeh's creative and fresh spatial approach leads to important insights. But *Provincial Passages* takes a narrow view of the origins of Chinese communism and does not distinguish between the cultural traditions of Zhejiang and of Hunan.[9] Her project may be extended by examining the ideological transformation of a group of radical intellectuals—those associated with Hunan First Normal School in the second decade of the twentieth century, important players in the founding of the CCP.

Hunan First Normal, like many new schools, transmitted new concepts.[10] Students tended to be from relatively humble backgrounds, the graduates of rural grammar schools in a quite insular province whose conservative culture was dominated by strong local elites. Those who arrived in Changsha in the early years of the Republic encountered a city that had been only recently, but rapidly, opened to foreign contact and then exposed to destructive political upheavals. They entered an institution that had been created by combining assets from an academy in the scholar-official tradition and several new schools in the Japanese style. The school was directed by earnest reformists who composed a cocktail of pedagogical ideas from Chinese, foreign, traditional, and contemporary sources. Teachers subjected students to rigorous physical as well as intellectual training, which emphasized both moral cultivation and political engagement.[11]

The historical, political, and intellectual milieu that surrounded those who studied at First Normal included elements shared by China and elements specific to Changsha and even the school itself. The entire nation, for example, experienced the changes, chaos, and humiliation of the last years of the Qing dynasty (1644–1911) and during the early Republican period. That intellectual milieu was shaped by radical ideological change. Because their country had been constantly subjected to the will of foreign powers, these Changsha radicals faced a national and a moral crisis. They were intent on finding the secret weapon that had enabled the West to overcome China. Intellectuals and activists all over China were engaged in the same search, but locally the search took on very different forms from place to place.

Hunan, an inland province, had been one of the most culturally sophisticated provinces in China for hundreds of years. Isolated, ruled by conservative elite, xenophobic, and comparatively backward economically, it became an intellectual hotbed for modern Western ideas, including Marxism and communism. One of China's great popularizers of Western knowledge, Wei Yuan (1794–1857), was from Hunan: It was Yuan who first urged the Chinese to adopt Western technology. His famous slogan, "Learn the superior techniques of the barbarians to control the barbarians," served as the driving force behind the nineteenth-century's Self-Strengthening Movement. The leading figures of that movement, Zeng Guofan (1811–1872) and Zuo Zongtang (1812–1855), were also from Hunan. Both believed that China must strengthen itself from within and learn from the West in industry and technology. In Hunan, this movement enabled Wu Dacheng (1835–1902), a governor of Hunan from 1892 to 1894, to transform the province from a center of anti-foreignism to one that promoted self-strengthening by means of industry and new style schools.[12]

The city of Changsha was both the provincial capital and the major commercial city of the region, with strong economic links to adjacent subregions. Traders and inhabitants benefited from an advanced riverine transportation network that linked the province north to Hankou and south to Guangxi. The leading students of First Normal all came from Hunan's peripheral agrarian counties. Those hilly areas suffered from poor soil, inadequate irrigation, and a scattered and sparse population. The people from such regions were often very conservative, cut off from intellectual innovation, and prone to strong faith in Confucian tradition. This volume will discuss how the curriculum that these men from the hinterlands encountered at First Normal affected their ideas and activities, and transformed them into radicals after they arrived in Changsha.

The radicalization of these youths would appear to confirm G. William Skinner's theory that the peripheries and regional frontiers have provided the personnel both for China's traditional rebellions and for its modern revolution. However, as Wen-hsin Yeh points out, provincial radicalism cannot be explained simply as hinterlanders expressing their frustration. In the specific case of First Normal, radicalization emerged out of the specific historical and intellectual circumstances of Hunan. These included the suppression of the Taipings, which left behind a powerful elite, the xenophobia that slowed Western penetration until after 1900, the local cultural traditions of Hunan, and the character of the new school system.

Although Changsha was opened as a treaty port only in 1904, by the time students arrived at the school in 1914 much had changed. New ideas and knowledge almost overwhelmed them. The great impact of the Western powers, largely invisible in rural areas, was obvious in the big city. The sharp differences between differing worlds, home and school, past and present, combined with the national crisis and moral crisis to inspire profound reflections. Many became cultural iconoclasts, then communists.

The situation in Hunan played no small part in this transformation. The effects of Western penetration, the Taiping Uprising, World War I, and conflicts between warlords were particularly acute. The province had produced a distinctive tradition, *Huxiang* culture with a unique emphasis on *jingshi zhiyong*, or "bureaucratic statecraft"[13] as an overlay on the classical Confucian tradition.[14] Beginning with Wang Fuzhi (1619–1692), Hunanese such as Wei Yuan, Zeng Guofan, Tan Sitong (1865–1898), and Yang Changji all made contributions to the ideas of statecraft. In the early nineteenth century, statecraft thought was taught by Hunanese scholars in Confucian academies. In 1827, Wei Yuan and He Changling (1785–1848) edited a book-length collection, *Jingshi wen bian* (A Collection of Writings on Bureaucratic Statecraft), devoted to statecraft ideas. In the mid-nineteenth century, the eminent national leader Zeng Guofan added *jingshi* to his work with the intent of rebuilding China's social-political order.

This cultural tradition was reinforced at First Normal by Yang Changji, the well-known Neo-Confucian who had decided to stay and teach there. Yang was an admirer of Wang Fuzhi and Wei Yuan. But he was also a scholar of Western learning, and had studied in Japan, Britain, and Germany for more than ten years. As an ethics teacher at Hunan First Normal, he became one of the institution's most influential and highly respected teachers. He urged his students to study all aspects of Western thought and institutions, but he never let them forget their own national heritage. While guiding his students toward the radical Westernized and iconoclastic magazine *New Youth* (*Xin Qingnian*), he also directed them to scholars from the Chuanshan Association who sought inspiration for a rebirth of their country within Chinese tradition itself, in the writings of the great Hunanese scholar of the early seventeenth century, Wang Fuzhi (also called Wang Chuanshan).[15]

Another important influence was Liu Renxi (1840–1917), Tan Sitong's teacher, founder of the Chuanshan Association in Changsha (1914) and its main lecturer. First Normal students often went to hear him speak of the need for a national renaissance that honored tradition. In such a setting, serious-minded young men, including Cai Hesen and Mao Zedong, focused on weighty matters such as the nature of man, human society, and China's situation in the world. In 1918 they formed a close-knit organization called the *Xinmin xuehui* (New Citizens' Study Society), which played a leading role in the May Fourth Movement in Hunan and had a broader influence as well. More than half of the seventy-four members of the association eventually became members of the CCP.[16]

That same year, 1918, First Normal students sent a large delegation to France, where they founded a study association and confronted the realities of Western society. Mao traveled to Beijing to help organize the trip, making connections with radicals during his time in the capital. Letters and articles circulated among centers of reform in Changsha, Beijing, and Paris. The Russian Revolution of 1917 had provided the radicals with a concrete model to imitate: They were convinced that Leninism was a practical path for China as well. Then the May Fourth Incident in 1919 released a storm of political agitation. Although the trip to France ended somewhat ignominiously—Cai and other Chinese students were deported after joining protests in Lyon—the lesson had been learned.[17] They returned to China to participate in the May Fourth debates over the nation's future.

The May Fourth Movement, much studied, has often been considered the turning point in China's modern cultural-intellectual transformation, a complete break with the past. In China, the Communist official view is that the movement led by iconoclastic students and intellectuals started as an expression of patriotism, evolved into severe attacks on Confucian tradition, and sowed the seeds of revolution.[18]

Some scholars in the West have looked beyond these themes to analyze deeper questions about the country's cultural-intellectual transformation. In his study of Yan Fu (1853–1921), Benjamin Schwartz describes the inner dynamics of the Chinese traditional values system in terms of self-transformation. A study of Liang Qichao (1873–1929) by Hao Chang also examines the inner dynamics of Chinese tradition, in that case the Neo-Confucian tradition, proving that China's modern cultural and intellectual transformation had begun by 1890.[19]

No matter how much scholars may disagree in their interpretations of the May Fourth Movement, no one denies its vital importance in modern Chinese history. But most research has examined the movement on the national level and focused on events in major cities like Shanghai and Beijing. In this study, a focus on the First Normal School will show how May Fourth ideas changed the context in which the students studied exposing them to the latest theories, including Marxism.

Although it is clear that a complex set of influences contributed to the intellectual formation of First Normal students, in the People's Republic of China (PRC) studies done on this period usually center around Mao Zedong.[20] Such studies typically present a history in which the thoughts, actions, lives, and memories of the Hunan radicals evolved into the thought of Mao, eventually to become the official orthodoxy of the PRC.[21] Outside of China, no scholar has yet examined the story of Hunan First Normal School.

This study provides a new look at the sources of the Chinese Revolution. The May Fourth Movement in Hunan differed from movements in Shanghai and Beijing. For example, many arguments broke out among Hunanese intellectuals about political activism. Some believed that the main goal of activism should be cultural enlightenment, whereas others wanted to revitalize society. Those who embraced communism were only one of many competing groups. Within the May Fourth Movement, supporters of each school of thought pursued their own goals.

After the *Xinmin xuehui* split in 1920, the majority of the members embraced communism.[22] Many became founding figures and important leaders of the early CCP, including Cai and Mao. It was the fate of most of the *Xinmin xuehui* members to be killed by the Nationalist Party (Guomindang) in the 1927 White Terror. However, the intellectual influence of those people on the Chinese Communist movement continued.

The educational reforms instituted by early republican leaders such as Cai Yuanpei between 1895 and 1919 produced new institutions, which became channels for the distribution of new and revolutionary ideas.[23] They also produced young scholars with new skills who sought fresh solutions to the nation's intractable problems. This one school produced an exceptional body of students just at the time that China entered a crucial era. The Hunan First Normal School nurtured one of several nuclei that coalesced to form a tiny communist minority in 1921. Because of their numbers and shared experience, the radicals from Changsha were the most influential group in shaping Chinese Communist ideology.

Chapter 1 examines the history of reform in Hunan up to 1900: growth, climax, and defeat. Hunan's late Qing modernization movement was driven by both national and local developments. Although reactionary gentry turned back the political reforms of the 1890s, reformists retained ultimate control over education. Some of these reformists were transformed into revolutionaries by the failure of 1898. The surge and reversal of the reform movement in Hunan were followed by a rapid opening of the province to foreign interests, which in turn spurred a renewal of nationalism. Hunan First Normal School was founded in a political landscape that would have been unthinkable forty years earlier.

Chapter 2 considers the transformation of Chinese education during the late Qing and early Republic, gradually focusing on the transformation of the Confucian Chengnan Academy into First Normal. China's traditional educational system was heavily weighted toward Confucian scholarship and study for the all-important civil service examinations. Success in the examinations depended on an intimate familiarity with the classical canon and subsequent commentaries, particularly those of the Song philosopher Zhu Xi (1130–1200). Among the special intellectual and cultural features of Hunan were an emphasis on bureaucratic statecraft, "the unity of knowledge and action," "investigating fundamental principles," and on searching for the truth that could contribute to national salvation.

When educational reforms were promulgated by the imperial government in 1901 as part of its New Policies (*Xinzheng*), Hunan's officials barely reacted. Real reform began in 1903—the year First Normal came into being—and made uneven progress in the volatile political atmosphere. One effort at reform was the adoption of a Japanese-style curriculum in 1905. When the liberal Tan Yankai (1876–1930) became military governor of Huanan, his regime encouraged further reform until such efforts were stemmed by a chaotic period of military rule. The New Culture Movement began to influence education at First Normal in the late 1910s, and the school flourished despite provincial and national upheaval.

The intellectual atmosphere of First Normal between the fall of the Qing dynasty and the beginning of the May Fourth Movement (1912–1919) is the subject of Chapter 3. Despite its links to the old regime, the school survived the collapse of the Qing. And it changed: Curriculum, policy, practice, and philosophy adjusted to the new circumstances. Amid a remarkably wide range of practical and "Western" subjects, during the Republic the school clung to traditional literary and moral training. This chapter treats the school's philosophy and curriculum, the composition of its faculty, and school regulations governing study, examinations, and student conduct.

The nature of the institution owed much to its progressive and learned faculty. Adherents of the Self-Strengthening and New Culture movements, these men believed in intellectual inquiry as the basis of national renewal and education as the method of national salvation. First Normal students inhabited a world of old-style literati culture rich in poetic imagery and historical allusions, which placed a high value on aesthetic pursuits and metaphysical reflection. And their teachers also guided them in the study of all aspects of Western thought and institutions and the intensive application of Western science and technology. The staff consciously tried to fashion the students into a community of the like-minded who would go out to reform the country. The principal, Kong Zhaoshou (1876–1929), shaped the school to this end, though he was for a time forced into political exile. The writings of both teachers and students demonstrate the profound impact the school had on the students' lives and intellectual development. Chapter 4 examines the contributions of Principal Kong, pedagogy teacher Xu Teli (1877–1968), director of studies Fang Weixia (1879–1936), mathematics teacher Wang Jifan (1884–1972), and history teacher Li Jinxi (1890–1978).

Chapter 5 looks at ethics teacher Yang Changji, because his influence on young radicals was so striking. Yang was a well-known Neo-Confucian writer specializing in the school of principle (li)—he also held degrees from Japanese and British universities. Renowned throughout Changsha for his Confucian erudition, he did not hesitate to blend Western philosophy with traditional ideas and forcefully rejected many aspects of Confucian society. Yang became a mentor to Mao Zedong, Cai Hesen, and Xiao Zisheng, inculcating in them a belief in resolution and individualism with public responsibility to society.

In Chapter 6, the focus shifts to the students themselves. The young men trained at First Normal during the early years of the Republic underwent an ideological transformation as shown in their writings and their lives. Curriculum, environment, staff, and the political and social forces at work in the school, city, and countryside were central to the transformation of the students. Involvement of the exchange program with France also affected the students' outlook. Xiao Zisheng stands as an interesting contrast to Mao Zedong and Cai Hesen, as an example of someone who joined the *Xinmin xuehui* but never took the final step of the journey to communism.

Chapter 7 is an intellectual biography of Cai Hesen. The credit for shaping the Chinese Communist Party, both organizationally and ideologically, usually goes to Mao Zedong. The contribution of Cai Hesen tends to be undervalued. Cai's firm belief that national salvation could be found in Russian communism influenced a generation of Chinese radical youths. Like Mao, Cai was prepared for his conversion by his training at First Normal and the *Xinmin xuehui*. His story is that of an intellectual transformation that parallels and supplements the better-known example of Mao.

The May Fourth Movement was the final catalyst for turning the radicals of the *Xinmin xuehui* into communists. The concluding chapter considers how the case of Hunan First Normal School can help us reinterpret the May Fourth Movement. Far from Beijing and Shanghai, different influences were felt and different conclusions were reached. Examining First Normal School reveals the complexity and flexibility of the movement; it suggests that political history is anything but monolithic.

Chapter 1

Reform in Hunan, 1895–1900

On October 1, 1949, following the Communist victory in the Chinese civil war, Mao Zedong proclaimed the establishment of the People's Republic of China (PRC) at Tiananmen Square. Education played an important role in shaping the man who then stood at the pinnacle of power. Just as communist cadres would have a profound influence on subsequent Chinese history, so they themselves had been influenced by their schooling. During their youth, in a period of political upheaval and intellectual ferment, a "modernized" school system had supplanted the traditional Chinese educational system, which had been centered on the classical canon and directed toward the civil service examinations. Many important communist leaders, including Cai Hesen and Mao Zedong, had been educated at the Hunan First Normal School in Changsha, the capital city of Hunan province, in the second decade of the twentieth century. How could this apparently ordinary normal school have fostered so many radical intellectuals who became early leaders of Chinese Communism? How had the end of the old examination system and the emergence of this new "modern" school system in the early part of that century affected both mentors and students?

To answer these questions, we must explore the link between the reorganization of the educational system and the growth of communism. We must examine the backgrounds not only of those radical students who formed the first generation of communist leadership but also of their teachers, the intellectual reformers, the curriculum of the school, its environment, the political and social forces in the school and in the surrounding city, and the contribution of these factors to the transformation in the thinking of radical students. Long before Mao stood at his moment of triumph in 1949, he and many of his allies had been heavily influenced by the First Normal School and their mentors there. The effect of that educational experience would have worldwide ramifications.

The origins of that educational experience lay in the reform movement in Hunan during the last decade of the nineteenth century, in the conservative opposition to reformist ideas, and in the nationalism that developed in response to the intrusion of foreign influence into Hunan.

Reform Reaches Hunan, 1895–1896

The Chinese people are well known for their great cultural pride. China, with its vast territory, large population, and long history, was the core civilization in East Asia for centuries. It served as a role model for its neighboring nations in cultural affairs, politics, institutions, and economics. In the middle of the nineteenth century, however, Chinese pride was seriously shaken by a series of humiliating foreign military incursions, beginning with the Opium War of 1839–1842. Worse came when China was defeated by Japan, seen by the Chinese populace as a "petty oriental barbarian," in the Sino-Japanese War of 1894–1895. As a result, China was forced to sign the humiliating Treaty of Shimonoseki, which clearly exposed the weakness of the Qing regime, and infuriated the nation. It also greatly shattered national prestige and traditional self-confidence. Externally, these setbacks invited further encroachment in the "scramble" for concessions, and internally they encouraged movements for reform and revolution. They made Chinese intellectuals pay serious attention to the reform of their country with the goal of standing up to the imperialist powers. Chinese intellectuals realized that if China were to survive in the modern world, it would have to relinquish some of the old and assimilate some of the new.[1] What to keep and what to change was the subject of considerable controversy, not least in the field of education.

In Hunan, the reforms began in 1895, three years before the Hundred Days Reform. Joseph Esherick, in his *Reform and Revolution in China*, argues that the late Qing reform program catered chiefly to elite interests whom he characterizes as the "urban reformist elite" and that the new local government institutions strengthened gentry power. The reforms in Hunan were encouraged, as Charlton M. Lewis points out, by a fortunate combination of reform-minded officials. First, Zhang Zhidong (1837–1909), the governor-general of Hunan and Hubei from 1889 to

1897 promoted educational, railway, mining, and industrial projects. In 1895, he supported Kang Youwei's (1858–1927) Society for National Strengthening (*Qiangxue hui*) and his newspaper, the *Qiangxue bao*. He had close connections with a number of reform-minded officials and elites in Hunan. He worked closely with Chen Baozhen (1831–1900), who served as the governor of Hunan between the years of 1895 and 1898. The third important official was the education commissioner, Jiang Biao (1860–1899). A native of Suzhou, Jiang received the highest *jinshi* degree in 1889. Deeply versed in classics, Jiang was also familiar with Western learning. He was interested in foreign affairs and had studied at the Interpreters College (*Tongwen guan*) in Beijing. He was a founding member of the Society for National Strengthening in 1895.[2]

Early reforms in Hunan accorded with the national atmosphere of the Self-Strengthening Movement (1861–1894). In 1895, Gov. Chen Baozhen established a mining bureau to exploit Hunan's extensive mineral resources. In the following years, Hunan also established a telegraph line between Changsha and Hankou, a police bureau, an arsenal, a chemical company, and a company that provided electric lighting for schools and examination halls. The electric company, however, lasted only until 1899, when it went bankrupt.[3]

More impressive was the attempt made to reform the educational system. As soon as Jiang Biao took the position of education commissioner of Hunan in 1894, he began to reform the traditional Confucian academies by emphasizing *jingshi zhiyong* (bureaucratic statecraft). He added geography and mathematics to the classical subjects required in the civil service examinations for the lowest *shengyuan* degree.[4] Jiang also introduced classes in foreign languages, and purchased instruments for the study of chemistry and electricity. He established the Hunan Reform Study Society (*Xiangxue hui*), and a reform newspaper, *Hunan Reform News* (*Xiangxue bao*), to promote a cautious program of reform. *Hunan Reform News* mainly introduced Western politics, laws, and culture, which included news and knowledge of history, geography, mathematics, business, diplomacy, and science.[5]

By 1897, the reform movements in Hunan were flourishing and Gov. Chen Baozhen diligently sought to implement a thoroughgoing program of reform in the province. At first, his reforms received a broad consensus of support. Even the senior Hunanese elites welcomed the approval of young activists like Tan Sitong and Tang Caichang (1867–1900). However, those senior Hunanese elites, the "conservative" faction in provincial politics, later adhered to the traditional pragmatic conservatism of Hunan that emphasized *jingshi*. Pragmatic conservatism had revived and enjoyed considerable success under the leadership of Zeng Guofan during the Tongzhi Restoration.[6] Since then, *jingshi* had remained a very important element in the culture of Hunan and its Confucian tradition. Those senior elites followed the statecraft theorists in stressing the importance of increased gentry involvement and power in local government. For instance, they invested heavily in new industrial enterprises.

Wang Xianqian (1842–1917) was the most prominent member of this group. He was a former compiler of Hanlin Academy and Jiangsu education commissioner. He had held posts in the State Historiographer's Office (*Guoshi guan*). In 1889, he retired from government service and returned to Hunan to be president of the famous Yuelu Academy in Changsha.[7] Although he was a famous scholar, known for his classical commentaries, massive compilations, and extensive private library, Wang energetically advocated commercial investment by the gentry. He personally invested in commercial enterprises. Wang even supported the initial moderate educational reforms of Jiang Biao. He encouraged his students to read the reformist *Current Affairs News* (*Shiwu bao*), edited in Shanghai by Liang Qichao.[8]

The Climax and Failure of Reform, 1897–1898

Marianne Bastid claims that the "modern gentry" effectively initiated and played a vital role in educational reform. Paul Bailey agrees with Bastid's argument and states that the Confucian legacy fostered support for educational modernization among the gentry.[9] The Chinese placed great emphasis on the transformative power of education.

The reform movement in Hunan reached its climax in September 1897, with the opening of the Current Affairs School (*Shiwu xuetang*). Wealthy Hunanese financed the school's buildings and equipment, and the government mines were expected to provide additional funds for the school. The Hunanese literati widely supported the school, as is evident from its endowment (an annual fund of $20,000 was subscribed by early July) and the keen competition for admission. In the initial round of entrance examinations, more than four thousand candidates applied, although only forty were accepted for the first class.[10]

The goal of the Current Affairs School was to train students to become "capable men" of an entirely new type. Students were educated in traditional Chinese as well as Western subjects. Because the phi-

losophy and the curriculum of the Current Affairs School was totally
new at that time, the school played an enlightening role in Hunan's
educational reform.

It was also in 1897 that the Hunanese gentry began to perceive
a radical dimension in the educational reform program; this in turn
destroyed the elites' support for reform one year later. The first radical
shift apparent to the gentry was the appointment of Huang Zunxian
(1848–1905) in 1897 as salt intendant and later as the judicial commissioner. A native of Guangdong, Huang was a distinguished diplomat. He
had twelve years of government service in Tokyo, San Francisco, London, and Singapore. Deeply impressed with Japan's success in the Meiji
period, he was eager to apply the lessons to China. He wrote a book on
Meiji Japan that was widely read in Hunan. This book later helped to
inspire the Guangxu Emperor's Hundred Days Reform of 1898.[11]

In fall 1897, Huang suggested that Xu Renzhu (1863–1900) replace
Jiang Biao as educational commissioner. Xu, then 34 years old, was a
son of a prominent Hanlin compiler and a good friend of Tan Sitong.
An active reform advocate in Beijing, Xu took Jiang Biao's place as
educational commissioner in fall 1897, and introduced Kang Youwei's
teachings to Hunan. Xu also was a good friend of Liang Qichao; he was
able to mobilize considerable government support of Liang's work at the
Current Affairs School.[12]

Huang Zunxian, the judicial commissioner of Hunan, was also a
good friend of Liang Qichao. In 1896, Huang and Liang worked together
to set up the Current Affairs News (*Shiwu bao*) in Shanghai. Soon after
he arrived in Changsha, Huang suggested that Liang Qichao be invited
to accept the post of dean of Chinese Studies at the new Current Affairs
School; he also proposed that Li Weige,[13] a translator for the *Current
Affairs News* be appointed as dean of Western Studies.[14] When Liang
arrived in Changsha, he brought with him three of Kang Youwei's students, Han Wenju (1855–1937), Ou Jujia, and Ye Juemai, who became
assistant deans at the school.[15] The appointments of the faculty at the
Current Affairs School were approved by the provincial elites. The
school was soon dominated by Liang Qichao's Cantonese friends and
his Hunanese followers, a group of young Hunanese gentry activists such
as Tan Sitong, Tang Caichang, and Xiong Xiling (1870–1942). These
people were remarkably young. In 1897, Tan, the oldest, was 32; Tang
was 30; Xiong was 27; and Liang Qichao was only 24.

Xiong Xiling, a native of Fenghuang, Hunan, was the son of a
military officer. Called the "boy genius of Hunan," he obtained the highest *jinshi* degree in 1895 at the remarkably early age of 24. Xiong had

entered the political life of Beijing with a three-year appointment to
the Hanlin Academy in 1894, but he was obliged to return to Hunan
because of his series of memorials opposing peace with Japan.[16]

Tan Sitong and Tang Caichang were the most radical reformers
among the Hunanese activists. Both were brilliant scholars and ardent
reformers. They represented a new type of patriotic idealist that was
just starting to appear in China. Tan was born into a leading Hunanese
gentry family in Beijing in 1864. He had a traditional education but
was attracted to knight errant ideals. Although his native town was the
turbulent district of Liuyang, in Hunan, most of Tan's time was spent
outside Hunan. He traveled extensively throughout China. Shocked by
China's defeat in the 1894–1895 war with Japan, he began to read works
on Western science and technology; he also contacted Kang Youwei and
began to study Buddhism. He wrote his best-known work, *Renxue* (*On
Benevolence*), as an attempt to synthesize Confucianism, Buddhism, and
Western science into a worldview. Tan believed that *ren* (benevolence)
was the source of everything. He saw the inequality of traditional society,
the "three bonds and five relationships," and the autocratic system of
government as being in basic conflict with *ren*. His views were among
the most extreme of the reformist group.[17]

Tan took the civil service examination several times, but earned
only the first, or *shengyuan*, degree. He did not receive an official position in the government until the last three years of his life. In 1896,
he received a supernumerary appointment in the local government at
Nanjing. The following year, he returned to Hunan at the invitation of
the governor Chen Baozhen to take part in a reform program.[18]

Tang Caichang had a background similar to that of Tan Sitong.
Also from Liuyang, both he and Tan studied under a local scholar,
Ouyang Zhonggu, who was a devotee of the Han learning and of the
late-Ming Hunanese Confucian scholar, Wang Fuzhi.[19] Tang, too, spent
a great deal of time traveling outside Hunan and was exposed to the
New Text scholarship.[20] In 1896, Tang and Tan launched study societies in their home districts, where they earned a reputation as the "two
heroes of Liuyang." In 1897, Tang went back to Changsha to join the
provincial reform movement. In Changsha, the two worked together
in setting up the new-style Current Affairs School. They also cooper-
ated in establishing a military academy and a newspaper, *Hunan News*
(*Xiangbao*) in Changsha.[21]

By November 1897, Hunan's reform movement had new leadership, headed by Tan Sitong, Tang Caichang, Liang Qichao, Huang Zunxian, and Xu Renzhu. Changsha was now ready for more radical reform.

Their movement coincided with the German occupation of Qingdao and Jiaozhou Bay in Shandong in November 1897 and the beginning of the "scramble for concessions" by the foreign powers. The weakness of the Qing government during these events fostered a sense of crisis. The fear that China was about to be sliced up "like a melon" and partitioned among the great powers haunted the reformers and strengthened the belief of these young patriots that radical solutions would be needed if China were to be saved.[22]

As this new patriotism swept through Hunan, a sense of alienation from the Qing government spread quickly. At the Current Affairs School, Liang Qichao conducted lectures on current events and "new learning." Liang and his colleagues also distributed literary materials revived from the Ming resistance to the Manchu conquest in the seventeenth century. Although racial consciousness began to appear frequently as Liang reminded the Chinese race of the alien rule of the present dynasty and called for "people's rights" (minquan), Charlton M. Lewis argues that it is misleading to insist that the main goal of these radical reformers was to overthrow the Qing dynasty. The proof was that as soon as the Guangxu emperor attempted a national reform, Liang and his Hunanese friends immediately rallied around him, and continued to do so even after the Hundred Days Reform ended.[23]

The most striking radicalization was Liang Qichao's suggestion to Gov. Chen Baozhen in December 1897 that in order to preserve a base from which to secure the future regeneration of China, one or two centrally located and prosperous provinces should declare their independence (zili) and reform themselves as an example to the rest of the nation.[24] Liang held that once Hunan was reorganized independently it could become a catalyst for the recovery of China. Liang argued that although this advice might sound disloyal or rebellious, it was a necessary action to prepare for the day when all other provinces would be ceded to or stolen by foreign powers. Thus, it was China's only hope.[25] Liang was not promoting provincial independence on the romantic ground of "Hunan for the Hunanese." He believed that the province was a perfect place to implement ideas that could eventually save the nation. Liang's proposal for provincial autonomy and local self-government was never opposed to by the provincial elites, although they soon attacked his radical teachings at the Current Affairs School. The proposal for provincial independence echoed in Hunanese politics for nearly thirty years.[26]

Liang hoped to popularize radical reform. As soon as he arrived at the Current Affairs School, Liang began to teach Kang Youwei's interpretation of Confucianism. He emphasized the origins of the Chinese political reform in ancient times. His lectures were based on the *Mencius*, the *Gongyang Commentary* (a New Text document), and Kang Youwei's book, *Datongshu* (The Book on the Ideal of Grand Unity), which regarded Confucius as a reformer. When students showed their notes to relatives and friends during the New Year vacation, a great stir was set off throughout the entire province. People were shocked by the radical ideas taught at the Current Affairs School.[27]

About the same time, Tan Sitong, Tang Caichang, and their literati friends were urging the governor to approve the creation of a study society of a new type: the South China Study Society (*Nan xuehui*). The South China Study Society started as an officially sanctioned gentry debating society. To Liang Qichao, study societies embodied the secrets of national power and wealth in the West, where scholarly organizations existed in each different field. Liang observed that they had also appeared in ancient China during Confucius' time. Because they were not new to either China or the West, study societies were the places to cultivate an eclectic search for knowledge and the kind of egalitarian philosophy that represented the main threads of Kang Youwei's writings.[28]

The South China Study Society also was regarded by Liang as the predecessor of a provincial legislature, which would help protect the independence of Hunan. He later recalled:

> As the theory that the great powers were partitioning China arose, Hunanese men of purpose all made plans for the period after the disaster. They thought to preserve Hunan's independence, but the independence movement could not be simply empty talk. It was first necessary that the people be versed in the art of politics and experienced in self-government. Thus, we established this society to discuss the matter and as a foundation for the future. Later [its example] could be spread to the other provinces of the South so that even in the event of future partition, South China would escape destruction.[29]

Many of the debates of the South China Study Society were published in the *Hunan News*, a new daily newspaper. Planned by Xiong Xiling in 1897, it was launched in March 1898 under the editorship of Tang Caichang and Tan Sitong, with subsidies from Gov. Chen Baozhen. Newspapers were crucial to the educational mission of the reformers, and the *Hunan News* became an important addition to such organs as *Current Affairs News* in Shanghai and the *Hunan Reform News* (*Xiangxue bao*) in Changsha. The *Hunan News* was distributed throughout the province and its stated purpose was to "spread the new trends and expand awareness."[30]

The *Hunan News* published theories linking parliamentary government, political parties, and people's rights to ideas in the classics and the examples of the ancient sage-kings. *Hunan News* also published some more moderate and concrete proposals by Tang Caichang, Tan Sitong, and others for military academies, a modern Western-equipped army and navy, and improved training of government officials.[31]

Stimulated by the newspapers and the South China Study Society, other reform institutions proliferated in Hunan during the spring of 1898. New associations with more specific reformist objectives advocated marriage reform, a ban on foot binding, and a kind of program for women's liberation. Another urged people to simplify the wedding ceremony and to end fancy forms of dress and expensive ways of entertaining guests.[32] The young reformers were questioning basic social norms and the very style of gentry life.

Clearly, Liang Qichao, Tan Sitong, Tang Caichang, and the young reformers were using the new-style schools, study societies, and newspapers as instruments to launch a major reform movement. At the time, there were fifty-one new-style schools, study societies, and newspaper publishing houses in China, and sixteen were in Hunan.[33] The formation of the Current Affairs School especially inspired the enlightened intellectuals and young students. Gentry elites in the province vied with each other to reform the old system of Confucian academies into modern schools and to create new-style schools in Hunan. In this regard, the Current Affairs School was a pioneering experiment in Hunan's educational reform.

In the thrilling atmosphere of the day, students and faculty at the Current Affairs School were occasionally allowed to criticize the autocracy and misgovernment of the Qing dynasty. Some forbidden works of the long-deceased Ming loyalists were reprinted. "The atmosphere in the school," Liang wrote later, "became more radical day by day."[34]

In the South China Study Society, Liang Qichao and his reformer colleagues were talking about "equality" among all members of the study society and within the elite. The South China Study Society became part of the grand plan that Liang was preparing for Hunan. In a letter he sent to Gov. Chen Baozhen in January 1898, Liang defined the goal of reform and outlined his ideal institutions. The Current Affairs School and the South China Study Society made the people enlightened; this popular knowledge *(minzhi)* should be extended as a basis for the people's political rights *(minquan)*, and the people should share equal power with the local elite and government officials under a system of American-style checks and balances.[35] These young reformers, especially Tan Sitong, exhaustively studied the ancient writings of *Mencius*, the *Gongyang Commentary*, the *Six Classics*, and other classics, to show that people's rights really were inherent in the Chinese tradition.[36]

Although the young reformers worked hard to search Chinese antiquity for reform precedents, some of their radical theories and ideas began to alarm the powerful and more orthodox members of the Hunanese elite. Originally supporters of reform, when they realized how fundamentally Kang's ideas and the radical theories of the young reformers threatened the core values and institutions of the social order, opposition began to form. According to these critics, the reforms and the theories of these radicals were not aimed at a defensive self-strengthening of China, but were aggressively subverting Chinese tradition and making revolutionary changes in the social order. They saw the ideas, institutions, and traditional sociopolitical structure under attack.

In summer 1898, the opposition was headed by Wang Xianqian and Ye Dehui (1864–1927). They gradually gained the support of reform-minded officials like Zhang Zhidong and Chen Baozhen. A good friend of Gov. Chen Baozhen, Wang had done much to support the initial moderate reforms in Hunan. According to Wang himself, it was only in February 1898, when he attended the inauguration of the South China Study Society that he began to doubt the course of the reform movement. The event took place at the Changsha Hall of Filial Purity *(Xiaolian tang)*[37] on February 21, 1898. More than three hundred people attended: commoners as well as provincial officials and gentry.[38] The opening address was given by the new chairman, Pi Xirui (1850–1908). Huang Zunxian, Tan Sitong, and Gov. Chen Baozhen also spoke. Wang was alarmed by the unorthodox tone of the speeches. Articles subsequently published in the *Hunan News* sounded even more threatening. Later, when Ye Dehui brought him materials from the curriculum of the Current Affairs School, Wang was completely convinced that Kang Youwei and his followers were plotting rebellion.[39]

Ye Dehui, a native of Xiangtan, Hunan, was only 34 years old in 1898. He was quite different from Wang Xianqian but equally important. Ye was a brilliant scholar and bibliophile and had earned the highest *jinshi* degree in 1889.[40] He had served on the Board of Civil Appointments before he retired on a large inheritance. He spent much of his wealth on books, and he was also a connoisseur of painting. He firmly believed that study was the gateway to moral cultivation. As for the nation, Ye believed that China's best hope was to avoid all kinds of Western influence, so he had never taken any part in the self-strengthening projects in Hunan's reforms. His extreme rightist views, which conflicted with those of the young reformers, forced the Hunanese gentry to find a middle ground, a quest that became the conservative reaction of 1898.

Actually, when the radical reformers spoke of "equality" in the South China Study Society, they meant equality within the elite. Their explicit goal was to expand gentry power. Many of them were influenced by such early Qing thinkers as Gu Yanwu (1613–1682), who had suggested that hereditary magistrates serve in their own provinces. Kang, Liang, and the young reformers often expressed opposition to the "law of avoidance" that prohibited it, which clearly showed their attempt to extend local gentry influence.[41]

Wang Xianqian and the senior Hunanese elite sought to preserve the gentry's position and also to fight the radical reformers' theory of "equality" within the elite. They found utterly unacceptable the idea that young men like Tan Sitong and Tang Caichang should be treated the same as the senior Hanlin scholars. The emerging conservative gentry felt the essence of Confucianism was opposed to such new theories that challenged the hierarchic order of society. Wang and the senior gentry were also disturbed by the young reformers' new interpretations of the classics. However, they were also inclined to defend Confucian orthodoxy on the basis of pure self-interest. With Kang Youwei rising to pre-eminence in Beijing and Liang Qichao uniting young Hunanese in schools and study societies in Changsha, the long-established gentry domination of Hunanese society and politics was threatened. They were also concerned that the prominence of the Hunanese in the imperial bureaucracy would end. Even worse to Wang and the conservative elite was the likelihood that Kang, Liang, and their new Cantonese group already controlled the youth of Hunan. As one Hunan conservative put it, "Above, they [the reformers] have Cantonese support; below, they have a factional mob."[42] Wang Xianqian himself also warned Gov. Chen Baozhen:

> Kang Youwei's sentiments are perverse and rebellious. This everyone knows. His sworn partisans from Guangdong province support him most strongly. The situation is particularly difficult to fathom. They use Western studies to make themselves

cultured and contact Western individuals to make themselves important. Their basic intention is to move north into Hunan, and their activities (to this end) have not changed.[43]

It was clear that the Western learning that Kang, Liang, and their devotees from Guangdong advocated also threatened the Hunanese conservatives and enhanced their resistance. First, conservative gentry like Ye Dehui firmly believed that keeping Chinese learning untainted by Western influences was the best hope for China. Second, the conservative Hunanese gentry never forgot how fiercely Hunan had resisted the pseudo-Christian Taiping rebels from Guangdong and Guangxi provinces half a century before and how courageously the *Xiang jun* (Hunan Army) under the leadership of Zeng Guofan had finally put down the rebellion. They often seemed to see a reincarnation of the Taiping rebellion in Kang and Liang. Although charges that the reformers were spreading both Western learning and Christianity were somewhat paranoid, it was plausible that a "factional gang" of New Text scholars from Guangdong could gain control of the educational apparatus of Hunan. If Kang's or Liang's theories eclipsed the conservative orthodoxy, Wang and his colleagues and students would be cut off from participation in the educational or political bureaucracy. The relationship between scholarship and political power in China had been institutionalized through the civil service examination system for centuries, and the linkage was strong.

Tensions and accusations gradually increased in Changsha. In early June 1898, a group of students at the Yuelu Academy petitioned Wang Xianqian to request that Gov. Chen dismiss Liang Qichao as dean at the Current Affairs School. They condemned Liang's unorthodox ideas of "people's rights" and political "equality." "If the authority (of the emperor) is brought down, who will govern?" the students petitioned. "If the people can govern themselves, what is the function of the emperor? These (political ideas) will lead the empire to chaos." "[These radicals] will mislead the students to become rebels with no respect to their fathers and the emperor."[44]

The petition from the students at the Yuelu Academy elicited an angry response from students at the Current Affairs School. Xu Renzhu, the educational commissioner, initially supported the students at the Current Affairs School and attacked those at Yuelu. But Wang Xianqian sided with Yuelu and Xu's voice was suppressed. Wang Xianqian, Ye Dehui, Zhang Zhidong, and seven others petitioned Gov. Chen to replace Liang Qichao.[45] The Hunanese gentry not only petitioned the governor but took their protests to Beijing. Xiong Xiling, therefore, recommended replacing all the conservatives (academic heads) with "enlightened, upright, universal scholars" so as to keep the conservatives "out of touch with current affairs."[46]

Xiong's suggestion was not adopted. Bitter debates continued, but the conservatives soon increased the pressure, and the radical reform leadership began to fall apart. One by one, the young reformers left Hunan. Some were virtually driven out; some, like Liang Qichao and Tan Sitong, found that even as reform sputtered in Hunan, greater opportunities were available in Beijing, where the imperial Hundred Days Reform was just starting.[47] On June 8, 1898, Pi Xirui resigned his chairmanship of the South China Study Society and left Hunan for his native Nanchang. In the middle of June, Xiong Xiling resigned his directorship at the Current Affairs School, and the assistant deans who came to the school with Liang Qichao also left for Guangdong. Later, Gov. Chen Baozhen enforced stricter censorship of the *Hunan News*, at the insistence of Zhang Zhidong. Late in summer 1898, Tang Caichang also headed for Beijing, at the invitation of Tan Sitong, but he had only just arrived in Hankou when he learned of the death of his friend. Tan had obtained a job in the Grand Council and played a key role in the Hundred Days Reform: He was one of six reformers executed when the reform movement was suppressed by the Empress Dowager Cixi's coup d'état in September.

After the coup, the imperial court wiped out the remnants of radical reform in Hunan, bringing changes in the province to an abrupt end. The imperial government then appointed the conservative lieutenant governor, Yu Liansan, to replace Chen Baozhen as governor of Hunan.[48] The Empress Dowager Cixi issued a decree on October 6, 1898 in which she ordered Zhang Zhidong to close down the South China Study Society and the Police Bureau (*Baoweiju*) and to burn all reform documents from the Study Society.[49] The Current Affairs School lingered for a short time under the supervision of Wang Xianqian. However, only about forty students remained, and all the progressive faculty and students left or were expelled. In 1899, the school was moved to another location in Changsha, and its name was changed to the Academy for Practical Learning (*Qiushi shuyuan*). The *Hunan News* had already ceased publication in August. Of the important reform institutions, only the Police Bureau (*Baoweiju*) was maintained intact: The new governor explained that actually it was only a different name for *baojia*, the traditional system of neighborhood security.[50]

Aftermath of Reform: Division and Revolution

It was easy to expel the radical reformers of 1898 from Hunan and to close down the institutions they established in the province, but the reform controversy over Confucian doctrine persisted. The province became divided into two groups, conventionally known as the "new faction" (the radicals) and the "old faction" (the conservatives).

The controversy over doctrine hardened into political divisions. Influential senior gentry like Wang Xianqian and Zhang Zhidong, who had supported the initial stage of the reform movement, now joined with those conservatives who believed that the change had gone too far. They pledged their loyalty to the Empress Dowager Cixi after her coup and took up the task of reaffirming Confucian orthodoxy while strengthening the traditional social and political order.

Although exiled and suppressed, the young Hunanese radical reformers of 1898 held onto their vision of sociopolitical progress and national power. The young patriots with new ideas were determined to break into or destroy the established gentry domination of local social and political power. However, repudiation of reform by the Qing court made the radical reformers rebel against the legitimate government. Their political status was now no different from that of the revolutionary, Sun Yat-sen, or from the more powerful leaders of illegal secret societies. Because their regular road to advancement and their usual access to legitimate sources of political influence were cut off, the radical reformers of 1898 joined Kang Youwei, Liang Qichao, and other Cantonese as exiles in Japan.[51]

In 1900, Tang Caichang and other Hunanese radical reformers of 1898 recruited a large army from the secret societies in Hunan and Hubei provinces for a revolt against the Qing government, with the encouragement of Kang Youwei's *Baohuang hui* (Protect the Emperor Society). Lewis argues that the cooperation between the radical reformers and the secret societies helped to attract the masses' participation in the movement for change.[52] Tang's uprising was suppressed. He and his followers were beheaded on the Wuchang execution grounds. Tang died a martyr to reform as had his friend, Tan Sitong. Tang's head was displayed outside a Wuchang gate the following day, on Zhang Zhidong's orders. It was reported that his eyes remained open, staring outward.[53]

The hope of many young Hunanese reformers to establish a strong and reformed imperial China died with Tang Caichang. The surviving Hunanese reformers were disheartened and turned toward a revolutionary violent overthrow of the political system. On the other hand, the conservative Hunanese gentry, threatened by Kang-Liang heterodoxy, backed up the provincial officials in their effort to maintain the conventional social political order and to cultivate orthodox values.

The Opening of Hunan

After 1898, foreigners began to penetrate into Hunan. Hunan was a province long known for its anti-foreignism. Throughout the nineteenth century, Hunanese had fought fiercely and successfully to prevent any foreigners from entering the province. However, conservative forces could not overcome the impact of the British belligerence of 1891, the Japanese victory in the Sino-Japanese War of 1894–1895, and the scramble for concessions in 1897–1898. Traditional Hunanese xenophobia was clearly out of date. Even in the early 1890s, Hunan's provincial officials were able to moderate the xenophobia of the Hunanese literati. During the reform controversy of 1898, xenophobia was rationalized intellectually by both radicals and conservatives. As anti-foreignism began to break down, imperialist penetration into Hunan proceeded rapidly. Missionaries hoped to convert the Hunanese and save their souls, while merchants were eager to open the resources and markets of central China.

In the eight years from 1899 to 1906, four treaty ports, Yuezhou (1899), Changsha (1904), Changde (1906), and Xiangtan (1906), were opened in Hunan.[54] The opening of Changsha was the key to Hunan, not because of Changsha's economic importance, but because it was the political and cultural center of the province. The Hunanese resistance to foreign entry was based on political and cultural xenophobia; thus, the opening of the capital city signified an overcoming or at least a neutralizing of Hunanese anti-foreign influence.

Meanwhile, foreign commercial interest in Hunan increased rapidly. As foreign commercial expansion got underway, it accompanied and assisted the missionary intrusion into the province. Powerful gunboats on the rivers of Hunan protected and reinforced the privileges and the treaty rights of the Western merchants and missionaries. Large amounts of cheap manufactured goods were imported to Hunan, which interrupted the traditional pattern of trade and threatened the authority of the local gentry. More important, it helped to awaken Hunanese consciousness of their economic rights. However, the expansion of foreign interests did not meet the traditional hostilities in Hunan, which were confined to remote areas of the province after 1900. Instead, expansion was facilitated by the protection and cooperation of government officials and provincial elites.

The earlier absolute anti-foreignism, based on faith in orthodox Confucian doctrines, gave way to political nationalism. The Hunanese realized that the security of China did not depend on doctrinal ortho-doxy but on industrial changes, on demands for material power patterned on the West, and on the recovery of Chinese economic rights. The new China would not be built on moral principles but on railways and mines. Unlike the old literati-based anti-foreign movement, the emerging politi-cal nationalism that tried to turn back the imperialist tide called for a different response to confronting the foreigners. Instead of fearing and injuring the foreigners, the political nationalists advocated that the Chi-nese argue with them in a friendly way to recover their rights. Unlike the reform movement of 1898, which was confined to radical patriots, the newly emerging nationalism involved many varied groups of people.

As foreign penetration extended into Hunan, the provincial elite strengthened reform programs that had begun in the 1890s. The provin-cial elite had to embark on industrial and commercial activities, which in many aspects were identical with the goals of the imperial court. By 1907, a strong reform movement led and dominated by the provincial elite partially restrained foreign expansion in Hunan. This next wave of reform fit right into the atmosphere of the new nationalism.

Chapter 2

From Confucian Academy to Modern School

Educational Reform in Hunan, 1900–1911

After 1900, the growing threat of imperialism became the dominant concern of Hunan's external relations, while education reform became the major focus of internal debate. Suppression of the reform movement of 1898 and the uprising of 1900 re-established the conservative gentry as the dominant power in the province.

Yang Nianqun's[1] chapter on Hunan and Daniel McMahon's[2] article make great contributions to the study of the Yuelu Academy and its place in Hunan literati activism. Yuelu remained as a traditional Confucian academy until 1919 when it was incorporated into Hunan University. Therefore, I focus on Hunan First Normal, which was converted into a modern school from Chengnan Academy in 1903.

Members of the provincial elite became leaders in the new nationalist movement to recover provincial rights to mining, railways, and industrial and transportation enterprises.[3] Although they were in relative agreement on promoting technological and economical reforms, they still held different views about issues of education reform. Some advocated Western-type curricula, new types of schools, and the abolition of the civil service examinations. Others, including the conservatives who had participated in suppressing the radical reform movement of 1898, defended the traditional values and institutions against the rapid expansion of Western learning. Initially, they had the support of the conservative governor, Yu Liansan, who launched a reactionary attack on the new educational policies. However, the conservatives were no more successful than before in preventing the forceful reintroduction of reforms. In fact, they were driven from the center stage in 1905 when the civil service examinations were abolished by Beijing.[4]

In the early twentieth century, when the Hunanese conservative elites were reacting against the educational reforms in the province, the central government and public opinion elsewhere were favoring reform in response to the catastrophe caused by the Boxer Rebellion.[5] In the meantime, educational reform projects became very popular: New-style schools, new types of study societies, and newspaper publishing houses kept springing up around the country. The Qing court, therefore, announced a political reform known as the New Policies (*Xinzheng*) in 1901.[6]

Directed by the proposals of Zhang Zhidong and other high officials, the central government set up a national school system, sent students for overseas study, formed a modern army, built railways, promoted industry, abolished the civil service examinations, reformed the bureaucracy, and finally, in 1906, prepared for constitutional government.

The most significant aspect of the New Policies was education reform. One of Beijing's first decrees in this regard was an edict issued in September 1901 ordering all Confucian academies to be converted into new-style schools. In 1902 and 1903, the Qing government issued additional new decrees on education reform.[7] These new policies were aimed at abolishing civil service examinations, reinforcing the establishment of new-style schools, and sending students overseas to study. Under the reform decrees, all the Confucian academies were to be converted into a regional hierarchy of modern-style schools at the provincial, prefectural, and counties levels. The provincial academies were to be converted into upper-level universities (*Da xuetang*), the academies of the prefectures to middle-level universities (*Zhong xuetang*), and the academies of the counties to low-level universities (*Xiao xuetang*).

Changsha had three Confucian academies at that time. Chengnan Academy was typical of the educational approach and history. Chengnan was founded by a famous Southern Song Confucian, Zhang Shi,[8] in the twelfth century. The teaching method of the Chengnan Academy combined independent study, questions and answers among students, and gathering for public lectures. Its main curriculum was the study of the Confucian classics. The students also occasionally had discussions on current affairs. The Chengnan Academy had a profound impact on the development of Hunan's academic thinking and culture. "It is the place where former great scholars had visited and offered instructions and enlightenment; where young scholars with great potentials gather; where the youths of Hunan are vying to come and study" (*xixian guohua zhidi, lanzhi shengting, qizi rushi, ze xiangzhong zidi zhenglai jiangxue zhiqu ye*).[9]

In 1822, Emperor Daoguang (r. 1821–1850) wrote four Chinese characters, "*li ze feng chang*," in his own handwriting to praise the Chengnan Academy. The characters mean: "Classmates temper and challenge each other in learning, and the place is imbued with scholarship." The emperor's inscription hung on a framed board at the main lecture hall of the academy.

When the New Policies decrees on education were issued, Hunan governor, Yu Liansan, supported and encouraged by conservative gentry like Wang Xianqian and Ye Dehui, resisted them as far as he thought possible. In response to the call for converting traditional academies (*shuyuan*) into modern universities (*xuetang*), Gov. Yu and his subordinates, with the support of the local conservative elite, argued that the education at the three main Confucian academies in Changsha was too classical and the students were too old to adapt their classical studies to a new curriculum. Yu and his supporters simply wanted to maintain the three leading academies unchanged. They turned only the former Current Affairs School into the modern school.[10]

In response to the call for sending students abroad to study, Gov. Yu and his subordinates permitted twelve students to be sent abroad to study for six months. The twelve students were carefully selected. All were mature degree holders and were most likely well grounded in traditional Chinese learning.[11] In June 1902, when the provincial Bureau of Education (*xuewuchu*) was established, the governor announced a set of pedagogical principles:

1. Nurture a virtuous character so as to produce loyal and obedient (students).

2. Encourage knowledge for practical use.

3. Stimulate ambition so as to shake off lethargy.[12]

These educational principles sounded similar to the spirit of the Self-Strengthening Movement of the nineteenth century, and were not even close to the essence of the twentieth-century reform movement.

Although the conservatives were able in some degree to subvert the intentions of Beijing's educational reform edicts in Hunan, the new-style schools proliferated throughout the nation. New kinds of teachers were urgently needed. In 1902, regular teacher training was mandated by the Ministry of Education.

Under the pressures of these circumstances, Gov. Yu established the Hunan Normal School (*Shifan guan*) in February 1903. The mission of the new provincial normal school was to train county elementary school teachers. The Normal School was located in the Changsha mansion of a rich member of the gentry. Gov. Yu appointed Wang Xianqian, a leading provincial conservative and Yu's key advisor on educational affairs, to be the director of the school. He hoped that although the educational structure was new, the content would remain unchanged.[13]

In its first year, the Hunan Normal School had only sixty students, all in the same class. Its curriculum included mathematics and other scientific subjects. It had fifteen or sixteen subjects in total but it still adhered to the philosophy of "Chinese learning for essentials, Western learning for practical use."[14] One-fourth of the curriculum consisted of reading the classics in the old-fashioned way and developing literary skills. Its teaching method and administration mainly followed that of the Yuelu Academy and the Chengnan Academy. However, it trained its students in mathematics, arts, and other "Western" subjects that had never been taught in Confucian academies before. Therefore, the school functioned as a model for educational modernization in the province. The founding of the Hunan Normal School also marked the beginning of teacher training education in Hunan.

The Formation of the Hunan First Normal School

Not until early in 1903, when Yu Liansan was replaced by a new governor, Zhao Erxun (1844–1927), did effective reform measures take hold in the province. Zhao Erxun was a Hanlin scholar, Chinese bannerman, and an official whose word carried some weight. Zhao was committed to a modern curriculum. He soon converted the Yuelu and Chengnan academies in Changsha into modern schools. He ordered the building of many new primary and secondary schools, introduced Western subjects and Western-style curricula, and saw to the purchase of modern textbooks.[15] In November 1903, Zhao sent a memorial to the throne to convert the Chengnan Academy into the Hunan Provincial Normal School. His proposal was approved. Zhao appointed the reform-minded scholar Liu Diwei to be the principal of the new school.

The conservative gentry did not like Zhao's reform measures at all. In particular Wang Xianqian and Liu Caijiu, the respective heads of Chengnan and Yuelu academies, protested the reform measures vigorously. Wang and the conservatives were unhappy about the curricula of the new school system and condemned the helter-skelter pace of classroom training. Wang wrote:

> Whenever the bell rings, students rush into the classroom and pick up books to recite. How can they expect to obtain true comprehension through this kind of training? It is said in the *Great Learning* that 'only with calmness of mind can one attain serene repose; only in serene repose can one carry on careful deliberation.' Now the classroom instruction is broken into several sessions and many students are crowded into one room. How can students in this kind of situation possibly have any 'calmness of mind' or 'serene repose,' not to mention 'careful deliberation?' "[16]

Wang urged that the new schools be closed and that students "study at home for the civil service examinations so that Chinese learning can at least be preserved. . . . The vast amount of money now being spent on these schools can perhaps be better used in developing our industry."[17]

The conservatives also deplored the new schools' stress on lectures to large groups of students, which to them seemed structurally closer to Christian churches (*Jiaotang*) than to any traditional Chinese system of education.

However, the conservative elite as represented by Wang Xianqian had no influence with the new governor, who would not listen to Wang's suggestions as had the previous governor. In protest, Wang resigned his position as director of the Hunan Normal School and "sat and looked on while the atmosphere daily deteriorated."[18]

Gov. Zhao appointed the reform-minded scholar Liu Diwei to take Wang's place as director of the Hunan Normal School. When the Chengnan Academy was converted into the Hunan Provincial Normal School in November 1903, Liu was also the principal of that school. In March 1914, the provincial government combined the two schools into one modern school, called the Hunan Provincial First Normal School, which eventually became the Hunan First Normal School.[19] Liu was active in reforming the school's philosophy, curriculum, and administrative system. In the following year, the school had 130 students, divided into three classes.

Evolution of First Normal and Political Culture, 1903–1912

In the first few years of the twentieth century, there was an alternating pattern of progress and back lash in Hunan's government leadership. First came the reform-minded governor Chen Baozhen, followed by the conservative Yu Liansan, and then the energetic reformer Zhao Erxun. In May 1904, Zhao was replaced by Lu Yuanding, an educational obscurantist. First events moved ahead, then the pace of reform was retarded. This frustrating situation lasted until 1907. During these years, there was no consistent policy of reform.

Advised and supported by the conservatives, Gov. Lu suppressed a newly opened girls' school, condemned the loss of moral cultivation in the converted Yuelu Academy, now a new-style high school, and established a more conservative school, which required its students to have a strong background in the Chinese classics before moving on to Western learning. Although Lu's governorship in Hunan slowed down the pace of educational reform, the damage was not great, as he only stayed for six months. Lu was succeeded by the energetic Manchu reformer Duan Fang, who himself only stayed in Hunan for seven months until summoned to the capital in the summer of 1905.[20] During Duan Fang's short stay, reforms, and especially educational reforms, were carried out earnestly.

By 1907, because of the rapid change of governors and the inconsistent policy of reform, the development of the Hunan school system was uneven and limited to major cities, especially to the capital city of Changsha. At 419, the number of lower primary schools was small.[21] Hunan, however, had made great progress in secondary education, such as the upper primary grades, middle school, normal schools, and technical schools. Most of these modern schools were concentrated in urban areas.

The Hunan First Normal School developed rapidly during the first years of its existence, although several principals followed each other in rapid succession. In September 1905, Tan Yankai became principal. During his tenure, the auditorium and student dormitories were built. In 1906, the school was enlarged to 250 students, divided into six classes. Tan was the first to adopt a Japanese-style curriculum. After that, the First Normal School continued to use the Japanese-style curriculum until

1925. Tan also established an accelerated Normal School (*jianyi shifan xuetang*),[22] which was the equivalent of a junior normal school, on the Miaoguo Hill. Liu Renxi succeeded Tan in November 1906, continuing Tan's reforming policies and practices.

In October 1908, Qu Zongduo assumed the job as principal. Qu formally clarified the mission of the school as training county elementary school teachers. He standardized the program into a five-year format whose first year was a one-year preparatory period. Students had to be older than 14 years to enroll in the Preparatory Department (*yuke*) for the first year and older than 15 to register in the Undergraduate Department. After 1909, First Normal became a formal secondary normal school with a unified admission system, training goals, and length of schooling. First Normal has remained a secondary normal school down to the present.

The curriculum changed very little during the first nine years of the school's history. Included in the curriculum, were sixteen subjects: Chinese literary skills, Confucian classics, moral cultivation, education, English language, translation (from Manchu into Chinese), history, geography, mathematics, physics, chemistry, science, crafts, drawing, music, and physical education. Many of the courses were Western subjects new to the Confucian academies.

Teachers were chosen by a strict selection process; only those who were well educated could be hired. Although the Principals of First Normal in the first nine years of the school changed rapidly, the teachers and curriculum established reformist continuity at the school. Besides, these principals were all regarded as "the best learned persons in their own times" (*jie biaobingguan yishi*), although some of them were politically conservative. The first principal of the school, Wang Xianqian, was a well-known scholar of the Han school of classical philosophy who wrote and edited large numbers of influential books. Principal Tan Yankai was a member of the prestigious Hanlin Academy. Principal Wang Da (1872–1927) was a famous scholar of geography. Principal Wang Fengchang was a well-known specialist in education. The teachers were academically accomplished also. This was especially true during the period of Tan's headmastership when he hired a whole group of reform-minded gentry to conduct classes at the school. Tan even invited two foreigners to be teachers, one from Japan and the other from the United States.[23] The teaching staff of the school was small in number, but highly professional and capable.[24]

First Normal was generously funded by the provincial government and attracted the best students in the province. The school enlarged its physical plant and new teaching materials for history, geography, and science were purchased. A larger library also served a growing student body. From 60 students in 1903, the school grew to 252 students in 1911. After 1904, the enrollment quota was fixed at about 250. During the year when Tan Yankai was principal, however, enrollment reached 400. The school graduated about 450 students during the first nine years of its existence (1903–1912). Among these 450 graduates, about 40 went to Japan to study, about 100 pursued advanced studies, and many became leading figures in Hunan educational reforms.[25]

Education in the First Normal School in the first nine years was always subject to a reforming process, but continued to manifest various inconsistencies and contradictions. On the one hand, the school was converted from an old-style Confucian academy into a modern school by adopting new teaching methods and the new Japanese-style curriculum, which taught a lot of Western subjects; on the other hand, the school still emphasized the educational philosophy of "Chinese learning for essentials, Western learning for practical use." Its curriculum focused on literary courses but underestimated scientific subjects. Confucian classics, moral cultivation, and translation were required courses for all students. Confucian classics were especially important as they made up a large part of the curriculum. Even so, the First Normal School was still one of the most distinguished academic institutions in the province because it attracted well-known scholars and the best students from Hunan. The educational reforms enacted by the school and the resulting political culture there in the first decade of the twentieth century laid a favorable foundation for further evolution under the Republic, one that would infuse in the students a philosophy and an ethics of commitment to social change and that would contribute to the growth of radicalism.[26]

Upheaval in Hunan and Reform Under the Republic

The Qing dynasty collapsed after the Republican Revolution in fall 1911. The First Normal School, which had been relatively closely linked to the old regime, survived to play a formative role in the society that followed, although a backdrop of political tumult continued from 1911 to 1917.

Tan Yankai, formerly the principal of First Normal, replaced Jiao Dafeng (1887–1911) in the post of military governor of Hunan in October 1911. Tan undertook a policy of political stabilization in Hunan and actively supported the national revolutionary cause. His priority was to avoid turmoil. To this end, Tan Yankai formed a provincial government made up of members of the Provincial Assembly and returned students from Japan. All the appointees essentially shared Tan's views. Also, all the appointees were residents of Changsha during the revolution. The returned students were sons of well-to-do gentry families. Thus, the new provisional government was very much a regime of the new urban elite.

With the support of the most important provincial gentry, the reformist elite, Tan Yankai forced hostile elements, particularly military leaders to submit. One of his first acts was to trim the swollen military. Tan also launched a reform on the three-hundred-year-old tax-collection system, which allowed him to refill the empty treasury. These accomplishments demonstrated the efficiency and competence of decentralized, federalist government. They also showed Hunan's strenuous objection to Yuan Shikai's efforts at bureaucratic and financial centralization.

With aggressive political manipulation and campaigning, Tan's government sought republican legitimacy in the elections of 1912–1913. In party politics, Tan's regime opposed Yuan Shikai but supported the Nationalist Party. The Nationalist Party had been formed in Beijing in August 1912 from the old revolutionary *Tongmenghui* (Revolutionary Alliance) and four other smaller parties. Meanwhile, those who generally supported Yuan had come together in the Republican Party (*Gonghe-dang*), which was also formed in August 1912.[27] Tan was invited by the Nationalist Party in Beijing to be chairman of the Hunan branch. Tan accepted and brought the entire Hunan urban elite with him to the Nationalist Party. The goal of the Nationalist Party was to unify the opposition to Yuan Shikai and to check his power by gaining a parliamentary majority in the elections scheduled for 1912–1913. The Nationalist Party, in the end, did win an overwhelming victory in Hunan. It did so not as a popular revolutionary party, but as the representative of the liberal urban elite and its opportunist allies.[28]

With the departure of Tan Yankai, Tang Xiangming became governor of Hunan. Tang was a foreign-trained naval officer from Hubei province. In October 1913, Yuan Shikai appointed Tang to succeed Tan as governor of Hunan. Tang's task was to uproot "disorderly parties" and strengthen central control over Hunan's administrative machinery. In August 1913, Yuan had already closed down the provincial assembly and other representative bodies. When Tang arrived at Changsha in October, he selected his own men to take all the important positions. He even arrested sixteen former officials of Tan's government who had spoken or acted against Yuan, to win favor with Yuan's central government.[29] Yet Tang realized that the hostile relationship between his force from the

North and the local elites could not be allowed to remain for the long term. He needed cooperation and support from the provincial elites. For their part, some members of the provincial elites were prepared to cooperate with Tang for the sake of preserving peace and order and for maintaining their power and advancing in their careers. Therefore, it was not surprising that some of the provincial elites joined the Peace Planning Society in late 1915 to support Yuan's imperial ambitions.[30] The seventy-one so-called "Hunan people's delegates" even voted to "respectfully ask our great president to assume the emperorship" on October 28, 1915.[31]

During Tang's rule in Hunan (October 1913 to July 1916), the Hunanese experienced a degree of terror imposed by Yuan Shikai's followers. For instance, special detectives conducted house-to-house searches looking for pro-Nationalist Party elements. They were said to have used all kinds of tortures, such as forcing bamboo splinters under fingernails, forcing prisoners to lie on hot coals, pulling off the scalp, and so on. One of Mao Zedong's biographers, Li Rui, maintained that Tang killed about five thousand people during his governorship in Hunan.[32] Others report lower figures. Tang's cruelty and dictatorship did not intimidate the Hunanese; on the contrary, it provoked strong rebellions, especially from the oppressed lower orders of the society.

When Tang Xiangming left Hunan, Tan Yankai assumed for the second time the formal leadership of the province as civil and military governor. Tan's second administration lasted a year, from August 1916 to September 1917.[33]

The Educational Policy of the Republic

The new Republican government began to issue a series of reform policies in 1912. Provisional President Sun Yat-sen appointed Cai Yuanpei the Republic of China's first minister of education in January 1912. This clearly showed that educational policy would change profoundly under the new regime. Cai had earned the highest civil service examination degree of *jinshi* in 1890, at the age of 23, one of the youngest candidates ever. In 1892, he was named to the prestigious Hanlin Academy, and in 1894 became a compiler there.[34] Cai thus had the best scholarly credentials available under the imperial system.[35] In 1906, disillusioned with the revolutionary politics he had once supported, Cai Yuanpei left to study in Europe: He received a bachelor of arts degree in 1910 from the University of Leipzig.[36] With such deep exposure to both Chinese and Western education, Cai was an ideal candidate to run the Ministry of Education for the new Republic.

Cai assembled talented young scholars for his staff. He appointed Fan Yuanlian (1875–1927) to be vice minister. Fan, as an assistant professor, had helped organize anti-Russian demonstrations at the Imperial University of Peking (*Jingshi daxue tang*) in 1903. Cai appointed Jiang Weiqiao (1873–1958) to be chief secretary. Jiang had been involved in the China Educational Association and later served as principal of the Patriotic Girls' School. Cai invited Lu Xun (Zhou Shuren, 1881–1936), who had studied medicine in Japan and become the best-known writer in China, to serve in a junior position at the Ministry of Education.

In February 1912, Cai published his proposals for the Republic's new educational codes in an article entitled "Opinions Concerning Educational Principles" (*Duiyu jiaoyu fangzhen zhi yijian*).[37] In that article, Cai maintained that education in the imperial Qing dynasty had been subordinate to politics, and that education under the new Republic had to be based on the people's will, and therefore beyond government control. Cai opposed the educational principles laid out in 1906 by the Qing. He pointed out that the imperial emphasis on loyalty to the emperor was totally incompatible with the essence of Republican government. Similarly, its reverence for Confucius contradicted the spirit of freedom in belief.

Cai advocated that education should proceed from creating happiness in the world while finally realizing the "world of reality" (*shiti shijie*) or the "world of substance" (*guannian shijie*). He held, however, that the Qing emphasis on military, utilitarian, and moral education should be retained. He said these and "education for citizens' morality"[38] were the basis for creating "happiness in this world" (*xianshi xingfu*). He also called for "education for a worldview" (*shijie guan jiaoyu*) and "aesthetic education" (*meigan zhi jiaoyu*). "Education for a worldview" was intended to break the monopoly status of Confucianism by emphasizing the importance of non-Chinese philosophies, as well as other native Chinese thought. Cai believed that "education for a worldview" amounted to seeking the "world of reality." "Aesthetic education" posed an alternative to the religious spirit of Confucianism by teaching students the Kantian idea that beauty and solemnity can link the phenomenal world and the world of reality, therefore allowing people to feel closer to the force that created the universe.[39] Cai held that "aesthetic education" was a means for reaching the "world of reality."

Cai Yuanpei's educational viewpoint provided the essential pedagogical foundation for the Republican government to work out its educational principles. At the Provisional Educational Conference in 1912, Cai advocated reforming schools by changing the length of the school year, having boys and girls study at the same elementary schools, and abolishing the course on intensive reading of the Confucian classics. Soon after that, the Ministry of Education issued a series of principles dealing with comprehensive school education, collectively known as "The School System in the Years 1911 and 1912" (*Renzi. guichou xuezhi*).[40] By the time these principles were promulgated in late 1912, Cai Yuanpei had resigned to protest Yuan Shihai's dictatorship.[41]

Educational Reforms at First Normal, 1911–1919

Cai Yuanpei's national policies provided a favorable context for educational reform in Hunan. Moreover, the spirit of literati reformism had never really ceased in Hunan. The provincial literati dissidents had consciously detached themselves from their own heritage; beginning in 1898, they first became known as radical intellectual reformers. They then became known politically as anti-Qing revolutionists, and eventually, in an ideological and social context, they became Marxists and Marxist organizers of the masses. After the revolution of 1911, although the conservative politics of stabilization still dominated the province, there was an obvious advancement of the "liberal regime" headed by Tan Yankai. This liberal regime made great efforts in education, judicial reform, and modern industrialization; collectively they should be regarded as an extension of the late-Qing reforms.

Tan Yankai's continuation of the Qing reforms is most strikingly apparent in education, where Tan and his elite reformist associates had won an enormous triumph over their conservative adversaries. Thus, the way was open for the large-scale establishment of modern schools. Several professional training schools, such as an engineering school, law school, and business school were set up in the province. The new schools were so numerous and opened so quickly that one reporter described the situation as equivalent to their "growing like trees in a forest."[42]

The general atmosphere of educational reform in the province permitted the First Normal School to explore and develop modern education according to its own practices. The fact that the First Normal School could initiate educational reforms in Hunan province was the

result of the victory of the provincial reformist elite over their conservative opponents. It was also the result of the First Normal's implementa-
tion of Cai Yuanpei's reformist ideas and of the national educational
principles of the Ministry of Education.

After the revolution of 1911, First Normal had a four-month
interruption and resumed instruction in February 1912.[43] In April 1913,
reformist educator Kong Zhaoshou replaced Zeng Peilin (1878–1939)
as principal of the First Normal, and began to implement the reforming principles of the Ministry of Education. However, in January 1914,
military governor Tang Xiangming ordered the arrest of Kong Zhaoshou
for his opposition to Yuan Shikai. Kong fled to Japan.

In March 1914, the provincial government ordered the Fourth
Normal School merged into the First Normal and renamed the school
Hunan Provincial First Normal School. Zhang Gan, the mathematics teacher at First Normal, was appointed principal. Zhang not only
retained but expanded Kong's educational reforms in the school. Zhang's
principalship lasted only until August 1915, and three more principals
followed in rapid succession. By September 1916, Tan Yankai was governor once more, and he reappointed former principal Kong Zhaoshou,
who had just returned from exile in Japan. Kong's second principalship
lasted two years. During this period, the New Culture Movement began
to exert strong influence around the country. Kong was an ardent supporter of the New Culture Movement. Under his leadership, the First
Normal School quickly entered the mainstream of the movement. Kong
used what he had studied abroad to further reform education at First
Normal, making it more regular and systematic.[44]

The years between the 1911 revolution and the May Fourth Movement of 1919 were the best in the history of First Normal. During this
period, First Normal had the reformist, energetic educators Kong Zhaoshou and Zhang Gan as its principals, and also boasted a group of progressive and learned teachers. The intellectually dynamic school had
become the largest and most distinguished public academic institution
in Hunan and played an important mediating role in the transmission
of new ideas.

Chapter 3

The Milieu of Hunan First Normal, 1912–1919

The Setting of First Normal School

The Hunan First Normal School was located outside the south gate of Changsha city at the foot of a hill known as Miaogao Feng. The Hunan First Normal School was the only really modern building in Changsha in the early years of the Republic, and local people used to call it the "occidental building."[1] The school was surrounded by a wall, and outside the main gate was a road from which branched out several lesser streets. The city itself lay to the north, while to the south was a flight of some five hundred stone steps leading to the railway.[2]

The Xiang River, the largest in Hunan passed at some distance in front of the school. It was navigated by a constant stream of boats of varying sizes. In the middle of the river lay a long island, where thousands of orange trees had been planted, earning the island its popular name *Ju Zhou (Juzi Zhou)*, or Orange Island. When the oranges ripened, the isle looked from a distance like a golden-red cloud floating on the water.[3] Students from First Normal often composed poems referring to the "orange clouds" and the "orange-cloud isle." The beautiful Yuelu Mountain and the First Normal School faced each other across the Xiang River. With green undulating hills behind and the surging river in front, the First Normal School merged into a very picturesque scene.

The first fifteen years after the Republican Revolution of 1911 was a period of full bloom for the First Normal School. Before the Revolution, the school had been converted from a Confucian academy to one offering a Japanese-style curriculum combining traditional Chinese and

43

modern Western subjects. In 1926, the First Normal School, together with other Hunan secondary institutions, converted the Japanese-style curriculum (a double-track system that separated the ordinary middle schools from normal schools) into an American-style curriculum for comprehensive secondary education.[4]

During the period between 1911 and 1926, the First Normal School had Tan Yankai,[5] Kong Zhaoshou, and Zhang Gan (1884–1967) as its principals. During their terms as headmasters, they launched reforms in the school's policies, philosophy, practices, and curriculum. The First Normal soon stood among the foremost educational institutions in the province and attracted many well-known and highly respected teachers, such as Yang Changji, Xu Teli, Li Jinxi, and Fang Weixia. The school had a large faculty and student body comparable to other educational institutions in Hunan. Its admission policy was strict: Students took several entrance exams, and only those with top scores were admitted. During the first decade of the Republic, First Normal became the most distinguished academic institution in Hunan and functioned as major transmission routes for new ideas and political movements. It graduated about one thousand students during this period (1911–1919). Many became prominent figures in the Chinese Communist movement and in the Chinese educational field.

Contextualizing the education at First Normal into the larger changing circumstances of China at that time, shows the distinctiveness of this particular school and emphasizes how it shaped the students' thought and mindset and contributed to their intellectual transformation in the first decade of the twentieth century. In general, much of the school's curriculum followed the standard early Republican form, which included extensive Chinese-language classes that moved from more contemporary to classical readings, moral cultivation class, and physical education. However, First Normal reformed the standard early Republican curriculum to suit its own needs and added some more distinctive features, such as having students themselves pick moral exemplars from among their peers and holding regular essay-writing contests.

School Philosophy and Regulations

The mission of First Normal was to train teachers. It was assumed that school teachers were to function not only as educators but as leaders to promote a new civic spirit in the local community. The prevailing philosophy on the function of normal schools can be seen clearly in First Normal's advertisement for students. The first paragraph declared:

> The rise or fall of a nation totally depends on its people of talent; the increase or decrease of the nation's people of talent entirely relies upon the nation's education; whether the nation's education is good or bad is largely dependent on the education of normal schools. Normal schools offer education for educators; therefore, normal schools are the place to train models for the citizens to follow, In this way, normal schools can be regarded as the fountainhead for building up a young, strong, and wealthy society, the new China.[6]

First Normal made it clear that its purpose, its philosophy, its rules and regulations, its curriculum, its length of schooling, its admission system, enrollment, and assignment of graduates were centered on the goal of training elementary school teachers.

In September 1912, the Ministry of Education of the new Republic issued the "Decree on Principles for Education" (*Jiaoyu zongzhiling*),[7] which emphasized military, utilitarian, and moral education. However, moral education was deemed essential, whereas utilitarian and military education were subsidiary. Moral cultivation, the decree made clear, should be completed by means of "aesthetic education" (*meigan jiaoyu*). Based on this decree, First Normal put together its own principles for educating students, which were combined with its own principles for teacher training. The statement was named "The principle purpose of educating students" (*Jiaoyang xuesheng zhi yaozhi*). The main articles declared:

1. Since a healthy body provides the solid foundation for a healthy mind, we urge students to keep fit and to participate in sports.

2. Since building good character and having resolution are of the utmost importance in becoming a good teacher, it is important to train our students to be aesthetically aware and virtuous.

3. Being patriotic and law-abiding are the key element in becoming a good teacher. We should let students know the

fundamental importance of building up our nation, and let them understand that every citizen should take his share of responsibility and do his (or her) part of a task well.

4. Independence and universal love are of the utmost importance in becoming a good teacher, thus we should train our students to be morally cultivated and to develop their self-governing ability. We should train them to be humanitarian, to respect every individual, and to treat public affairs and the public interest as of the utmost importance.

5. Our Republic's philosophy of education emphasizes real practice, so we should let students understand the general situation of the current day, investigate the social realities, and seek truth from facts, so they can become people who work hard and contribute to society, and not become individuals who sit idle and enjoy the fruits of others' work.

6. Education for a worldview and an outlook on life is essential for spiritual education, so we should urge our students to study a philosophy of life so they can develop noble interests.

7. When giving lectures, the teacher should pay attention to his teaching methods, so when students become teachers in the future they will know how to teach.

8. When choosing materials for teaching, we should make sure that these materials are practical and useful to our students when they are teaching in the future.

9. Learning does not totally depend on professors' lectures. We should train our students to increase their interests in independent studies, so they can develop a capacity for individual initiative.[8]

These goals clearly show that First Normal focused particularly on moral, utilitarian, and military education, especially on moral cultivation. The school paid serious attention to aesthetic education and education on a worldview. The school also advocated voluntarism and self-governance. The emphasis on moral education, physical education, voluntarism, self-governance, and training for elementary school teachers became the tradition of the school.

First Normal adopted an educational policy that took the "people" as its essential focus, as articulated by decrees and officials of the Republican government. The school admonition or slogan (*xiaoxun*) was centered on "knowing or remembering the national humiliation" (*zhichi*). The admonition, which was rather reformist for its time, is outlined in Fig. 3.1. "Knowing the national humiliation" was placed at the center of the school's admonition, whereas public-spiritedness, sincerity, hard work, and thrift were subordinated to it. Education was divided into three parts: moral, intellectual, and physical. In order to thoroughly carry out the policy, First Normal added four requirements:

1. All professors should follow (and implement) the policy effectively in order to achieve a systematized and spiritual education.

2. One should constantly exploit "the national humiliation" to awaken the consciousness of the students.

3. All professors should advocate voluntarism.

4. Chinese is temporarily chosen as the united center of all departments.[9]

School authorities composed a school anthem.[10] There were only forty simple words in the anthem, which was easy for children to remember and sing. The purpose of the anthem was to arouse student interest and pride in becoming teachers, and to foster lofty ideals in them. First Normal also had a school flag, which was fringed with red tassels like the army flag of ancient times. There was a yellow dart in the flag; the flag itself was blue green in color, and in the middle was a white star. A black Chinese character *shi* (normal school) was embroidered in the center of the white star. The First Normal School also provided the students with school uniforms. All of these emblems and symbols indicate an effort to arouse the students' consciousness of patriotism and love of their school. It also showed the endeavor by school authorities to cultivate lofty ideals in the students.[11]

Under the direction of the "Regulations for Normal Schools" (*Shifan xuexiao guicheng*) from the Ministry of Education, which was issued in December 1912, and under the leadership of Kong, First Normal made some changes in the length of its school year based on consideration of its own state of affairs. There were two divisions in the Undergradu-

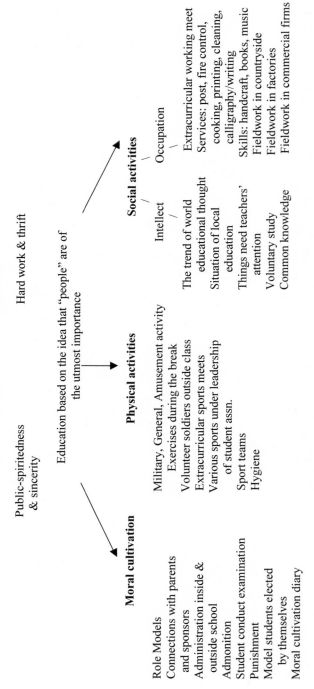

Figure 3.1. Hunan First Normal School Admonition (1911–1918).

ate Department of Teachers' Training (*shifan benke*), Division One and Division Two. The length of the course of study in Division One was five to five-and-half years. Before entering this division, all the students had to complete a one-year program of study, the first of five years, in the Preparatory Department (*yuke*) at the school. The graduates of the Preparatory Department would then be entitled to advance into the Undergraduate Department if they passed all their examinations. The length of study in Division Two of the Undergraduate Department was one year.

According to its own particular situation and needs, First Normal made some changes in the curriculum and course of study. They added four subjects to the Preparatory Department' original eight courses: history, geography, science, and handcraft. They believed that history and geography were the key elements of Chinese Language and Literature (*guowen*); science and handwork were considered essential to the direction of agriculture.

In the Undergraduate Department, the school's leaders also added subjects. To the first year's curriculum in the Undergraduate Department, they added geometry to the original mathematics class, geometric drawing to the original drawing class, as well as two new courses: physics and agriculture. They believed that charting/drawing was fundamentally important for working and regarded a clear understanding of physics and geometry as the basis for charting/drawing.[12]

Furthermore, Hunan was an agricultural province and agriculture deserved to be particularly emphasized. That was why First Normal added four subjects to the first year's curriculum in the Undergraduate Department. First Normal added two new subjects, economics and business, to the third year's curriculum in the Undergraduate Department, because China needed to compete in these areas to forestall European imperialism.

Because practice in agriculture and in industry was extremely important, First Normal made it a rule that each week all the students of First Normal, starting from the third year, should have three hours of practice either in agriculture or in industry after classes. The students could choose between the two. Because more classes were added to the original curriculum, the length of the course in the Undergraduate Department was extended by six months in 1913 (Table 3.1).

First Normal School, especially under the administration of Principal Kong in 1913, soon grew to be the key institution for carrying the Republic's educational reforms in Hunan. A public institution, funding for First Normal came from the provincial budget. All students had a

Table 3.1. Class hours per week by subject prescribed by the Curriculum of Divisions One and Two of the Undergraduate Department, 1913. (The History of Hunan First Normal School—1903–1949, p. 16.)

	Preparatory Dept.	Div. One Year 1	Div. One Year 2	Div. One Year 3	Div. One Year 4 Sem. 1,2	Div. One Year 4 Sem. 3	Div. Two
Moral Cultivation	2	1	1	1	1	1	1
Education	10	6	3	3	11	11	15
Chinese Classics	2	2	4	3	3	3	2
Calligraphy	2		2				
Foreign Language	4	4	4	3	3	3	
History	1	2	2	2	1		
Geography	1	2	2	2	1		
Mathematics	6	4	2	3			2
Science	1	2	2	2			2
Physics & Chemistry		1	2	3	3		2
Law & Economics				2	2	2	2
Drawing	2	2	2	2	2	2	2
Handwork	2	2	2	2	2	3	2
Music & Choir	1	2	1	1	1	1	1
Gym	4	4	4	4	4	4	3
Agriculture		2	2	2	2	2	2
Business				2	2	2	2
Total	36	36	35	37	38	34	36

tuition waiver. The school also provided each student a certain amount of money for necessary expenses at the school. However, all the new students had to pay ten gold dollars (*jin yang shiyuan*) as a guaranteed deposit and an additional sum for their school uniforms and membership fees in the students association when they enrolled at the beginning of the school year. If a student withdrew from school, he had to repay the tuition fees and board expenses. The ten gold dollars served as a guarantee.

First Normal accounted for one-third of Hunan's advanced normal school students. In 1912 and 1913, the school admitted students from twenty of seventy-five counties in the province. In 1914, its territory was enlarged to twenty-five counties.[13]

First Normal had a very strict admission process. Candidates[14] had to be physically healthy, possess a good character, and have top scores academically. Additionally, candidates had to have applied voluntarily to First Normal. Candidate had to apply to their county government first to take the primary examinations held in the county. The county magistrate then chose ten to twenty qualified candidates to recommend to First Normal. Those candidates would take another entrance examination at the First Normal School.

The entrance examinations consisted of written, oral, and physical examinations. The written examinations included the Chinese classics, mathematics, history, geography, science, and English language. The written examination was divided into two parts: a preliminary examination and a re-examination. Only those who had passed the preliminary examination were able to take the re-examination. And only those who had passed the re-examination were able to take the oral examination and physical examination. Admission was based on the candidates' total scores (the written examinations accounted for 75 percent of the total; the oral examination and physical examination constituted 25 percent together). In the first decade of the Republican years, the First Normal School admitted approximately one hundred students from a pool of several hundred applicants each year.

Because the school provided students with a tuition waiver, free board and lodging, and financial aid, First Normal was very attractive to families of modest means. However, it was still unrealistic for those who came from really poor families to be admitted by First Normal, because of their finances as well as the school's strict entrance examinations. For instance, of the 120 students admitted to the Preparatory Department at the school in fall 1917, only 32 percent came from peasant families;

45 percent came from the families of scholars, and 21 percent from the merchant class.[15]

New students endured a four-month trial period. During the trial period, any student could be expelled for bad conduct, poor health, missed classes, or fraud in connection with the entrance examinations. After the trial period, the students were guided by the school's rewards and punishments regulations.

Graduates were expected to serve society after completing their studies. Students from Division One had to teach for seven years in the county elementary schools of Hunan; the graduates of Division Two had to teach for two years in an elementary school in the province. If for some exceptional reason a graduate could not do so, he had to obtain a service waiver from the provincial authorities or refund the sums expended on tuition and other expenses while at the school.

Admitted students were guided through a demanding curriculum in the classics (Table 3.1). Chinese classics took more class hours than any other subject in the school's curriculum. Besides Chinese classics, the students also were drilled by the school authorities about an educated man's moral character and political responsibility. Moral cultivation was a required course each semester from the first year in the Preparatory Department through the fifth year at the Undergraduate Department. Physical education was greatly emphasized and took a large portion of the curriculum, too. During the five school years, the students had four class hours of gym every week. Therefore, during the first decade of the Republic, First Normal continued to promote old-style moral and literary teaching. Its aim was to train future educators who should set moral examples for their students and the local community.[16]

Course Content and Examination Regulations

During the 1910s, First Normal also became a model for integrating modern Western subjects into its curriculum. There were seventeen subjects all together. Besides the modern Western subjects, such as mathematics, physics, chemistry, and science, the students also had to master a demanding curriculum in moral cultivation, as well as in Chinese classics.

A course in ethics (*xiushen*) was required each semester. The gist of this moral cultivation course at First Normal was to foster lofty moral values in the students. Moral cultivation, actually, was something of an intrinsic value that stood on its own.[17] It was autonomous and seen as free of all utilitarian considerations. In that sense, it differed greatly from the newly added Western subjects, which were more concretely defined and were intentionally designed for the future "vocation" (*zhiye*) of the students. For instance, ethics teacher Yang Changji believed that "quiet sitting" (*jingzuo*) an approach to self-moral cultivation was based on the view that the human mind could combine with the universal mind or the ultimate *li* (principle). He enthusiastically recommended it to his students and colleagues and kept this practice all his life.[18]

The ethics class encouraged students to practice in their daily conduct what they learned in class. Because the students would become elementary school teachers in the province, it was very important for them to know and to live in accord with the lofty moral values. Teaching in those days was highly respected by the public. Teachers were regarded as having an important social mission: to set a good moral example for his students and community. Therefore, students of the First Normal School were expected to embrace a public activism that affirmed the meaning of social action. The ethics course also would teach students classroom layout and pedagogical techniques for the teaching of moral cultivation in elementary schools.

Chinese classics also was a required course for students at every grade. During the first year at the Preparatory Department, students had ten class hours of Chinese classics per week. During the following four-and-half years in the Undergraduate Department, six class hours per week of Chinese classics were taught during the first year at the Undergraduate Department, four class hours per week the second year, and three class hours per week in each of the remaining three years.

The essence of the Chinese classics course was to help students understand and master the Chinese language. In that way, students could cultivate an interest in literature, which in turn would enlighten their moral and intellectual consciousness. The professors also helped the students to understand and master the pedagogy of teaching Chinese classics in elementary schools. For example, at that time, the First Normal students competed after school to see who could read the greatest amount of material. However, they had the habit of reading fast but failed to fully understand what they were reading. Xu Teli, the education teacher, put forward a solution to this problem: "Do not read without taking up the pen."[19] He told them the main thing was to understand what they had read. They should assess the value of the book through thinking, mark down the key words of the book, and take down the main points as well as make their own comments while reading. Therefore, they would remember what they had read, fully understand it, and also reach the goal of studying for the purpose of application.[20] Xu's advocacy greatly influenced his students. Mao was one of the students who effectively put Xu's views into practice. During the years he studied at First Normal, Mao wrote *Jiangtang lu*[21] (class notes), *Dushu lu* (notes taken from reading), *Suigan lu* (informal essays), and *Riji* (diaries). He wrote down 13,000 words of annotations and comments on the *Lunlixue yuanli*. He also copied several books.

Modern literatures would be taught first; premodern literatures second; then medieval and ancient literatures. The origins and development of Chinese characters, Chinese grammar, and the history of Chinese literature were taught also. Students were able to familiarize themselves with and master the language; thus they were able to make practical use of the language both in daily life and in future classroom teaching.

There were specific requirements for selecting the readings and poems to be taught in class. The readings should contain certain aspects of the nation and a general knowledge of the world, and they should have some connections with other subjects. The readings should be about the way of the world and the heart of human beings or about moral courage. They should be about brave and steadfast warriors, about people adept in the martial arts whose examples gave rise to chivalrous conduct and the like.[22]

Reading materials were supposed to be given to students according to their level of education. For instance, the students in the Preparatory Department were introduced to narrative essays, then to letters, and finally to argumentative writings. Readings in poetry (*ci*) and rhapsodies (*fu*), as well as ancient poetry (*gushi*; a form of pre-Tang poetry) were supposed to be taught in the fourth year. The policy, however, called for only a few poems and rhapsodies to be introduced. The narrative essays had to be clearly complete and accurate. The argumentative writings and letters had to be simple, natural, and smooth in style. The rhapsodies (*fu*), poems, and folk songs were supposed to be elegant but not flowery, straightforward but not vulgar. There were specific requirements for teaching the selected readings, which included punctuating texts.[23]

There also were specific requirements for students in writing essays. The topic of the essay was given in accordance with the students' intellectual level. It also had to relate to other subjects. The content of the essay needed to be associated with modern events. The students should practice writing narrative essays first, letters next, and argumentative essays last. When they wrote narrative essays, their arrangement of ideas were to be clear, unified, and coherent. Writings fabricated from pure imagination were disallowed. Argumentative essays and letters were required to be practical, reasonable, convincing, and systematic. The students were asked to write some *wuyan guti* poems (a form of Pre-Tang poetry, usually having five characters per line) only when they were in their fourth year.

When grading papers, the professor was supposed to point out the weakness of each paragraph and make comments, suggestions, and corrections on the side. All wrongly written or mispronounced characters, improperly used words and phrases, as well as slang were corrected. Fourth-year students were asked to grade elementary school students' papers as a kind of practical training. During both summer and winter vacations, students were required to write on provided essay topics.

There were three noticeable characteristics in the teaching goals and in the specific requirements for teaching all subjects: reflection of the Republican educational philosophy, which advocated democracy and science; emphasis on moral, utilitarian, and military education, which would enable the students to develop morally, intellectually, and physically; and attention to the vocational training of elementary school teachers.

During the first ten years of the Republic, First Normal faithfully carried out the educational principles of the Ministry of Education. To train qualified graduates for the new Republic, First Normal not only had its own systematic and complete curriculum, syllabus, and teaching contents, it also had its own strict and comprehensive examination system. Examinations emphasized three aspects: moral, intellectual, and physical education, which were named "evaluation of student conduct," "examination of students work," and "physical examination."

The evaluation of student conduct covered twelve items: etiquette, appearance and manner, speech and deportment, disposition, ability, hobby, sociability, academic work, community service, vocation, sports, and cleanliness and neatness. Student conduct was graded (*jia, yi, bing,* and *ding*; A, B, C, and D) at the end of each month or at the end of each semester. The grade was given by the faculty in accordance with each student's conduct based on the aforementioned twelve items. The principal, the dean of studies, teachers, parents, sponsors, and fellow students all had the responsibility to check the students' conduct. The principal, the dean of the studies, and other faculty members were responsible for writing down the students' good or bad conduct on their conduct reports. Parents and sponsors were required to report their sons' conduct to the school when they were asked to do so. As far as the students themselves were concerned, they were asked each year to select model students from among themselves who met the required standard. This became one of the traditional methods for evaluating students' conduct at the First Normal School.

The standard for selecting model students among students themselves focused on three aspects: moral, intellectual, and physical education. Expectations regarding moral cultivation included honesty and sincerity, self-government, self-restraint, eagerness to learn, thrift and simplicity, and volunteer service. "Honesty" and "sincerity" meant having a sense of honor and of shame, moral courage, care in choosing friends, and having the will power to refuse outside temptation. "Self-government" meant observing discipline, paying attention to etiquette, and being careful about one's speech and jokes. Ability to learn meant not being absent from classes, being diligent in one's studies, frequently reviewing what one had learned, and willingness to use reference materials. "Self-restraint" included stopping bad habits and bad desires, such as laziness, drinking, gambling, and womanizing, and being able to bear hardships and stand hard work. "Thrift" and "simplicity" included not being too fastidious about one's food and clothing and valuing an economical, simple life.[24]

The requirements and contents of physical education included the quality of courage, as well as skill in gymnastics, martial arts, and other sports. "Courage" and "insight" included being adventurous and always forging ahead or keeping alert. The quality of hygiene included living a regular life, being clean and tidy, and having a shower or bath regularly. Gym included being skillful at setting up exercises during the break, being fond of sports, and so on. Martial arts included being good at Chinese boxing/*gongfu* and swordplay. Sport included being skillful at ball games, track and field sports, and swimming.

The requirements and contents of intellectual education included literature, science, aesthetic perception, profession, ability, and speech. "Literature" meant being good at Chinese classics, poetry, prose, and the like. "Science" required being good at English, mathematics, physics, chemistry, history, and geography. "Aesthetic perception" required being good at calligraphy, drawing, and music. "Profession" referred to taking the practical training in agriculture, industry, and business seriously. "Ability" applied to having the ability to deal with an emergency or complicated situations, being capable and careful in handling affairs, and the like. "Speech" included being good at public speaking, at debates, and at repartee.

The election of model students was probably created by Principal Kong Zhaoshou in 1913 and probably had never been done before in Chinese schools. Every student could cast three votes, and each vote was only good for one person. They could select the candidates from their own class or from outside their class. When voting for a candidate, the detailed items and contents of the standard that the candidate had met was listed on the vote. No one was allowed to vote for a candidate out of gratitude. Because the standard was high and the requirement was strict, not many students were selected. For instance, in the election of 1917, there were 575 students in twelve classes who participated in the election, but only 34 students were elected as model students. Among the 34, Mao Zedong received the highest votes and Zhou Shizhao (1897–1976), the second highest. Others who were elected included Li Weihan, Zhang Kundi, Zhang Guoji (1894–1992), He Guo (1896–1990), and Jiang Zhuru (1898–1967).[25]

The determination of grades was divided into two parts: daily schoolwork and examinations. Grades for schoolwork were based on answering questions and stimulating their interests in studies. Students were encouraged to prepare, review, and think independently for each course. Preparation for a course required students to read the material before going to class. Before teaching the material, the professor would ask the students to explain the main ideas of the material. They believed that would help the students understand the material better. Review required the students to go over what they had learned. When a new lesson was taught, the professor would ask the students to answer the major points of the old lesson, in order to help the students see the connection between the old and the new. Independent thinking referred to the professor's questions from what the students had learned or what they were going to learn. When the professor raised a question, students were free to decide how to answer it. They could do some research on the question before answering it. The professor would let students talk about the question before giving them his explanation. In this way, students were encouraged to think independently.[26]

Second, the grades of daily schoolwork came from homework. For instance, every essay, every mathematics assignment, and every calligraphy homework assignment was graded by the instructor. In the third category were practical training grades, such as teaching training, volunteer service, volunteer soldiers, sport activities, choir and orchestra, and practical training in agriculture, industry, and business. Fourth, students were graded on taking lecture notes and writing diaries. The professor would check students' notes at least once every semester. Examinations were administered at the end of each semester, each school year, and just before graduation.

The grading policy of First Normal was strict and clearly defined. So, the students were very serious not only about their examinations, but also about their daily schoolwork from the first day they began to study at the school, because daily schoolwork constituted 60 percent of the total grade.[27]

In order to promote academic exchange, to encourage students to learn from each other, and to enhance interests in their studies, it became an annual activity at First Normal for the school to hold a schoolwork exhibition. The schoolwork exhibition included examination papers of students who did the best work. It would exhibit the best essays from both Chinese classics and English classes, the best drawing and handcraft works of students, the best lecture notes, excellent book reports, commentaries, and writings about what they had gained in studies, and practical trainings. At that time, although the best works from all the subjects in the curriculum were exhibited, essay writing from the Chinese classic class was considered all important. If the essay was good, then the student was regarded as a good student.[28] The exhibition was usually held in the schoolroom. Each student in the fifteen or so classes at the school was required to write an essay once a week. The best essay from each class was sent to a teachers' committee, which chose three to five to be hung in the glass-covered exhibition cases in the large display room for all the students to read as models. Xiao Zisheng's and Mao Zedong's essays were often honored in this way.[29]

Besides the schoolwork and essay exhibitions, there was a proficiency test on essay writing every semester. During the test, students were not allowed to bring anything except brush (pen) and blank papers; there was to be no plagiarizing, no talking, and no one was allowed to leave the classroom. The test lasted for five hours. During the proficiency test on essay writing in July 1917, 414 students of 575 passed the test. Among the 414 students, only 30 received a grade of A. This test system showed that First Normal was very strict in student training at that time.[30]

In addition to tests on moral cultivation, conduct, and academic works, there were specific requirements on the newly added Westernized physical examination, which included checks on height, weight, chest measurement, vital capacity, vision, hearing, spinal column, physique, teeth, arm wrestling, and illness. Physical examinations usually were done by the school doctor (probably a Western medical doctor), physical education teachers, and the dean of academic studies. One of four grades was assigned to a physical examination: *jia*, *yi*, *bing*, and *ding*; A, B, C, and D. When checking students' height, weight, chest measurement, vital capacity, and arm wrestling, the examiners were asked to consider the examinee's age before giving him a grade. In that way, grading was supposedly fair to everyone.

Although First Normal had set a high standard with respect to evaluation of students' moral cultivation and intellectual and physical education, most students could still meet the standard and pass the tests, due to the school's strict admission system and its efficient teaching policies and practices. The examination result for the grade of which Mao was a member in 1917 provides an example. There were 173 students in that grade who took the examinations, and 166 passed the moral cultivation test, 172 passed the academic test, and 155 passed the physical examinations. The goal of First Normal was to train virtuous educators and leaders of a new civic spirit.[31]

Requirements for Faculty and Staff

In order to maintain high academic standards, run a competitive athletic program, and cultivate the students' moral life, First Normal considered the role of the faculty to be very important. The school faithfully carried out the spirit of the "Decree of Instructions to School Administrators and Faculties" issued by the Republic's Ministry of Education in September 1912. They firmly believed that:

> On campus, the schoolteachers and staff members should be reserved and dignified in front of their students. While outside school, they should set themselves as a public model for others in society to follow. They should possess a noble, determined, and faithful spirit, and take pleasure in fulfilling their lifelong duties.[32]

The First Normal authorities stated:

> If all the school teachers and staff members could do these things, then the time when our nation's academic development,

the transformation of our corrupt customs, and our ability to develop at the same pace as the Western powers would arrive soon.[33]

Therefore, all the teachers and staff members at the First Normal were required

to do their utmost to fulfill their duties as long as they were at their posts, so as to take the responsibility of intellectuals, who were considered to have foresight. They were required to treat students as good friends, and to love students as their own children or younger brothers. They should also set examples for students to follow, exert favorable influences on students' characters, and foster students' abilities of independence and self-control.[34]

In the first decade of the Republic, there were only two staff members at the First Normal who were appointed directly by the provincial government: the principal and the accountant. The staff consisted of four directors of studies (*xuejian*), one person in charge of general affairs, one accountant, one secretary, one librarian, one equipment administrator, one school doctor, and several office clerks. This division of labor was borrowed from Japanese schools. Based on the class size and teaching load, the principal submitted proposals to the provincial government calling for either increasing or decreasing the number of teachers. As an example, in the second semester of 1917, there were 549 students divided into twelve classes, and 45 teachers at First Normal. Seven teachers devoted themselves to Chinese classics. There were five teachers for math and gym, three for English and drawing, and two each for moral cultivation, geography, physics, and agriculture. Three of the faculty taught history, but one of these taught geography as well, and another taught both history and Chinese classics.

In order to let every staff member discharge his responsibilities, First Normal laid down not only general principles for all staff members to follow, but also detailed working regulations for people in different departments. The general principles were enumerated in fourteen items. It was stipulated that "all teachers and staff members were to be hired and appointed by the principal. They should discuss their work with the principal. They should be responsible, have good conduct, be honest and sincere, and set a good example for the students. They should be interested in the study of education, and be committed to their work."[35] The general principles included specific requirements regarding leave time or absence without pay. The detailed working regulations included eleven items regarding the responsibilities of the principal, fifty-eight regarding the responsibilities of the directors of studies, and thirteen dealing with the responsibilities of the teachers. The obligations of and requirements for each were written clearly and specifically in the detailed working regulations of the school.

The First Normal School had routine meetings on administrative affairs every Friday evening. The principal, directors of studies, secretary, accountant, and those in other administrative positions were required to participate in the meeting. All suggestions and proposals regarding the school's administration were discussed and decided at these meetings. If something urgent happened, a provisional meeting would be called.

In addition to the administrative meetings, First Normal had educational administration meetings. All the school's teaching work was under the direction and guidance of the educational administration meetings, which were attended by all teachers and was held at the beginning of each semester. Before the meeting, the principal or directors of studies would collect the professors' opinions and suggestions about the school's curriculum or teaching and prepare an agenda. The draft agenda would be distributed to each professor. The principal then convened an administration meeting to discuss and decide the proposals. A resolution was passed when more than half of those in attendance voted for it. (The idea of voting probably came from the West.) As soon as a resolution passed, it would be issued to the public and put into practice. The meeting system of the First Normal School thus conformed to the requirements of the Republican educational principles. It also was supposed to help strengthen the school's teaching and administration so that First Normal School could maintain its distinguished status.[36]

Regulating the Behavior of Students

First Normal also had specific requirements for supervising the students. Copies of the national "Edict on Educational Reforms in Normal Schools" distributed by First Normal included a "preface" added to the decree: "In governing the people, we should establish law and order. Without law and order, there is no way of governing the people. The law is something that people can rely on and is regarded as the governor."[37]

From this, it is clear that First Normal was committed to the regulations and rules of the Ministry of Education. Furthermore, First Normal also required its students to devote themselves to academic studies and train themselves to be physically and mentally healthy. Everybody was free, yet "freedom is within the boundary of law. Everybody was equal, yet equality did not allow disorder. Everyone must follow the school's orders. If anyone did not fulfill his duty as a student but went off into wild flights of fancy, he wasted his young life. That means he did not strive to make progress, but gave himself up as hopeless. In that way, even if he realized his error and showed repentance later on, it was too late for regret."[38] Therefore, the school "expected that all the students maintain a sound character, and was prepared to enhance his strength of independence and self-government. The future of our Republic is entirely dependent on promising young people."[39]

Although the school rules and regulations were rigid and rather conventional, they were in keeping with Republican educational principles. They also were in accord with the entire social, economic, and educational atmosphere of China at the time. Xiao Zisheng recalled,

> The daily routine for students of the First Normal was very rigid and their activities were strictly scheduled to the last minute: the times for entering classrooms, the reading rooms, dining room, and the dormitory were all fixed and were indicated by sharp blasts on a trumpet, in imitation of the army bugle. When the trumpet sounded, the thousand or more students all gathered like so many ducks and they were directed by ten disciplinary officers.[40]

The First Normal's regulation of student behavior contained six aspects dealing with etiquette, conduct and discipline, service, schedule, public places, and rewards and punishment.

Rules of "general etiquette" stipulated that the student should take off his hat and bow before coming in and leaving the faculty and staff offices, before the teacher started the class and after he finished his lecture, and when meeting a teacher at other times. Specific etiquette applied to these events: congratulations, beginning of school, end of school, graduation, and commemoration. The expectations of etiquette on special occasions included instructions (for all students, teachers, and staff) about taking off hats and giving three bows to the national flag, and bowing to each other (for students and faculty).

Etiquette for special occasions covered events arranged by the principal, for example, when a government inspection group arrived or some special guests or organizations came for a visit. The general requirement in such situations was that no one was allowed to be absent from these ceremonies without a reason.

Rules of conduct and discipline included school order and hygiene. "School order" referred to the school's discipline, which could be summarized as the "twenty-eight forbidden practices."[41] There were eighteen clauses on hygiene. The regulations for hygiene detailed, for example, how students should act when they were sick, as when suffering from an infectious disease. Regulations also stipulated that students should sit up straight in class; they should leave the classroom only at breaks between classes; they were not allowed to drink alcohol or smoke; spitting was forbidden; they should keep themselves clean, and keep their bedrooms, classrooms, and public places clean. Although some of the regulations were somewhat rigid and reflected the limited views of the time, adherence varied notably from person to person or from one administrative regime to another. For instance, during the years when the reform-minded Kong Zhaoshou was principal (April 1913 to January 1914; September 1916 to September 1918), he did not enforce several of the clauses of the school's discipline, such as clause 1. The students were not allowed to engage in managing any kind of non-academic enterprises; clause 2. The students were not allowed to join any kind of non-academic organizations or educational associations.[42]

Services referred to the work of service workers (*fuwu sheng*) at the First Normal School. Those appointed included students on weekly duty from each class, the auditor at the student association, student volunteer soldiers, group leaders when working at the school farm and school garden, assistants at the school shop, and those who were temporarily appointed to help at sports contests or academic exhibitions.

Their responsibilities included "passing on the orders of the faculty and staff to fellow students; representing the students' opinions to the faculty and staff; taking care of public property; helping maintain the school's discipline; arranging students to clean classroom."[43] The school was trying to train the students to handle various activities, as well as their abilities to work independently and be self-governing.

A fourth section of the principles on the management of students dealt with daily work and rest schedules and explicit regulations for requesting absence. According to the historical record of First Normal, there were no students who broke the rules for requesting an absence during the first decade of the Republic. For instance, the average absence from school of 120 students enrolled at the Preparatory Department in 1917 was only six class hours.

The fifth section was called "public rules." It applied to the discipline the students were expected to follow in public places, such as offices, classrooms, labs, playgrounds, the library, reading room, exhibition room, telephone room, tearoom, dining hall, study hall, and bathroom. There were specific regulations for the students to observe at each public place. Those regulations also made it clear what kind of punishment a rule breaker would receive; usually one or two points were taken off a certain subject. The main purposes of the regulations were to emphasize school spirit and school discipline, to carry forward a proper style of study, and to keep the order at the school.

The last section of these principles dealt with rewards and punishments. There were six kinds of rewards: adding grades, exhibiting excellent academic work, praise in written or oral form, financial reward, and certification of merit. Regarding punishments, there were seven types: taking off points, oral criticism, a warning note, writing a self-criticism, public criticism in print, failing to go up to the next grade, and expulsion. Conditions for rewards and punishments were very explicit. In the first decade of the Republic, there were no class advisers (*ban zhuren*) or political personnel at the First Normal School. The major way that First Normal managed students and maintained order was to rely on its rigid code of discipline and its strict system of rewards and punishments.

The rules of the school were to train students to be disciplined, to maintain a sound character, and to become virtuous and responsible persons. Those students were future educators and "China's survival in a hostile and competitive world depended on the quality of its people."[44] Therefore, the educational reforms implemented at First Normal produced reconfigured philosophy, policy, practice, course content, and school regulations that provided favorable circumstances for the First Normal students' intellectual transformation.

Illustration 1. Hunan First Normal School, which was reconstructed in 1968 (based on the original feature of the school in 1912).

Illustration 2. The well where Mao and other students came to have cold water baths year round.

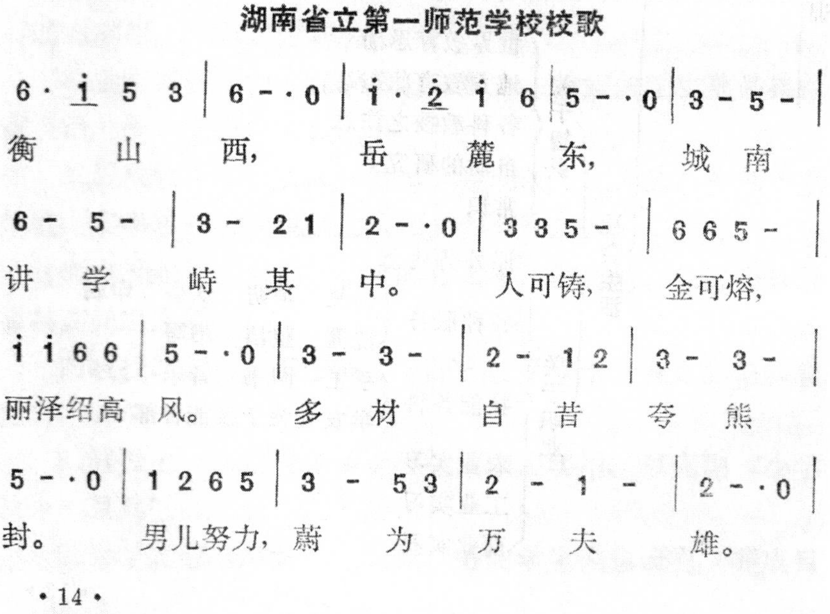

湖南省立第一师范学校校歌

6·<u>1</u> 5 3 | 6 - ·0 | 1· <u>2</u> 1 6 | 5 - ·0 | 3 - 5 - |

衡　山　西，　　岳　麓　东，　　城　南

6 - 5 - | 3 - 2 1 | 2 - ·0 | 3 3 5 - | 6 6 5 - |

讲　学　峙　其　中。　　人可铸，　金可熔，

1̇ 1̇ 6 6 | 5 - ·0 | 3 - 3 - | 2 - 1 2 | 3 - 3 - |

丽泽绍高 风。　　多　材　自　昔　夸　熊

5 - ·0 | 1 2 6 5 | 3 - 5 3 | 2 - 1 - | 2 - ·0 |

封。　　男儿努力，蔚　为　万　夫　雄。

· 14 ·

Illustration 3. School anthem translated into English by Yan-shuan Lao.

Mt. Heng to the west, Mt. Yuelu to the east,
Chengnan Academy soars up in the midst.
People are capable of being molded,
Just as gold can be cast.
Herein students are carrying on the lofty tradition.
Since the olden days, we are always
　　Proud of our abundance of talents in the realm.
Ye men, exert yourselves, so as to be future leaders of the multitude,
　　On a grand scale.

Chapter 4

Teaching the New Culture
First Normal's Faculty

Mao Zedong once said during an interview with Edgar Snow in 1936: "I was a student in the First Normal for five years, . . . during this period my political ideas began to take shape. Here also I acquired my first experiences in social action."[1] Mao's words reflected the common experience of many radical students at First Normal. For instance, He Shuheng, one of the oldest students of the school in 1914,[2] wrote several letters home and asked the women there to unbind their feet. Because his advocacy sounded too radical to his family members in the conservative village, none of the women of his family actually did what he asked. In 1913, however, he went home for summer vacation, asked his third daughter to collect all foot-binding bandages and all three-inch golden-lily[3] shoes from home, and destroyed them in public. After that, all the female members of his family freed their bound feet, an event that gained much attention in the local area.[4]

Although the students' radicalization was not without connections to the changing world with which they interacted, the more immediate origin of their intellectual and political transformation was within the school itself. The students' radicalization was inseparable from the impact of very effective, progressive teachers. As Paul Bailey[5] and Sarah McElroy[6] point out, the educators made great contributions to the educational reform and made great effort in transforming the quality of the people. Those instructors at First Normal helped bring about an intellectual transformation during the second decade of the twentieth century.

The Teachers' Generation

According to a First Normal's school history written in 1918, the school had fifty-two employees at that time. Of those, thirty had graduated from, or had once taught at Hunan Higher Normal University (*Hunan gaodeng shifan*). Only a few of the teachers had graduated from Hunan *Youdeng* Normal University (*Hunan youdeng shifan*). Generally speaking, those graduates of the Higher Normal University took comparatively radical stands, whereas those from *Youdeng* Normal University represented a relatively conservative viewpoint.

All the teachers were of a generation that had witnessed the ebb and flow of reform. Hunan had emerged as the most active province in the Hundred Days Reform Movement of 1898. At the beginning of the twentieth century, Hunan stood high among the provinces that sent the largest number of students to study in Japan. Among these overseas students, many went to Japanese normal schools. After graduation, they returned to Hunan and became active in the province's education reforms. These returning students established distinguished secondary schools like Chuyi, Mingde, Xiuye, and Zhounan in Changsha. Many of the same returned students were active in the New Culture and May Fourth movements.

The teachers' radical and progressive influences on their students' intellectual and political life was immense. A few of them, like Kong Zhaoshou, Yang Changji, and Xu Teli, not only enjoyed a good reputation in Hunan, but also became very influential in the New Culture Movement in the country as a whole.

At First Normal, the unique role that teachers played and the kinds of experiences that they created for their students revealed that they had exerted a powerful, positive, and lasting influence on the lives of the young men. At the school, the teachers' involvement did not begin or end at the classroom door. Their influence reached beyond the classroom and was formative in the students' personal and academic development. They taught the students something of value—not only in the given subjects, but also about themselves. They opened the students' minds, changed their lives, and made them think more deeply. They were like a bridge, not an end point for all the students who came into their lives. Therefore, those teachers *de facto* altered the trajectory of their students' lives and greatly affected the young students in their intellectual transformation and radicalization. Of the many distinguished teachers who taught at First Normal in its heyday, the following deserve particular attention.

Principal Kong Zhaoshou

Kong Zhaoshou, also known as Jingcun, was a native of Liuyang, Hunan. A graduate of Hunan Higher Normal University, Kong also went to study at the Tokyo Institute of Political Science and Law and graduated with a bachelor's degree in law in 1916. Twice he served as principal of First Normal, in 1913 and again from 1916 to 1918.[7]

Kong was one of the most influential educational reformers of the early Republican period. During his first term as headmaster, Kong supported the reformist educational principles issued in 1912 by the Ministry of Education. Kong proposed that a comprehensive set of school regulations be set up governing students' conduct, academic study, and physical examinations. He also advocated student volunteer and self-government activities. For instance, in September 1913, students established a Skill Society (*jineng hui*) under his leadership.[8]

The Skill Society (the name was changed to *Xueyou hui* or Student Friendship Society in 1915) sought to promote virtue, study, and education. Members also wanted to advance learning and promote industriousness, mold the body, and create a sense of fraternity among students. Four times during the period from 1915 to 1917, students elected Mao Zedong as its secretary. In 1918, during his last semester studying at First Normal, Mao was elected manager of the society and head of its section on educational research.[9] The society had fourteen departments and sponsored various activities corresponding to the needs of the student and teacher members. Young men could join a debating department or groups that discussed questions concerning educational subjects and current affairs. The society frequently invited famous people to give lectures. In the war between the southern and northern warlords of the 1920s, the society led the students in policing the campus to guard against thieves and assaults.

Because of his reputation as an educational reformer, Kong attracted generous support from the provincial elites, faculty, and students, as well as opposition and even staunch animosity from antagonists. During Kong's time as principal in 1913, Tang Xiangming was appointed governor of Hunan by Yuan Shikai, leader of the national government at the time. Kong opposed Yuan Shikai and his conservative advocates in education, who wanted to restore Confucianism as the essential element in the curriculum. Therefore, in January 1914, Gov. Tang gave the order to arrest Kong Zhaoshou. One battalion of soldiers surrounded First Normal. However, Kong was tipped off, disguised himself as a water-seller, and escaped by a side door of the school. After that, he quickly left China for Japan.[10]

When Kong reassumed the position as principal following Yuan's death and Tang's removal, he assembled a group of learned and progressive men as faculty. He rehired those who had displayed a "sense of justice" and were unhappy with "Butcher" Tang's rule. Fang Weixia and Wang Jifan became directors of studies. He also hired Yang Changji as the school's ethics teacher, and Xu Teli as the education teacher. Kong further engaged an American as the English teacher and a German as the music teacher.[11] He hired forty-five teachers. Most had graduated from higher normal universities. Six were students who had returned to China from Great Britain and Japan.[12] Incorporating what he himself had learned during his exile in Japan, Kong energetically promoted a full-scale education reform at First Normal and led the school into the mainstream of the New Culture Movement.

Kong worked on school regulations, revising old ones and formulating new ones. He rearranged the curriculum and changed various teaching methods. For instance, the school's meeting system, the obligations and responsibilities of the faculty and staff, course requirements, and the regulations concerning students became formal written regulations under the leadership of Kong Zhaoshou.[13] His educational philosophy included an emphasis on moral, military, and utilitarian education, which he believed to be the only way to save China and to make the country strong and wealthy. His educational philosophy accorded with the Republic's 1912 "Decree on Principles for Education."

Kong strongly advocated patriotism. At his suggestion, the focus of First Normal's school admonition was changed from "sincerity" (cheng) to "knowing the national humiliation," reflecting a reaction to the historical circumstances surrounding China at the time. Like many other Chinese intellectuals of this period, Kong was outraged by the fact that Japan had issued the Twenty-One Demands from China in 1915.

On May 7, 1917, First Normal held a commemorative meeting in memory of the "national humiliation day."[14] Kong gave a long speech on fostering patriotism and the spirit of upward mobility. Afterward, Li Weihan and three other students prepared their respective notes for publication. Their work appeared as a 13,000-word article, which addressed ten themes. Those included the important geographical position of China, Japan's aim to dominate China, Yuan Shikai as a traitor, the Twenty-One Demands, boycotts of Japanese goods, a comparative analysis of China and Japan in politics, military power, education, finance, and national salvation. Kong had summarized these themes in his speech and argued that in order to save the nation from extinction, every Chinese should be aware of the national humiliation. He argued that if everyone would take the cause of expunging the national humiliation as a matter of personal responsibility, China could be saved and the various insults avenged.[15]

Kong believed that education represented the ultimate means of solving all these problems and saving the nation. "If everyone knew the national humiliation, and disciplined himself, especially cultivated his personal morality," he maintained, "society would become good; if society were good, people with talent would come forth in large numbers; if the nation had a large number of people with extraordinary ability, the country would certainly become strong and powerful."[16] Thus, he called on his students to exert themselves while remembering China's national humiliation.

Kong firmly believed that the educational philosophy of moral, military, and utilitarian education best suited China. Moral education was deemed essential, with utilitarian and military education having a lower priority. However, Kong took military education very seriously, too.

In October 1916, soon after he reassumed the headmastership of First Normal, Kong submitted a proposal to Gov. Tan Yankai concerning the establishment of a student volunteer army. He argued that establishing that group would be an appropriate response to the Ministry of Education's decree, "Emphasis on Military Spirit" (*Zhuzhong shangwu jingshen ling*). It also would conform to current trends, he noted, because in the modern world, all great powers emphasized military education. He advocated changing or abandoning some of the old customs like "Good iron is not used to make nails; good men do not become soldiers." In his proposal to Gov. Tan, he wrote: "If we emphasized military education, if our citizens were to cultivate a strong and healthy body and had the ability to defend their country when it was bullied, this would change the international image of China as the 'sick man of East Asia.'"[17] He maintained that military education could prepare young students to be useful once they were needed to fight for their country. Therefore, he asked Tan to supply weapons in numbers sufficient for use by a company.

After Tan's approval of Kong's proposal, a student volunteer army was established at First Normal. According to the monthly "important events" recorded in First Normal's 1918 history, the student volunteer army did an excellent job of policing the campus in wartime. In November 1917, when war broke out in southern Hunan, people panicked. Students from the volunteer army patrolled the campus to guard against assault. In March 1918, when panic and confusion occurred in the city of Changsha, students from the volunteer army calmly guarded their school and policed the city in cooperation with other schools in Changsha. In April 1918, when war broke out in Eastern Hunan, students from the volunteer army again organized to police both the campus and the city, as well as assist city residents.[18] They also set up a team to provide special relief for women and children.

In his capacity as the principal of First Normal and as an activist in education reform, Kong Zhaoshou rose to be a prominent voice in educational affairs not only within Hunan province but also nationally. In November and December 1917, Kong Zhaoshou attended the national educational conference held in Hangzhou. At the conference, he presented a 10,000-word "Proposal," suggesting that Chinese secondary and higher education reform their curriculums. He pointed out that the current curriculums, borrowed from Japan, were inapplicable to modern Chinese schools. He called for a thorough reform in curriculum and teaching methods, and the creation of a profession of new-style educators. For instance, he maintained that the typical normal school's curriculum was overloaded with more than twenty subjects. He suggested that these schools either drop some courses or divide themselves into two colleges separating the science majors from the humanities majors. Because he was heavily influenced by John Dewey's pragmatic philosophy of education, he advocated the idea that education would be the best way to achieve national salvation.

Because of poor health, Kong resigned his position as principal in summer 1918, and soon thereafter died in Changsha.

Education Teacher Xu Teli

Xu Teli, also known as Xu Maoxun, was a native of Changsha, Hunan. He came from a poor peasant family. His mother died when he was 4 years old, and his father and 10-year-old brother had to work in the fields to support the family.[19] Xu attended a private tutorial school in his native village between 1886 and 1892 but stopped at the age of 15 because of poverty. Xu tried to continue his grandfather's occupation as doctor of traditional Chinese medicine.[20] However, he gave it up after two years of reading Chinese medical books because he found them too hard. At the age of 18, he became a private tutor and continued in that occupation for ten years.

In 1905, Xu took the regional examinations held in Yuezhou to test the results of his studies. He placed nineteenth among the more than three thousand examinees.[21] He thus enjoyed a reputation in the province, and schools contended to invite him to join their faculty. In the same year, in order to improve himself, he entered the Ningxiang Short-term Normal School in Changsha, graduating after four months. During his study there, he encountered many new subjects and concluded that Western technology was superior to China's. He also learned and accepted the revolutionary ideas of Sun Yat-sen, for the principal of the school, Zhou Zhenlin, was a member of Sun's *Tongmenghui* (Revolutionary Alliance) and often introduced Sun's revolutionary views to his students.

After graduation, Xu established a primary school in Changsha and studied algebra, geometry, trigonometry, and analytic geometry during his leisure hours. In 1906, he taught at the Zhounan Girls' Middle School in Changsha and used the school as an arena for propagating revolution. He organized student strikes in opposition to the Manchu government. Once while lecturing to the students on foreign aggression against China, he broke into a loud lamentation and cut off the end of one finger, using the blood to write eight Chinese characters, "*qu chu da lu, hui fu Zhong hua*" meaning "drive out the Manchus and restore China."[22]

In 1910, already a highly respected and well-known teacher, Xu went to study at the program for elementary school teachers founded by the Jiangsu Provincial Board of Education in Shanghai and soon went to Japan on an inspection tour of educational facilities. After returning, he continued to work in the Zhounan Girls' Middle School, both as its principal and as a teacher. An ardent supporter of Sun Yat-sen, he took part in the 1911 revolution. He was then selected as the section chief of the Department of Education at the Hunan Provincial Government. The Hunan Provisional Assembly elected him its speaker in 1911. The next year, he established the Changsha Normal School, which provided short-term normal classes. The following year, he founded an elementary school in his home village.

In 1913, he was invited to join the faculty of the Hunan First Normal School; there he taught education, pedagogy, and moral cultivation until 1919. A humble man, he also was iconoclastic in both his words and actions; he drew much attention to himself by walking rather than riding a rickshaw between his teaching jobs at various Changsha schools. At that time, not many secondary educational institutions existed in Changsha, and the teachers of these schools held high social status. As a result, most of them came to school in rickshaws. Xu was simultaneously principal of the Changsha Normal School, located at the north gate of Changsha, and a teacher at First Normal, at the south gate. The distance between the two schools was ten Chinese *li* (about four miles). He always walked between the two schools, even on rainy days.[23] Such actions not only had a great influence on his students but also affected other teachers. For instance, Huang Shutao, a drawing teacher at First Normal, had a large family to support. He used to ride a fancy rickshaw to school, even though his family's finances were very tight. After observing Xu's example, he told Xu one day: "You don't ride rickshaws, yet the students still respect you. I will learn from you."[24] After that, he never rode a rickshaw to school again.

Xu specialized in pedagogy. He edited all the teaching materials he used for his classes. In 1914, he published an article entitled "The Study of the Pedagogy of Chinese" in the *Gongyan* journal.[25] Together with other First Normal teachers, Yang Changji, Li Jinxi, and Fang Weixia, Xu founded the Hongwei Publishing House to publish elementary and middle school textbooks. Hongwei published two volumes of *Pedagogy for Elementary School Courses* in China.

Xu always lectured in a stentorian voice and displayed an infectious appeal. In his talks, he paid special attention to the connection between social life and the students' actual thinking. Students highly praised his classes. They said his practical lectures were easy to understand. Xu liked to use exemplary persons of both the past and the present as models. He also used his own experience to guide his students. Once, in a moral cultivation class, when he was talking about thrift, he told his students that living a thrifty life could not only save money but also promote a strong spirit, train an adamant will, and mold a noble character. He said: "I'm used to the thrifty life. I feel only frugality can make me feel happy."[26] He continued:

> I'm very pleased with myself about one thing. That is, I have never been the victim of a thief. I don't have leather suitcases, a fancy wardrobe, or any valuable furniture and goods in my house. Usually, my money is casually stored in old books in baskets. Thieves would never figure out that the money they wanted was located in a pile of old books, so I've never lost

money. When I walk in the street, thieves see me wear such shabby clothes, they walk away from me quickly because they are afraid of being robbed by me.[27]

Students liked his class not only because of his lively lectures but also because he would answer their questions very lucidly. His student Xiong Jinding recalled: "Mr. Xu's lectures never stuck to conventions and were never cut and dried. He always avoided the stale and brought forth the fresh in his lectures. And he always explained profound things in a simple way. Therefore, his lectures were very enjoyable and vivid."[28]

Xu advocated that students develop a proper approach to study. He told them to make certain they understood what they had read and take down the main points while reading. In this way, each book they read would count.[29]

Xu had a strong sense of justice, which greatly influenced his students. As early as 1911, he organized student strikes in opposition to the railway policy of the Manchu government. That year, the Qing government decided to nationalize the privately owned major railways and use them as assets for huge, hidden foreign loans. When this news arrived in Hunan, Xu was teaching at the Zhounan Girls School. Indignant, he contacted other schools in Changsha and called for a student strike. A few days later, all the schools in Changsha responded favorably to his call. This was the earliest student strike in the history of Changsha.[30]

In 1915, when Yuan Shikai was intent on making himself emperor, his followers organized a Peace Planning Society in every province to support Yuan's imperial ambitions. An ethics teacher of First Normal named Liao Mingjin (Hutang, 1867–1927), was a member of the Chuanshan Association. At the lectures at the association, Liao, like all the other members, often talked about the incompatibility between the monarchical system, public opinion, and the situation of China, and called on people to stand up against Yuan's imperial ambitions. However, in his classes at First Normal, Liao proclaimed that the monarchical system accorded with the interests of the people as well as the nation. Xu and other teachers like Yang Changji, Fang Weixia, Wang Jifan, and Yuan Zhongqian were disgusted by Liao's hypocrisy and set themselves against him. Xu even wrote a letter to Liao in the name of the students. He wrote:

At the *Chuanshan Association*, you opposed the monarchical system, but at First Normal you approved of it. Sir, you are

one person, how can you have two faces? . . . [Since we
are your students and] under your authority, we don't have
anything with which to repay you now; when opportunities
come in the future, we will not forget your instruction [and
will repay you then.][31]

After he received this letter, Liao realized that his actions enraged the
community, so he never publicly supported the monarchical system again.

In June 1915, the Hunan Provincial Assembly declared that, beginning with the fall semester, normal school students should pay ten *yuan*
for their tuition fee and other incidental expenses. Ten *yuan* was not a
small amount to most of the First Normal students, who did not come
from wealthy families. They complained to Principal Zhang Gan. Mao
even organized a strike among the students to drive Zhang from the
school. Zhang angrily ordered Mao and another sixteen students leaders expelled. However, Xu, Yang Changji, Wang Jifan, and Fang Weixia
energetically interceded for Mao and the other students. The principal
rescinded the order.[32]

In 1918, Zhang Jingyao, a native of Anhui province and Baoding
military school graduate, was appointed military governor of Hunan.
During his governorship, he took Hunan's economy to the edge of collapse. He used various ways to get money for himself. For instance, he
even used the death of his mother as an excuse to wrench more from
the overburdened merchants. Besides selling opium, imposing higher
taxes, and forcing arbitrary fines on the Hunanese gentry, he opened the
Yuxiang Bank in Changsha and it printed a huge amount of paper currency, which circulated throughout the province. Then the bank refused
to redeem the currency for other forms of money. Zhang Jingyao then
ordered those who had the paper currency to buy the lottery tickets
he issued. In this way, he embezzled almost all the money equal to the
amount of the paper currency he had circulated.[33] He also confiscated
the limited educational revenues from tuition, which meant that the
teachers did not get paid for five or six months, while students in the
public schools went without food.

Zhang Jingyao totally depended on his military power to retain
office. He made his three brothers, Jingshun, Jingyu, Jingtang, officers in
his army; their troops engaged in widespread extortion and the robbery
of private homes. The troops also raped women wherever they went,
while their officers demanded daughters of gentry families as concubines.
There was a saying about the four brothers among the Hunanese, "*Yao
Shun Yu Tang, hu bao chai lang*" (Yao, Shun, Yu, [and] Tang [were the]

tiger, leopard, jackal, [and] wolf).[34] The Hunanese understandably hated the Zhang brothers.

Xu vigorously participated in the Hunan student movement to oust Zhang Jingyao. He pointed out: "Until Toxic Zhang (*Zhang du*) is driven out [of the province], Hunan has no hope."[35] He called on both the students and the citizens of Hunan to join the movement. Zhang ordered Xu arrested in summer 1919. Xu had already been in the process of arranging traveling expenses to study under the work–study plan in France promoted by Cai Hesen and Mao Zedong in September 1919.

Xu studied at the University of Paris for three years and the University of Lyon for one. During his student days in France, he also served as an apprentice in a metal plant and acted as a cook for workers. He then worked in factories in Germany and Belgium for one year. In 1924, he returned to China from France and established the Changsha Girls Normal School, also known as Daotian Normal School, and served as its principal as well as a teacher. He said:

> I'm a man who is not interested in political activities. I really
> enjoy being wrapped up in reading. Because of foreign pressure
> and internal political corruption, I drifted into the patriotic
> movement, and felt that if the masses did not participate
> in the movement it was because of their ignorance. I thus
> believed that education was the first and foremost means of
> national salvation.[36]

Therefore, during the White Terror of 1927, the most severe time for the Chinese Communists, Xu joined the CCP. In January 1937, on his 60th birthday, a special celebration party was held for him, and Mao Zedong called Xu one of the two most beloved and respected teachers he had at First Normal.[37] Mao also wrote Xu a letter to congratulate him on his birthday. In the letter, he wrote: "You were my teacher twenty years ago; you are still my teacher now; and you will continue to be my teacher in the future."[38]

Xu worked in the educational field his whole life and died in Beijing on November 28, 1968, at the age of 91.

Director of Studies Fang Weixia

Fang Weixia (Zhuya), a native of Pingjiang, Hunan, became a leading figure in the early CCP. He also influenced a generation of Hunan students.

Fang graduated from First Normal's short-term department in September 1906 and soon enrolled at Hunan Youji Normal College. He studied at the Normal College for three years and graduated in 1909. Then he went to Japan to study for two years. On his return in 1911, he worked at First Normal until 1918, first teaching science and agriculture and then becoming director of studies at the school.[39] From 1916 to 1918, he played a particularly important role at First Normal. His status and function at the school placed him next to Principal Kong Zhaoshou in importance.

While he was working at First Normal, Fang became an ardent supporter of Sun Yat-sen's revolutionary views and firmly opposed the dictatorship of Yuan Shikai. In 1915, when Yuan Shikai tried to assume the emperorship, Fang joined First Normal teachers Xu Teli, Yang Changji, and Wang Jifan in opposing Yuan's attempt. He stoutly opposed Yuan's Hunan followers like Ye Dehui, who organized the Peace Planning Society and supported Yuan's imperial ambitions. However, he supported the reform-minded Tan Yankai. That was why Tan Yankai became governor of Hunan the second time in 1920, he appointed Fang as chief of the Education Department of the Hunan Provincial Government.

While teaching science at First Normal, Fang tried to enhance students' interests by having them do fieldwork. He often took his students to the Yuelu Mountain to collect specimens of plants, minerals, and rocks.[40] While serving as director of studies, he represented Kong as head of the Student Friendship Society (Xueyou hui) and supervised its activities.

After Kong Zhaoshou reassumed the position of principal in 1916, he made Fang director of studies. The two men not only shared political views and educational philosophy but also were good friends. While serving as director of studies, Fang stipulated the specific curriculum for each subject in all five grades.

Fang was a prominent voice in educational affairs and enjoyed a high reputation in Hunan. During his time at First Normal, he was elected a member of the Provincial Assembly and made chief of the Education Department of the Hunan Provincial Government. Because of his radical and reform-minded views, he often attracted opposition and ridicule from provincial conservatives. However, he also received support and respect from his students as well as from his colleagues. In his capacity as the director of studies of First Normal, Provincial assemblyman, and chief of the Education Department of Hunan, Fang, together with Principal Kong, embarked on a full-scale education reform at First Normal, which had a long-lasting effect on the administration, curriculum, policymaking, and the students and teachers of the school.

In 1920, when Mao Zedong opened a bookstore in Changsha, Fang used his capacity as Provincial assemblyman to support and publicize it. Besides providing financial aid, Fang also organized the Pingjiang Branch of the bookstore, an action that contributed to the spread of Marxism in Hunan.[41]

In 1924, Fang joined the CCP and began to work as a political adviser in Tan Yankai's Xiang (Hunan) army and thus contributed to fostering CCP membership in the army. During the Northern Expedition, he worked as a CCP representative in the national revolutionary army. After the split between the Nationalist Party and the CCP, he participated in the Nanchang Uprising of 1927.[42] Then he was sent to study at Sun Yat-sen University in the Soviet Union. He returned to China from the Soviet Union in 1931 and worked as the director of the political department in a Red Army school in Fujian province. After the Red Army began the Long March,[43] he stayed in the Hunan-Jiangxi border region and led guerrilla warfare. Arrested by the Nationalists (the KMT or *Guomindang*) in southern Hunan in 1935, he was executed the same year.

Math Teacher and Supervisor Wang Jifan

Wang Jifan, a native of Xiangxiang, Hunan, came from a well-to-do family. His father, Wang Wensheng, served for a time as a low-ranking official of the Qing government in Northeast China. Wang's mother was the sixth child of the Wen family of Xiangxiang and the elder sister of Mao Zedong's mother. Nine years older than Mao, Wang was the second son of his parents, but was number nine among his cousins, so Mao always called him "ninth elder brother."[44]

From his earliest years, Wang was considered hard working and very intelligent. He was admitted by the Changsha *Youji* Normal College at the beginning of the twentieth century. While studying in Changsha, he grew interested in the study of the New Learning and was influenced by the reformers. He considered reform and self-strengthening as the only way to change China's situation of accumulated weakness and poverty.

After graduation, Wang began to teach at First Normal. Because of his enlightened and reforming views as well as his scholarly accomplishment, Wang was welcomed and respected by his students. Mao Zedong especially received much help from him both mentally and financially since, apart from the teacher–student relationship, they were also cousins.[45] In a conversation with his old school friend, Zhou Shizhao, Mao also recalled: "I have never formally studied at a university; I have never studied abroad either; it was at the First Normal that the foundation of all my learning and all my intellectual knowledge was laid."[46]

When young, Mao lived with his maternal grandparents because his parents were afraid he would die young as had two earlier children. At his grandparents' home, Mao came to know and to admire Wang. Mao consulted Wang about all the things he did not understand. During the five years Mao studied at First Normal, Wang helped him in matters of money and of mind. Wang interceded when Mao encountered trouble, as in the matter of the strike to drive away Principal Zhang in 1915. Wang also provided help and advice to other students. He encouraged students to be interested in current affairs. He supported the Students Friendship Association, the Xinmin xuehui, and the Changsha bookstore, the latter two of which were organized by students. He also supported the movement to "Oust Zhang Jingyao of Hunan," the Hunan independence movement, and the work–study plan in France.

Wang worked in Changsha until 1937, first at First Normal, then as principal of Changsha Changjun Lianli Middle School from 1928 to 1936. In spring 1937, he went to Henan province and worked as the secretary-general of the Education Department of the provincial government. He only stayed in that position for three months and then returned to Hunan to be the principal of the Guanglan Middle School.

After 1949, Wang worked for a while as vice president of the Hunan Administration Institution. Then he took a post at the Hunan Provincial Archive. He also served as a representative at the First, Second, and Third National People's Congress. He died on July 11, 1972, in Beijing, at the age of 88. A memorial meeting was held. The words on the ribbon from Mao's wreath were: "*Jiuge qiangu*" (Eternal repose to my ninth elder brother.)[47]

History Teacher Li Jinxi

Li Jinxi (Shaoxi) was a native of Xiangtan, Hunan, and an eminent linguist. He earned his *Xiucai* degree at the age of 15, then was admitted by the Hunan *Youji* Normal University, where he studied in the Department of History and Geography. He graduated from the school at the age of 22 in the midst of the Republican Revolution of 1911. Li founded and became the chief editor of *Changsha Ribao* (*Changsha Daily*) and *Hunan Gongbao* (*Hunan Gazette*).[48] His newspapers published articles that introduced the Republican Revolution, commented on current affairs, and publicized the New Learning. While operating the newspapers, Li also had contacts with a few progressive youths who had helped him copy his manuscripts. In addition to transcribing, these young people also gave their comments on Li's work. Li once recalled that there were three young men helping him transcribe manuscripts, all quite different from each other. The first would copy out the exact manuscripts without questioning. The second would raise questions about them, and sometimes embellished the sentences for Li. The third would refuse to transcribe the draft article if he did not agree with the author's point of view. The second one became the famous playwright Tian Han (1898–1968). The third one became the leader Mao Zedong. The first one did not achieve as much, so Li declined to mention his name.[49]

In 1914 and 1915, Li taught history at First Normal. In September 1915, he was invited to Beijing by the Ministry of Education to be the chief reader-editor of elementary and middle school textbooks for liberal arts subjects. In 1919, he began to teach at Beijing Normal University, where he worked for fifty-nine years until his death in 1978.

Although Li did not teach long at First Normal, his influence on his students was profound. Only a few years older than most of the students, he was already an energetic and diligent scholar. Reform-minded, he had a very good relationship with his students. In 1914 and 1915, Li, Yang Changji, and four other First Normal teachers all lived in the same area called Lishi yuyuan (Li's quarter) in Changsha. In 1914, Li and Yang Changji organized a Study Group of Philosophy (*Zhexue yanjiu xiaozu*).[50] The student members of the Group were Cai Hesen, Mao Zedong, Chen Chang, Xiao Yu, Xiao San, and Zhang Kundi. They met regularly on Sundays at the homes of the teachers at Lishi yuyuan. At the meeting, the students often consulted with Li and Yang about their studies, introduced reading materials to each other, exchanged their views, and discussed current affairs.[51] Li Jinxi kept a precise record of the students' visits to Yuyuan in his diaries from April 1915 to August 1915; the entries show his interactions with the students:

April 4, 1915, Sunday. In the morning, Runzhi [Mao Zedong] came. I read his diaries and told him the reading method. . . .

April 11, 1915, Sunday. In the morning, . . . First Normal students Xiao Zisheng [Xiao Yu], Runzhi, and Kunfu [Xiong Guangchu] came. We talked about the reading method.

May 30, 1915, Sunday. In the morning, . . . Kunfu and Runzhi came. Then we met Jifan [Wang Jifan] and talked about how to reform society.

July 11, 1915, Sunday. In the morning, . . . Zhangfu and Runzhi came and asked about how to study the basics of *Xiaoxue* (philology and phonology). I told them to read the *Duanzhu shuowen*.

July 13, 1915, Tuesday. I came back at night and then explained the method of reading history books to Zhangfu and Runzhi.[52]

July 20, 1915, Tuesday. In the morning, . . . I sat in the entrance hall, reading part of the "Shanxing" from the *Qunxue yiyan*. I felt refreshed and comfortable, so Runzhi moved to read in this room, too.

August 15, 1915, Sunday. In the morning, . . . Runzhi and Zhangfu came. We went to Kunfu's place, in order to discuss reading methods.

August 29, 1915, Sunday. . . . In the morning, . . . Jifan came. . . . Zisheng and Runzhi came. We talked about [our] studies for a long time.[53]

Working together with his friends and colleagues, Yang Changji, Xu Teli, and Fang Weixia, Li Jinxi also helped organize the Hongwen Publishing House between 1914 and 1915. Hongwen published mainly elementary and middle school textbooks for the Republic. Li served as chief editor for the publishing house.[54]

Li's connections to his First Normal students continued after the May Fourth Movement. The letters Mao Zedong wrote to him from November 1915 to June 1920 reveal that Mao did not simply regard him as a teacher, but also as a close friend whom he could trust and "could consult with about academic studies as well as about the affairs of state."[55] For instance, in a letter of November 9, 1915, Mao complained about the curriculum of the school, then wrote:

I plan to leave such a school, look for a better plan, and make a lofty resolution. I long for [you] my elder brother to come back, so I can discuss this with you. I don't have many mentor friends, but I'm lucky to have you. I regret not to have known you earlier. I wish I could come to you and ask for advice every day.[56]

When rumors circulated that Li was working for Yuan Shikai in Beijing, Mao wrote to Li anxiously and in frank words asked him not to be deceived by Yuan and go astray. He asked Li "to come back quickly! Don't be reluctant to leave!"[57] From the letters and Li's diaries, we can see that the relationship between Li and his students remained close. After the founding of the People's Republic, Li kept in contact with Mao Zedong and Zhou Shizhao. He even mailed his will (*Yuli Yizhu*) to Zhou Shizhao in the later period of the Cultural Revolution (1966-76).[58] Li outlived both Zhou and Mao.

Li Jinxi devoted his whole life to the study of linguistics and made major contributions to the study of Chinese grammar and syntax, as well as to the reform of Chinese characters and the compilation of dictionaries. After 1949, Li, like Wang, was selected as a representative to the First, Second, and Third National People's Congresses. He also served as a member of the First, Second, and Third Chinese People's Political Consultative Conferences and of the prestigious Chinese Academy of Sciences in the Social Science Division. Besides holding these social and academic positions, Li worked at Beijing Normal University. He died in Beijing on March 27, 1978, at the age of 88.

Other Teachers

Other teachers, like Yuan Zhongqian (1868–1947) and Yi Baisha (1886–1921), had some influence and left their mark on the students at First Normal as well. Yuan Zhongqian, also known as Jiliu, taught the Chinese language and literature at the school. He was nicknamed "Yuan, the Big Beard." A holder of the *juren* degree[59] and deeply rooted in Chinese Classics, he required his students to take seriously their study of the classics. Yuan urged them to study the moral characters of the ancients and follow their examples. In his classes, he often named historians, writers, poets, painters, and calligraphers in Chinese history as examples and used their accomplishments and their resolution in pursuing their studies to inspire his students. He asked them to resolve that

"If [one's] literary talent cannot exceed that of his contemporaries, it cannot be called talent. If [one's] learning cannot exceed that of the ancients, it cannot be called learning."[60] Despising nonclassical writings like Liang Qichao's, he ridiculed Mao's style, based as it was on that of Liang Qichao. He urged Mao to take Han Yu, the famous Tang dynasty essayist, as his model. Mao worked seriously to do that. For instance, in his *Jiangtang lu*, Mao's notes came mainly from Yang Changji's ethics class and Yuan's Chinese classical literature class. Mao recalled in 1936, "Thanks to Yuan the Big Beard, therefore, I can today still turn out a passable classical essay if required."[61] Yuan also encouraged his students to attend lectures at the Chuanshan Association and study the writings of the early seventeenth-century scholar Wang Fuzhi. At his urging, many First Normal students like Mao Zedong, Cai Hesen, and Xiao San attended those meetings and absorbed that point of view.

Yi Baisha (original name: Kun), a native of Changsha, Hunan, had graduated from Shanghai Dewen School and then assumed the deanships of Huainingxian Middle School of Anhui and Anhui Provincial University. After the Wuchang Uprising of 1911, he organized a students' army in Anhui province to protect the public security of the capital city. After the failure of the Second Revolution[62] of 1913, Yi fled to Japan. In Japan, he and Zhang Shizhao (1881–1973) founded the *Jiayin* magazine. He published many articles like "Guang Shangtong" ("Advocate Grand Unity") attacking Yuan Shikai's dictatorship.

After the appearance of the radical iconoclastic magazine *New Youth* in 1915, Yi began to publish articles advocating democracy and science. For instance, he published "*Shumo*" ("Commentary on the School of Mozi"), "*Kongzi pingyi*" ("On Confucius"), and "*Zhuzi wu guilun*" ("Masters' Remarks on the Non-existence of Ghosts") in *New Youth*. His article "*Kongzi pingyi*" represented one of the first formal denunciations of Confucius in the May Fourth period.[63] He believed the Chinese worship of Confucius had allowed the imperial rulers to use Confucius as a tool to control people's thinking and take away people's freedom. In order to bring down absolutism in ideology and academia, Yi stated that truth became explicit after debating; learning was improved after competing.[64]

Yi taught Chinese and history at First Normal in 1917 and 1918, the period during which most of his articles appeared in *New Youth*. Yi also gave public lectures to the student body of First Normal. For instance, the First Normal's Historical Records indicate that on March 26, 1918, Yi Baisha was invited to give a public speech.[65] Yi Baisha grew especially interested in the school of Mozi.[66] He praised Mozi highly during his lifetime, a practice that likely exerted a profound influence on students like Cai Hesen, who in his youth adored Mozi.

During the second decade of the twentieth century, First Normal gathered a group of progressive and learned men on its faculty. They devoted themselves to intellectual inquiry as the basis of national renewal and believed that education stood as the best approach for national salvation. Education could "penetrate to the root of society's problems and provide the basis of a solution."[67] They tried to infuse in the school a sense of pride and to fashion the students into a community of the like-minded who could go out to reform the country. The teachers urged students to try to live up to the ideals of the school's motto. And, indeed, the students did change their world through the CCP.

In academics, students received solid training in the Chinese classics; thus, First Normal students inhabited a world of old-style literati culture rich in poetic imagery and historical allusions, which placed high value on a free-flowing life of aesthetic pursuit and metaphysical reflection. Meanwhile, teachers also guided the students to study all aspects of Western thought and institutions, including the intensive application of Western science and technology. Foreign knowledge was taught alongside homegrown wisdom, traditional ideals, and contemporary reformist ideology. The faculty profoundly influenced the students' intellectual transformation, which certainly helped shape the careers and thoughts of the students and contributed to their radicalization.

Chapter 5

Sage in Residence
Yang Changji

Of the many luminaries who taught at First Normal in its heyday, Yang Changji deserves particular attention. Yang Changji, also known as Yang Huaizhong, was a native of Bancang, Dongxiang, Changsha, which was located about fifty kilometers northeast of the city of Changsha. A well-known Neo-Confucian writer specializing in the School of *Li* of the Song and Ming dynasties, he was equally celebrated as a man of Western learning, spending ten years studying Western moral philosophy and education in Japan (1903–1909), Scotland (1909–1912), and Germany (1912–1913). Therefore, Yang incorporated the Western liberal and individualistic thought, such as Kantian and Neo-Kantian ethics, T. H. Green's concept of self-realization, the humanistic and liberal tradition instigated by J Rousseau, and Spenserian utilitarianism, into his sociopolitical and ethical thoughts and was able to reappraise Confucianism. He fiercely criticized Confucian moral codes, such as filial piety (*xiao*) and chastity (*zhen*), and the Confucian doctrine of the Three Bonds (ruler–subject, father–son, and husband–wife relationships), while maintaining the framework of Confucian humanism. Before the May Fourth Movement, Yang was an ethics teacher at First Normal, where by all accounts, he was one of the school's most influential and most respected instructors. He taught Mao Zedong and was the father of Mao's first wife, Yang Kaihui (1901–1931).

Traditional Scholar

Yang Changji drew widely and eclectically from traditional Confucian thought. Even before he encountered ideas of reform and revolution, he had a rich stock of earlier ideas in which to integrate them. Some of these ideas he kept or reshaped; others he discarded, according to the needs of the times. Yang was born into a family with a long-standing tradition of Neo-Confucian scholarship. During his formative years, he was influenced profoundly by his family background, as well as by the Hunanese intellectual heritage and by the ideas and values circulating at that time. Such an influence, as Hao Chang points out, can occur through both formal and informal channels of education.[1]

In the late seventeenth century, Yang's ancestors moved to Bancang from Putang village, also in Changsha county, where they had been farmers for several generations. Because they had broken away from the control of the *zongfa* (kinship) system—in Yang's own words, they "had gotten in touch with people from other lineage groups, acquired new points of view, cut off connections to their own clan, and cast off old, decayed conceptions"[2]—they began to pay attention to their younger descendants' education. Yang's great-great-grandfather and his great-grandfather were both "*taixue sheng*" (students of the imperial academy); his grandfather was a "*yixiang sheng*" (student of the county academy) who died ten years before Yang was born. Yang's father had the title of "*ligong sheng*" (a scholar recommended to the emperor) but he never held government office, instead spending his life as a private tutor in his own region.

Yang's mother came from an eminent literary family named Xiang. His maternal great-great-grandfather held the highest "*jinshi*" degree and was an official of the Qing imperial "*Xuezijian*" (equivalent to the Ministry of Education). His maternal great grandfather held the "*juren*" degree and served as educational commissioner in several districts. His maternal grandfather was also a Confucian scholar but died young.[3] The Xiang family was renowned for its knowledge of Zhu Xi's School of *Li*.

Influenced by this family tradition, Yang was deeply steeped in Neo-Confucianism. He began to study the Confucian classics at the age of 7. Under his father's guidance, Yang mastered the Confucian canon of the Four Books and Five Classics within a few years. He also read extensively in ancient Chinese philosophy, Chinese history, and ethics. When he was a little older, he began to study the works of such eminent Confucians as Zhou Dunyi (1017–1073 AD), the Cheng brothers, Cheng Hao (1032–1085 AD) and Cheng Yi (1033–1107 AD), Zhu Xi, Lu Jiuyuan (1139–1192 AD), and Wang Yangming.

Zhou Dunyi, a native Hunanese, has been regarded as one of the most important founders of the Neo-Confucianism in the Song dynasty.

He was a major influence on Zhu Xi, and a formative influence on the Cheng brothers (Zhou's nephews) who studied with him briefly when they were teenagers. Zhu Xi drew significant parts of his system of thought and practice from Zhou Dunyi and the Cheng brothers. Zhou's thoughts of moral metaphysics were summarized in his two major works: the *Taiji tushuo* (*An explanation of Diagram of the Great Ultimate*)[4] and the *Tongshu* (*Penetrating the Book of Changes*). In the latter, Zhou elaborated on his moral metaphysics, centering on *cheng* (sincerity), which to him, as the highest goodness itself, becomes the ultimate source of moral principles.[5] "*Cheng* is the foundation of the sage" (*shengren zhi ben*) and "sage-hood is nothing but *cheng*."[6] *Cheng* thus can be used to distinguish between good and evil and perfect oneself. Through identifying *cheng* with the sage, Zhou made the connection between the evolutionary process of the cosmos and the moral development of man, which became the very core of his moral philosophy, and provided the essential outline of Neo-Confucian ethics and of Confucian individualism.[7]

Zhou's doctrine of self-cultivation exerted tremendous influence on Hunan scholars, which was based largely on his dialectical approach to *cheng*. *Cheng* in its essence was assumed to be absolute tranquility and inactivity (*jiran bu dong*), while in its functional aspect it was seen as dynamic. "Being active without activity and tranquil without tranquility" demonstrated the ultimate state of the spirit of a human being, namely, of sage-hood or perfect *cheng*. Because absolute tranquility was the foundation of the sage in his metaphysics, Zhou approved of stillness in his method of self-cultivation.[8] According to Zhou, one had to "restrain one's wrath and repress one's desires"(*chengfen zhiyu*), "move toward good and correct one's mistakes" (*qianshan gaiguo*), before one could reach the state of "having no thought and yet penetrating all," and finally could achieve sage-hood.[9] Zhou's concepts of *cheng* and moral cultivation exerted a considerable influence on later Hunanese Confucians.[10] To later Confucians, Zhou personified the virtue of *cheng*, the full realization of the innate goodness and wisdom of human nature. Yang Changji drew significantly from Zhou of his moral cultivation and his concept of *cheng* and held to it throughout his life.

The School of *Li* in which Yang immersed himself was one of the two central Confucian schools of the Song dynasty and culminated in the great thought of Zhu Xi. Zhu Xi's philosophy saw the world determined by a dualism among a rational, natural, and moral order (*li*) and material force (*qi*). *Li* (principle) can be understood as the structure or organizing principle of everything in the universe. It is fully present in each thing that exists. The *li* determines why things are the way they are, and how they ought to be. *Qi* (material force) comes in varying degrees of clarity or turbidity.

Zhu believed that the Way (*Dao*) of Heaven (*Tian*) is expressed in principle or *li*. There is the purity of *li*, and the shifting turbidity of *qi*. Because our *qi* is so turbid initially, we cannot discover the *li* or principle for ourselves. To clarify our *qi* and achieve enlightenment, we must carefully study the *Four Books* and do "the investigation of things" under the guidance of a wise teacher. It is cleat that Zhu subscribed to the traditional Confucian ideal of moral self-cultivation.

Zhu's theory of personal cultivation and its principal teaching—to preserve the ultimate principle and destroy human desire (*cun tianli, mie renyu*)—ultimately aimed at the realization of good and the destruction of evil. He basically regarded *tianli* and *renyu* as contradictory and totally different. For Zhu, *tianli* meant a state in which a human mind was consistent with reason, and *renyu* referred to a state in which the mind had fallen into temptation. His theory of personal cultivation related questions of good and evil to desire. Zhu thus understood evil as the shortage of *tianli*, and his instruction "*cun tianli, mie renyu*" can be viewed as asceticism. Zhu Xi was a major inspiration for Hunan scholarship, due in part to his revival of the Yuelu Academy. He lectured there while serving as pacification commissioner of Jinhu South (*Jinhu nanlu anchashi*) based at Tanzhou (present Changsha) in spring 1194.[11]

As Yan-shuan Lao indicates, another contribution Zhu Xi made involved his emphasis on the concept of ruler–teacher unity. Zhu argued that the ruler as ideal ruler/sage-king, as teacher of antiquity and the Way (*Dao*), and as moral exemplifier had the obligation both to rule and to instruct his subjects. His theory of the ruler–teacher unity had made a strong impact on Mao, who had sought this unity throughout his life. Mao would long have a particular interest in being called great teacher among the four "greats" (great teacher, great leader, a great commander in chief, the great helmsman). That emphasis shaped the poems, articles, and mass campaigns he launched, including the Yanan Rectification Campaign (*zhengfeng yundong*), the anti-rightist movement, the Great Leap Forward, and the Cultural Revolution.[12]

In the nineteenth century, the years of Yang's schooling, Zeng Guofan and a group of Hunanese scholar-officials initiated the revival of the School of *Li*. Zeng was an eminent imperial official, statesman, and general, but mostly remembered as a prominent Confucian scholar who was responsible for the suppression of the Taiping Rebellion. Zeng was eclectic. Besides the Confucian *Lixue*, he drew on a wide range of ideas, such as *Hanxue* and the Hundred Schools.[13] His stress on personal cultivation was something that Yang drew from him, and retained through all the changes ahead.

The revival of the School of *Li* can be seen as a reaction against the indifference of the Empirical Research School to the sociopolitical commitment of Confucianism, and the *Lixue* scholars' deepening concerns about their intellectual world. Zeng and these *Lixue* scholars felt a pressing need to reaffirm the neglected Confucian idea of taking inner sagehood as the starting point of governing state. They perpetuated the idea of moral self-cultivation, drawing largely on Zhou Dunyi's concept of *cheng*. For them, self-cultivation focused on cultivating the mind, examining oneself daily, and using the approach of *xingshen rike* (a daily lesson of self-introspection) and a "character-building programme."[14]

The revival of *Lixue* was also a resurgence of a reaction against historical change. Although the Taiping Rebellion had been suppressed by Zeng Guofan's *Xiang jun* in 1864, the Qing court was still living in lingering fear, wondering how and why the rebellion could have happened. Zeng held that the emergence of the Taiping Rebellion from south China provided evidence that internal rebellion had been accompanied by foreign encroachment. He believed that the Taipings had appropriated "the doctrine of the heavenly ruler" from "foreign barbarians" and had used the "so-called teachings of Jesus" (who was said to be the brother of the Taiping leader, Hong Xiuquan), to destroy the principles of orthodox Confucianism.[15] Therefore, quashing the Taiping Rebellion, Zeng called for an urgent revival of Confucian orthodoxy, which for him was the School of *Li* of the Song and Ming dynasties. Zeng devoted his whole life to studying and promoting this school; he was also familiar with the Han Learning. Furthermore, he advocated incorporating valuable aspects of all the One Hundred Schools. His view that the School of *Li* provides the ultimate principle of the world, while other philosophical schools also contain insights with some value, deeply influenced Yang, who once wrote that he would never belittle and reject all the other philosophical schools, but only honor the Confucian teaching.[16] He continued, "Although I started as a student of the *Song xue*, I also recognize the contribution of *Han xue*'s textual research; although I started as a student of the Cheng-Zhu School, I also recognize the distinct insights of the Lu-Wang School."[17] The revival of Neo-Confucian moral philosophy was also accompanied by an emphasis on the ideal of practicality (*jingshi zhiyong*).

Scholars in the late Qing, especially those from Hunan, greatly admired Zeng, who came to be regarded as the *zhongxing mingchen* (famous courtier in the resurgence of the nation) and *yidai ruzong* (the master of Confucianism for a generation).[18] Yang Changji's father shared this enthusiasm for Zeng's writings. With his father's encouragement, Yang seriously studied many of Zeng's works and later praised him highly to the students at First Normal. Regarding philosophy, Zeng paid special attention to *cheng* (sincerity or authenticity) in the School of *Li*. Yang was even more influenced by Zeng's views on moral cultivation. Yang's diaries in *Dahuazhai riji* (*Diaries from the Dahua Studio*) revealed the close attention he paid to the types of books Zeng had read and even to Zeng's approach to dealing with people, his lifestyle, and his methods of study. When he was studying at home, Yang named his study room *Dahuazhai* (Dahua studio). Yang had particular praise for the way Zeng pursued his studies (or *gewu*), writing in his diary, "In the past, Zeng made his own study plans. He made himself read ten pages of history every day and continued this practice all his life. This study method should be followed by everyone."[19] He often cited Zeng Guofan as an example for his students to follow and as a model for motivating himself.

At the turn of nineteenth century, Wang Fuzhi's thought became another important source of inspiration not only for the Hunanese literati, but also for the entire Chinese literati world.[20] Wang developed an evolutionary, materialistic, and nationalist view of history and evinced a critical attitude toward despotism.[21] He rejected the prevalent Chinese idea that there once had been a "golden age." He asserted that the present was better than the ancient; ancient laws and morals did not necessarily apply to the contemporary world; each period had its own characteristics. A good ruler had an obligation to alter policies and institutions in order to meet changing times and his subjects' wants and desires. He believed that different cultures and geographical areas should keep to their own customs and should have their own rulers and forms of government.[22] His argument made an indirect attack on the Manchu regime. He argued that the Manchus did not belong in China. Both the reformers of 1898 and the nationalists and revolutionaries at the turn of the twentieth century were drawn to his writings and were particularly influenced by his passionate nationalism, his evolutionary idea of history, and his theory of necessary social and political change to meet the present needs, and to find guidance for the future.[23] His emphasis on distinction between Chinese and non-Chinese (*yixia zhibian*) undoubtedly became a building block for the kind of nationalism that Yang and Mao espoused.

Regarding the relationship between "Heavenly principle" and "Human desire," Wang argued that people's common desire was nothing but the satisfaction of their basic needs in life. He rejected Buddhists' renouncement of human desires; he also criticized the Cheng-Zhu School's doctrine that one needed to destroy human desires in order to exemplify the Heavenly principle. He advocated the unity of the Heavenly principle and human desires: The principle of heaven lies in nothing but what the people desire in common.[24]

Concerning the doctrine of the Three Bonds, Wang's view differed from that of Zhu Xi. As Yan-shuan Lao points out, Zhu Xi and his *lixue* School had made great contribution to the spread of the Three Bonds by equating it with the heavenly principle (*taiji*).[25] Wang's evolutionary view of history—Three Bonds should be changed to meet changing times—and his critical attitude toward despotism represented a veiled resistance against Zhu Xi's view of Three Bonds. Being selective and eclectic, Yang and Mao drew much more from Wang than from Zhu Xi regarding this issue because both of them attacked Three Bonds. Both also owed much to Tan Sitong who was most likely influenced by Wang on this topic as well.

Wang's thought was taught in Hunanese academies and formed a component of the curriculum for Hunan's Neo-Confucian students.[26] Some of Wei Yuan's key philosophical and reformist ideas, such as the evolutionary view of history and the condemnation of those who despised the present while exalting the past, owed much to Wang Fuzhi.[27] Two teachers of Tan Sitong were devoted students of Wang's philosophy. Tan himself was deeply influenced by Wang Fuzhi. Tan's ether-based monism, his metaphysical dynamism, his moral activism and radicalism, and his inclination toward "practical learning" all came from his study of Wang's teaching.[28]

Although choosing to live in solitude, Wang's thought was rather a reflection on, and passionate concern about, the events taking place in the world at that time.[29] In a period of dynastic decline and alien invasion, "for him Confucianism was nothing if not the philosophy of those morally committed to action relevant to the problems of the present."[30] This is why Wang's thought as a philosopher and historian of the seventeenth century was so attracted to both Confucian literati and revolutionaries at the turn of twentieth century when China was facing a similar crisis albeit in a different form. Yang Changji also greatly admired Wang Fuzhi who remained the source of his intellectual inspiration, manifested in the high frequency of his citation of Wang's work in his diaries, lectures, and essays.

All of Wang's works convey a strong inclination toward practical orientation. For Wang, the study of history and historical writing should aim to reveal the main principles of how to manage the world (*jingshi zhi dalue*) through the evaluation of historical events.[31] He took the study of the Confucian Classics as the essential starting point and the study of history as their practical application. This part of Wang's thought became one of the most important origins of the nineteenth-century revival of the Confucian ideal of practical statesmanship, with an emphasis on professional statecraft as the principal approach to achieve the Confucian moral perfection.[32]

The leading figures of the revival of Wang's thought were a group of Hunanese scholars, such as He Changling and Wei Yuan, who were concerned that inner moral cultivation and exemplary leadership were not sufficient to solve the problems China was facing. They believed professional statecraft and institutional approaches should be added.[33] This intellectual tradition started in the eleventh century and has been promoted by almost every director of Yuelu Academy since then. It had significant influence on shaping the minds of the nineteenth-century literati of practical statesmanship, who also demonstrated a special concern with the moral philosophy of self-cultivation and always regarded it as the foundation (*ben*).[34]

In the 1890s, Hunan was first the center of xenophobia, then the center of reform movement, with Hunanese gentry literati as the driving force. Confucian tradition remained the major source, whereas Western learning became important only during Hunan's reform movement period, which was the intellectual setting where Yang Changji's thought began to take shape.

Although Yang lost his mother when he was 8 years old, and his father when he was 14,[35] he was very self-driven and studied very hard. In 1889, he passed the civil service examination at the county level, earning the title of "*yixiangsheng*" (another name for *shengyuan*, equal to the first *xiucai* degree in the Qing dynasty). He failed the examination for the "*juren*" degree in the following year. Yang's father passed away in 1884. By 1888 when he was 18, Yang was married and with a wife and soon a daughter to support, he took up his father's career as a private tutor and began to teach at home.

In addition to teaching, Yang continued to pursue his own studies, putting great effort into learning about the School of *Li*. Zhu Xi's theory of personal cultivation and his teaching of *cun tianli, mie renyu* especially influenced him. Zhu held that "nature is the principle or the ultimate principle" and the Way of Heaven was expressed in *li*. Yang was a staunch supporter of Zhu Xi's view, and firmly believed in Zhu Xi's formulation that although *li* in itself was pure and perfect, base emotions and conflicts arose with the addition of *qi*; human nature was originally good, as Mencius had argued, but not pure unless action was taken to purify it, because the *qi* was initially so thick that it covered the *li*. Yang was convinced that it was imperative to purify *li* by destroying the *renyu* that blocked it. Only in this way could one "preserve *tianli*" and become a virtuous person. Therefore, Yang put Zhu Xi's teaching into practice and exemplified asceticism in his life. For instance, he was very careful about controlling desire (*zhi yu*). He wrote in his diary in 1894: "What has happened is the *kalpa* [a Buddhist term meaning predestined fate] (*yi chengwei jieshu*); what is yet to happen is the killing instinct (*wei chengwei shaji*). In the destiny of Heaven, it is the waxing of *yin* and waning of *yang*. In the human mind, it is the triumph of desire and the extinction of *li*."[36] Around the same time, he also observed, "Mind that follows desires leads to suffering, and following *li*, happiness."[37] Yang firmly believed that a virtuous person would deny desire, especially the selfish carnal desire caused by the distortion of temperament, keep a calm mind, and deal only with the ultimate *li*. Yang thus proposed the model of "following *li*" (*xun li*) and "destroying *yu*" (*qu yu*).

On moral cultivation, the Lu-Wang school was added to the mix. Yang was drawn by Wang Yangming's (1427–1529) School of Mind/Heart as well. He accepted the view of Lu Xiangshan (Lu Jiuyuan, 1139–1192) that "The universe is my mind, and my mind is the universe." Lu and Wang criticized Zhu Xi for focusing obsessively on the need for diligent study or "the investigation of things" to see *li*, claiming instead that *li* was in one's heart. Thus, there was no better place to seek it than within oneself. Yang thought that people could see what *li* required of them, if they cultivated and used their mind to that end.

Yang's preferred method of mental cultivation was "quiet sitting" (*jingzuo*), a popular form of meditation from the Song dynasty down to Qing times. However, Yang's practice of the so-called "floating mind" (*youxin*), a kind of exercise of breathing combined with inward envisioning, was not simply a matter of method, but part of his intellectual and spiritual quest.[38] As a young man, Yang was very interested in this meditation and enthusiastically advocated it, and he followed the practice of "quiet sitting" all his life. He often said that in "quiet sitting," the first step was to eliminate all sorts of random thoughts and desires. He would make his mind move about within his body, imagining the delight of blood circulating. He would make his mind travel beyond the great vacuity and imagine the purity and unity of the *qi*.[39] He believed that "quiet sitting" as an approach to self-cultivation was based on the view that the human mind could combine with the universal mind or the ultimate *li*. His "floating the mind" thus should be a seeking for intellectual and spiritual freedom from the convention. To him, the idea of mastery of one's self in oneness involved in a practice of vital energy and the realization of Confucian ideal was guaranteed by this method of "quiet sitting." In this way, Confucian ideals pervaded throughout the mental and everyday life of a Confucian student.

Yang was also very much attracted to other notions of the School of *li*, such as *cheng*, *jing* (stillness), and *jing* or *ju jing* (abiding in reverent composure), and frequently referred to them. Originally, the word *cheng* was a moral concept, the requirement to be authentic and sincere when dealing with people. However, Zhou Dunyi gave it a cosmological resonance when he linked cosmology and Confucian ethics. He maintained that being *cheng* was the foundation of the sage, the foundation of the Five Constant Elements of Virtues (*wuxing zhi ben*),[40] and the source of all human behavior (*baixing zhi yuan*). Thus, the concept took on independent substance. When discussing *cheng*, Yang usually approached it from a moral perspective. For instance, he wrote: "Being ultimately authentic (*zhi cheng*) to other people, one will receive the moral virtues of the sage and not be resented (by others)."[41] Yang believed that a noble man or a virtuous person could not engage in manipulative power for personal ends, but must undertake authentic actions. Doing so personifies the virtue of authenticity, the full realization of one's innate goodness, which in turn would change some of the old corrupt habits of the society.[42] In this way, Yang put forward the idea that *zhi cheng dong wu* (ultimate authenticity moves things). He saw morality and actualization of one's moral potential as extremely important, believing that being authentic would both create emotional connections with and physically improve everything.

Jing (stillness) and *jing* or *ju jing* (abiding in reverent composure) were originally self-cultivation methods used by the Neo-Confucians of the School of *li* in the Song dynasty to realize their aim of "preserving *tianli* and destroying *renyu*." Yang borrowed these methods and applied them to reading. He also followed the Song Confucians in the practice of *jing* (stillness) and *ju jing* (reverence) urging people to ignore what was happening in this complicated and ever-changing world, to destroy or limit desire, and concentrate on self moral cultivation. However, this goal was not easy to achieve, and Yang often felt frustrated at not being able to reach the desired states.[43]

Yang's intellectual and spiritual quest started with his extensive reading of classical and Neo-Confucian works from his childhood to his 20s. It was then that painstaking self-cultivation and search for sagehood began, a goal based on a threefold humanistic concern: man's ultimate potential as an individual, the individual's relationship to society, and the realization of man's ultimate potential.[44] His methodology was characterized by quietness, reverence, and the floating mind. During this time, Yang's metaphysical views of man, mind, and human nature formed, influenced mainly by Zhou Dunyi, Zhu Xi, Wang Fuzhi, and Zeng Guofan. He also drew heavily on the intellectual heritage of the Hunanese school. All those, plus his exposure to the reformist ideas prevalent in Hunan, helped greatly in shaping his thought—valuing the self and understanding the present reality based on Confucian concepts of man, universe, and society, and his belief that the inner moral strength of self was the basis of an individual's independence (*zili*) and self-realization. These ideas Yang took with him as China confronted the defeat by Japan and the rise of reform after 1895.

Intellectual Reformer

China's worst humiliation of the nineteenth century was its failure in the Sino–Japanese War, which greatly shocked and traumatized the Chinese, especially its intellectuals. China thus was pushed onto the track of increasingly radical change in almost every realm. Like many intellectuals of his time, Yang was very much concerned about the historical and political changes that China was undergoing. His worries about the fate of the country and his search for answers that could help to save China quickly, dispelled the dejection induced by his personal setbacks in the civil service examinations. In the 1890s, Yang studied at the two most prestigious Confucian academies in the province in order to prepare for the examinations for the *juren* degree, which were held every three years. In 1893, he attended the Changsha Chengnan Academy. In 1898, he studied at the Yuelu Academy.[45] He failed the examinations for a second time in 1893, an experience that profoundly depressed him. Yet his depression dissipated with the outbreak of the Sino–Japanese War in 1894.

The Hunanese Reform movement represented a decisive event in Yang's intellectual life. It provided him with a chance to interact with Western learning, which proved crucial to the formulation of his ethical, educational, social, and political thought, grounded in a synthesis of Chinese and Western thoughts. Particularly, his reformist thought, a syncretism of the Confucian humanistic principle of "Perpetual Renewal of Life" and Western liberal democratic ideas, such as "popular sovereignty," "people's rights," and "individual rights," enabled him to challenge the Chinese monarchical system and to call for political reform. However, because he had already reached his intellectual maturity (between late 1890s and 1902) before leaving for Japan, Yang's commitment to Confucianism never wavered. He regarded it as a universal truth and the source of his intellectual and spiritual life. He also was dedicated to an intellectualistic-educational approach for solving China's problem.

Driven by a desire to acquire "world knowledge" in order to provide guidance to society, Yang started his ten-year intellectual journey abroad in 1903. This experience was crucial to his intellectual and spiritual development. He integrated key ideas and values of Western liberal individualism, particularly Kantian ideas of autonomy, respect for the self and person, and subjectivity, into his thought of valuing the self, where the independence of the self or an individual was the core. Metaphysically, he still thought it in a Confucian way. His notion of comprehending the present reality shows his profound concern with reality and an overwhelming emphasis on "strenuous action." Individual's self-realization should be applied here and now. The Confucian ideal of sagehood still essential in his thought.[46] Young Mao Zedong embraced Yang's two ideas and interpreted them in his own terms as "individualism" and "realism," claiming to be committed to these two principles.[47]

The period around the turn of the twentieth century was a crucial period in Chinese history. After 1895, Western impact began to spread to the essential (*ti*) levels. The basic Confucian moral values—the doctrine of the Three Bonds—were challenged. The Confucian ritual code was broken down. Thus, the Chinese, especially the intellectuals, went through a crisis of identity, for the culture they had admired for so long now became problematic. They began to search for a new cultural identity based on nationalism. Furthermore, the Chinese notion of universal kingship, the core of a Chinese-centered cosmological order, also crumbled as a result of the Western and Japanese military threat and cultural penetration. Chinese intellectuals not only had to deal with a sense of crisis of the cosmological order but also had to reexamine the institutional foundation of the Chinese sociopolitical order. In this sense, Chinese intellectuals were searching for a new set of values to build a new order.[48] As Benjamin Schwartz points out in his book, *In Search of Wealth and Power: Yen Fu and the West,* these internal dynamics provide an important mechanism for the self-transformation of the traditional value system, permitting many age-old ideas and values to survive into the contemporary phase.[49] This intellectual background inspired a whole generation of Chinese intellectuals engaged in the struggle for modernization through philosophical thought.

Along with other like-minded intellectuals in Hunan, Yang found an outlet for his concerns in the reform movement of the late 1890s. At the national level, the reform movement was launched in spring 1895 with Kang Youwei's letter to the Guangxu emperor, signed jointly by more than 1,300 *juren* degree holders who were then taking the palace examinations in Beijing. In that letter, Kang Youwei asked the emperor to abrogate the treaty even though doing so would cost China its restored peace, and proposed various other measures for national salvation. He particularly emphasized the importance of political reform, which he believed was fundamental to the task of creating a strong China.[50] Kang's letter was disseminated quickly across the country and influenced many people. Yang was excited by it and became a zealous supporter of Kang's reform effort.

The reform movement went well in Hunan because it had sympathizers on the highest levels of government in Chen Baozhen, the province's governor, and Huang Zunxian, the province's judicial commissioner. It also benefited from the efforts of the Hunanese reformers. In 1898, the reformist newspapers, *Xiang bao* (*Hunan News*) and *Xiangxue bao* (*Hunan Reform News*) were launched by the Hunanese reformers Xiong Xiling, Tan Sitong, and Tang Caichang, with support from Gov. Chen. They also established the *Nan xuehui* (South China Study Society) and the *Shiwu xuetang* (School of Current Affairs) that same year.

Yang joined the South China Study Society and became a regular correspondent. One article he wrote for the society, "*Lun Hunan zunzhi sheli shangwuju yi xian zhenxing nonggong zhixue*" ("On how Hunan should take precedence in the promotion of studies of agriculture and industry over the establishment of a Commercial Bureau under the imperial order"),[51] drew high praise and was published in *Xiang bao*. Yang also frequently attended the society's lectures and was eager to familiarize himself with the new learning. Among the lecturers was Tan Sitong with whom Yang often consulted. Yang was much impressed by Tan's philo-sophical tract, "On Benevolence" (*Renxue*), especially its universalistic conception of **ren** and its sense of cosmic dynamism. He declared: "If a person does not know this *Renxue*, he has frittered away his life."[52] He thought very highly of Tan's philosophical and political views, especially the "energy of the mind," which I discuss in more detail in the section on moral education. Yang also supported Tan's criticism of the Confu-cian Three Bonds. Years later, in his diary of March 1915, Yang recalled:

> I have studied philosophy for over ten years. It has been very difficult. But when I read *Renxue* by Tan from Liuyang, I suddenly felt enlightened. In his preface, Tan wrote that there were so many restraints on people. People should first muster the courage to rip apart and burst the fetters of gains and interests; then, the ropes that the Confucian moral prin-ciple and human relationships created around them; next, the restraints of Heaven; and finally the constraints of Buddhism. He asked people to move forward [in life] with great mental effort and an indomitable spirit. He has captured my mind. I feel a thousand times stronger than before. . . . Now I realize that my former worldview was so parochial.[53]

These passages clearly show that Yang was fully convinced by Tan's philosophical ideas.

Like his contemporaries, Yang especially admired Tan's devotional spirit; indeed, Tan's legendary martyrdom gave him a special aura in the memory of modern Chinese intellectuals. Yang later wrote, "When disaster falls upon a family, if one man sacrifices his life and the whole family can be saved, a man of filial piety will do it. When catastrophe arrives in the world, if one man or one family gives up his life or their lives, and the people of the rest of the world can be saved, a man of benevolence (*Ren ren*) will do it."[54] Yang believed that Tan Sitong was a "man of benevolence" who had died for the sake of the people under heaven. He often said: "The spirit of a martyrdom of Tan from Liuyang fills the universe and will last forever."[55]

After the failure of the Hundred Days Reform Movement of 1898, Yang was totally disillusioned with Empress Cixi's court and lost interest in the civil service examinations—especially after hearing that another famous Hunanese reformer, Tang Caichang, whom he knew well and greatly respected, had been killed in August 1900. Meanwhile, one of Yang's close friends, Yang Yulin (1872–1911), began to advocate revolutionary ideas and establish ties to anti-Manchu activities. In 1902, Yang Yulin went to Japan to study and encouraged Yang Changji to do the same.

Yang Yulin, also known as Shouren, was one year younger than Yang Changji. The two Yangs were related: According to family history, Yang Yulin's father was Yang Changji's cousin. However, they became friends only when both were studying at Changsha Chengnan Academy in 1893. Yang Yulin's specialty was classical Buddhism, but he was also very knowledgeable about the major writings of other schools of philosophy. After several years in Japan, in spring 1908 Yang Yulin went to England to study. Following a series of failed revolutionary uprisings, in which numerous revolutionaries were killed, Yang Yulin became deeply depressed because many of the dead had been his close friends and comrades. In May 1911 he committed suicide in Liverpool, England, by drowning himself.[56]

After humiliating defeats from the West and Japan, from the mid-nineteenth century on, a group of Chinese scholar officials decided that the secret China lacked and the West possessed was technological expertise. Thus, an urge to borrow, to learn, and to master the Western technology began. In the early twentieth century, large numbers of Chinese students were sent overseas to study. Many of them picked up an interest in the most avant-garde European social and political philosophies. Thus, their borrowing went beyond modern science and technology and constitutional monarchy to nationalism (i.e., opposition to imperialism), republicanism (i.e., opposition to empire), democracy, anarchism, and eventually Marxism. For several reasons, Japan was the most popular destination. First, the Meiji Restoration showed that Japan was successful in learning from the West, making it a good example of a modern constitutional monarchy; second, Japan was closer than Western countries, so study there was much cheaper; third, the basic cultural similarities between China and Japan made study there easier for the Chinese students; and fourth, Meiji Japan was militarily strong.

The examinations for studying abroad were organized by the provincial government; Yang Changji took them in late 1902. His high scores earned him scholarships to study in Japan. Such government scholarships obligated their holders to serve the province for five years after their return. Yang had mixed feelings about going to Japan to study at that time. He was happy to have this opportunity to acquire the new knowledge that would help him to make China strong and wealthy. He was loath to leave his homeland and family, particularly his wife and children (by then he had a son as well as a daughter). However, he was more concerned about the fate of his country. Before he left China, he changed his name to Huaizhong, to show that while abroad he would "hold China in his heart."[57]

In February 1903, at the age of 32, Yang left for Japan. He traveled with more than thirty other Hunanese students. During their long voyage, they often talked about education, literature, and the Japanese language, which Yang apparently began to study before his departure. Zhu Deshang, one of the Hunanese on board, wrote in his diary on February 6, 1903: "After talking with Yang Bisheng (Changji) about Japanese language, I have a much better understanding of it now."[58] Yang and Zhu also made an agreement that after they arrived in Japan, besides taking classes, they would translate into Chinese what their countrymen needed most and immediately send the completed translation to a publishing house.

When he first arrived in Japan in February 1903, Yang studied at Tokyo's Kōbun College, which had been founded by the famous Japanese educator Kanō Jigorō (1860–1938). Because large numbers of Chinese students went to Japan to study during this period, and because many of them did not know any Japanese and had not previously received any modern Western-style education, the Japanese educators and businessmen established preparatory schools to equip the Chinese students for the regular universities. Kōbun College was the most prestigious preparatory school for comprehensive studies and teacher training.

In the beginning, Yang studied in the accelerated teachers' training department, which was set up to meet the urgent need for teachers for the newly emerged Western-style schools in China. The course of study was designed to last between six months and three years, and on its completion all the students were to go back to China to teach. Yang soon felt the curriculum was not sufficiently challenging and could not prepare him for the further studies in regular Japanese universities that he desired. Therefore, he transferred to the regular department to study education, psychology, ethics, and pedagogy. In 1906, he graduated from Kōbun College and entered Tokyo Higher Normal College, majoring in education.[59]

During his years in Japan, Yang believed that China's survival depended on education to raise the quality of its people. Chinese students in Japan at this time were intellectually active, and in Tokyo they founded more than twenty journals. *Youxue yibian* (*Study Abroad and Translations*), begun by the Hunanese students Yang Du and Yang Yulin, was among the best known. At Yang Yulin's invitation, in 1903 Yang Changji published part of his 1898 diaries in *Youxue yibian*, and these selections revealed what was then Yang's philosophical thinking.

Like many of his contemporaries, Yang was attracted to the Western concepts of individuality and personal independence. He wrote in his diary: "In the physical world, the center is my body; in the spiritual/mental realm, the center is my mind. In short, among the ten thousand things in the universe, I am the essence. The emperor is *my* emperor; the father is *my* father; the teacher *is* my teacher; the wealth is *my* wealth; heaven and earth are my heaven and earth. . . . Mencius said: 'All things in the world are complete in me.' . . . Everything in the universe is also my responsibility."[60] Here Yang was advocating the liberation of individuality and respect for personal liberties. In so doing, he was also challenging the Chinese concept of the Mandate of Heaven as the foundation of imperial rule and relocating sovereignty in the people themselves.

Yang not only embraced freedom for the individual, but also advocated taking people themselves as fundamental to change and through them making reforms in society, government, and corrupted customs. Because of the previous failure of the Hundred Days Reform Movement of 1898, which was imposed by the emperor from the top down, Yang believed that China needed a bottom–up reform movement. In order for it to succeed, he stressed the need to reform people's thoughts. He wrote in his diary: "Concerning the methods of reform, there are two. The first style is top–down reform. This style can be quickly implemented but easily altered. The other style is bottom–up. This particular method is slow to implement, yet when carried out successfully, its effects are long-lasting."[61] Yang believed that in order to reform the general public, one must first reform the education that shapes their mentality. He noted, "In the sky, the greatest source of power is the sun. On earth, the greatest power comes from electricity. In human beings, power comes from the mind. With a strong mind, what can't one do?"

As a student in Japan, Yang was diligent, studious, and austere. But he had a penchant for travel, embracing an old Chinese proverb: "Traveling ten thousand *li* is better than reading ten thousand books. Therefore, he ended up visiting many of Japan's travel destinations. Once when he was traveling with a friend, named Li Xiaodan, he confided that he really wanted to master philosophy, especially that of *Lixue*, and persuaded Li Xiaodan that he, too, should study these works. Yang said to his companion, "You read extensively, however, you have not yet studied the School of *Li*. Therefore, you have missed the foundation, the essence of knowledge. Japanese scholars have written a lot on the School of *Li*. Have you read any of them?"[62] Li recalled often going to Yang for discussion and advice—sometimes about Liang Qichao, sometimes about Wang Fuzhi—and over time he learned much from Yang. Yang concentrated on study and remained aloof from the radical political activities of Chinese students in Japan, although he also supported the republican ideal.

In Japan, Yang was systematically trained in Western educational psychology, pedagogy, philosophy, ethics, and world history. He was also greatly influenced by his teacher, Kanō Jigorō whose educational thought emphasized moral character (*deyu*), intellectual education (*zhiyu*), and physical strength (*tiyu*). That provided a source of inspiration for the formulation of his own educational thought, which emphasized both physical and mental strength (*shenxin bingzhong*).[63] Yang owed much of his perception of Western moral philosophy and its tradition to another teacher, Yoshida Seichi (1872–1945), a prolific writer on Western ethics.[64] Yang also drew largely from Fukuzawa Yukichi's (1834–1901) ideas about relationships between individuals and society for his interpretation of the idea of the individual's independence.[65]

While Yang was studying at Tokyo Higher Normal College, his close friend Yang Yulin became the secretary of Kuai Guangdian, who was the education commissioner for the Qing government in Europe. In spring 1909, at the strong recommendation of Yang Yulin and Zhang Shizhao, Kuai Guangdian sent Yang Changji to Great Britain for further study. Yang arrived in spring 1909 to enter the University of Aberdeen in Scotland, majoring in philosophy and ethics. During his stay at Aberdeen, Yang systematically studied the history of Western philosophy and ethics, as well as the theories of the major popular contemporary schools of philosophy. The intellectual influence of Aberdeen University can be seen in Yang's systematic exposure to the history of Western ethics and modern currents of British and German ethics, such as utilitarian and evolutionary ethics and T. H. Green's concept of self-realization.

The teaching of philosophy and moral philosophy at University of Aberdeen had a long history. Thomas Reid's (1710–1796) philosophy had a lasting influence at Aberdeen. His ethical thought emphasizing the application of ethical principles to moral practices is essentially similar to Yang's philosophy. Alexander Bain (1818–1903), who imbibed the philosophy of Reid, was one of the teachers who most influenced Yang's philosophy.[66] With the help of his teacher John Clark, Yang got the chance to see real primary school life in Aberdeen in winter 1910. The survey was resulted in two articles published in *Hunan Journal of Education* shortly after Yang's return home in the spring.[67]

While in Europe, through reading and personal observations, Yang also developed a view of a sound middle-class society, which became an important part of his social, economic, and political thought. Yang kept his penchant for travel in Britain and seized every possible chance to go deeper into British social and cultural life. He was utterly impressed by the wealthy and peaceful city life of Scotland, with its efficient government, free school education, and well-educated people with gentle manner. Therefore, social customs became his main concern. His later writings included topics on marriage, inheritance, the nuclear family, respect for individual rights, and freedom of thought. His social criticism is distinctive for its application of Western humanistic values, particularly the concepts of person and personality in Kantian ethical thought.

Its low cost of living made Aberdeen more attractive to Yang than London. Besides, his good friend Zhang Shizhao had already studied there. And by the end of 1909, Yang Yulin resigned his job as the secretary of the education commissioner and joined Yang at Aberdeen, majoring in English and bringing the total number of Chinese students at the university to four. Because they had few school activities outside of class, Yang had plenty of time to explore the British educational system, local culture, and life and customs more generally. In summer 1912, after three years of study, he graduated from Aberdeen with a bachelor's of arts degree.[68]

Yang then stayed in Germany for nine months as a visiting scholar and came to regard himself as a Neo-Kantian idealist, as is evident in topics he chose for teaching and translation at First Normal.[69] Studying with New idealist James Black Bailie (1872–1940) at Aberdeen certainly fostered his interest in German idealistic tradition, particularly in Kantian and Neo-Kantian ethic. The main goal of his stay in Germany was to study the German school system and German educational thought, particularly the educational philosophy of Johann Friederich Herbart (1776–1841).[70] Yang returned to China from Berlin in spring 1913 with guiding principles for social reform based on an amalgamation between Confucian and Western thoughts.[71]

After Yang's return to China, Tan Yankai, governor of Hunan, invited him to be the provincial commissioner of education, but Yang politely refused.[72] He did not like the dictatorial rule of Yuan Shikai,

whom he felt had grabbed the fruits of the revolutionaries' labor. He
believed that the government of Tan Yankai in Hunan was dominated
by men of wealth and position, and a commissioner of education who
believed (as he did) that China's political and social institutions and
ethics must change would draw their attack. His commitment to education was also deeply rooted in his sense of the Confucian *junzi*'s mission
of being a teacher for society. Yang therefore chose to make his career
the teaching of ethics,[73] first at Hunan Fourth Normal School, which
was combined into the First Normal School in 1914, and then at First
Normal in Changsha. In 1918, President Cai Yuanpei invited Yang to
join the faculty of Beijing University, where he taught ethics until his
death two years later. During his tenure at First Normal, Yang was both
teacher and mentor to young men who, decades later, became China's
leaders.

Moral Educator

At First Normal, Yang was teaching at an institution with an unprec-
edentedly complex curriculum, which combined traditional Chinese and
modern Western subjects during the first decade of the Republic. The
number of subjects taught rose to seventeen, including geometry, geometric drawing, physics, and agriculture. Besides the modern Western
subjects, such as mathematics, physics, chemistry, and science, the students also had to master a demanding curriculum in moral cultivation,
as well as in Chinese classics.

Yang was one of the most influential and respected teachers at
First Normal. In addition to ethics, he taught logic, philosophy, and
education. He was deeply rooted in the Chinese classics and had made
the philosophy of the Song and Ming dynasties his specialty. He was "a
very learned person and he was endowed with a strong personality that
kept him to very strict moral code," Xiao Yu (Siao-Yu) recalled. "His
conduct was at all times beyond reproach. He was so familiar with the
doctrine of Confucius that his friends and his students regarded him as
if he were a reincarnation of the great sage."[74] Thus, his students gave
him the nickname "Confucius" because of his impeccable conduct.[75] At
the same time, however, he was also deeply influenced by the Western
philosophers Kant, Spencer, and Rousseau.

Xiao San (Emi Siao), another former student, remembered that
Yang "was not a brilliant speaker, but neither did he have tiresome

mannerisms, and his audience was always most respectfully attentive."[76] Because Yang's lectures were based on his own study and experience, they were very different from those that were mere composites of others' books. Indeed, he often incorporated what he wrote in his *Diaries from the Dahua Studio*. To be sure, Yang's first lectures did not make a very good impression on some of his students.[77] Nevertheless, "within two months, everyone who attended Mr. Yang's lectures admired and respected him. Although he did not talk much in class, each short statement meant a great deal. Within a year, the entire school accepted him and he became the 'Confucius of First Normal.' Other schools in Changsha invited him and he conducted classes [in schools] as far [away] as the high school at the foot of Yuelu Mountain. Soon he was known to the students throughout the city as 'Confucius.' "[78]

While teaching in Changsha in the 1910s, various strands of thought prevailed in the Chinese intellectual world. Roughly two main groups existed: the cultural-radical stream led by Chen Duxiu and Hu Shi calling for the complete modernization of Chinese culture and literature, and the neo-traditionalist trend, represented by three currents: Zhang Binglin/Liu Shipei's "national essence," Liang Qichao's "national character," and Kang Youwei's for the institutionalization of Confucianism as a state religion. Both were motivated by a common concern to reevaluate the Chinese culture and create a new culture that would revive the Chinese nation. The latter group defended the core Chinese values against the total westernization of Chinese culture, but was willing to adopt certain Western ideas and values. Yang exposed his students to the prevalent trends of thought. He urged them to study all aspects of Western thought and institutions, but never let them forget their own national heritage. Yang imparted his view of cultural reform to his students in his teaching, which was now infused with nationalism, but still contained the old moral principles of Ming and Qing times. A statement that appeared in an article he published in Changsha in 1914 makes clear the spirit of his teaching and his disapproval for the total westernization of the Chinese culture:

> Each country has its own national spirit, just as each person has his own personality. The culture of one country cannot be transplanted in its entirety to another country. A country is an organic whole, just as the human body is an organic whole. It is not like a machine, which can be taken apart and put together again. If you take it apart, it will die.[79]

Therefore, Yang made sure that his students received not just some exposure to Western ethical theory but also a solid grounding in the writings of the principal Chinese philosophers of the Ming and Qing periods. Although he severely criticized certain aspects of Confucianism and rejected many conventional Chinese behavioral patterns, Yang did emphasize many traditional Chinese virtues, such as the Neo-Confucian core principles that *li* (principle) is eternal and fundamental, the energy of mind, as well as other virtues as self-discipline, patriotism, and resistance to alien rule. Yang firmly believed that *li* is ultimately fundamental (*ben*) and the organizing principle of everything in the universe. Because it is initially sheathed in our *qi*, we need diligent study or "the investigation of things" to discover it.

Yang was a great admirer of Wang Fuzhi.[80] After studying Yang's published works, Peng Dacheng has concluded that Yang widely read in both Chinese and Western philosophy, he devoted himself to and best understood the *Tongjian* (*Comprehensive Mirror for Aid in Government*) and Wang Fuzhi's *Du Tongjian Lun* (*On Reading the* Tongjian). These works accompanied him for his whole life.[81]

The period from 1895 to 1920 was a transitional era in Chinese history, during which the crises of values and identity were first challenged and then broken down as the Western influence spread more widely. The Chinese intellectuals thus had to find new values and new culture identities in terms of nationalism. When Liu Renxi founded the *Chuanshan xueshe* in June 1914 in Changsha, Yang directed his students to this group of scholars who were seeking insights on China's regeneration within Chinese tradition itself—more precisely, in the writings of Wang Fuzhi. Wang was one of the most prominent among several remarkable figures, who at the time of the Manchu conquest had refused to serve China's new foreign rulers. After he established the association, Liu became its main lecturer. Yang often encouraged his students to attend these lectures. Cai Hesen, Mao Zedong, and Xiao San often went to listen to Liu's lectures.

"The Association was named after [Wang] Chuanshan, so it certainly should teach the philosophy of Chuanshan. The greatest contribution that Chuanshan made was his advocacy of a nationalism, which regarded enslavement of the Han Chinese by alien rulers as an extreme humiliation and a cause of uttermost anguish," Yang wrote in his diary, "We should know that Chuanshan had attained this high degree of moral integrity. We should know this."[82] Yang also showed high regard for Wang Chuanshan's idea of patriotism and his deep concern about the invasion of China by foreign powers:

The nationalism Chuanshan advocated was centered on the Han Chinese, which would seem parochial in present-day China since China was [and is] now a federation of nationalities. However, the aggression of foreign nations like Great Britain, France, Russia, Germany, the United States, and Japan was worse than the alien rulers China had experienced in ancient times. We must therefore remember the importance of nationalism, even though China was a unity of nationalities.[83]

On another occasion, Yang observed:

Once I was taking a European history class at the Tokyo Higher Normal University, and the Japanese professor said that the Chinese were like the Romans. What they cared most about was their culture. Even though their country might be taken over by alien rulers, as long as the aliens accepted Chinese culture, the Chinese would accept the alien rulers. I thus realized that the Japanese were ill-disposed toward China. They had the ambition of taking over China after the Manchus lost power. We Chinese should always remember this.[84]

When Yang was teaching, he never confined his lectures to the textbooks but often incorporated what he wrote in his *Diaries from the Dahua Studio*. His views on foreign aggression, nationalism, and patriotism strongly influenced his students. For instance, in 1915, when the news that Yuan Shikai had signed the humiliating "Twenty-one Demands" with Japan arrived in Changsha, the enraged students of First Normal immediately launched a series of anti-Japanese attacks, which Yang and other teachers from the school actively supported. Yang's influence on his students was so profound, according to the American journalist Harrison Salisbury, that "Li Rui, after examining Mao Zedong's notebooks of the period [written while he was a student at First Normal], found it difficult to distinguish between Mao's own ideas and those of Professor Yang. The two seemed to meld into one."[85]

His ten years of study abroad in Japan, Britain, and Germany had not weakened Yang's belief in the Neo-Confucianism of the Song and Ming dynasties. His interest in philosophy had a great influence on his students. While he was teaching at First Normal, Yang worked with another teacher, Li Jinxi, to organize a philosophy study group; its members included Cai Hesen, Mao Zedong, Chen Chang, and Xiao San. The study group met regularly, and the students introduced reading materials to each other, exchanged ideas about what they had learned, and discussed some philosophical questions in which they were interested.[86]

"Yang was an idealist," Mao Zedong recalled, "and a man of high character. He believed in his ethics very strongly."[87] Yang was especially interested in the study of "mind energy," an idea he took from Wang Yangming and Tan Sitong. Yang believed that the energy for making a nation rich and powerful was hidden within the mind of each member of society, and that this energy could be released only by stimulating individual initiative:

> To have a fundamental reform, we must first save the fallen minds of our people. However, the citizens of our nation generally lacked morality, so, even if there were good laws, there would be no good results. Therefore, nowadays, only if the minority with virtue fights against the majority who are corrupted or conventional and who follow demoralized customs and habits can conditions be changed. Thus, we have very many important things to do in addition to politics. If we want to save our country from perishing, we must begin with the education of the citizens. This is the only path to national salvation to which I can attest.[88]

Yang's emphasis on subjective initiative, on human minds, and on the function of education had a marked effect on his students. For instance, before Mao Zedong and Cai Hesen, the founding figures of the CCP, came into contact with more radical Western ideas in 1919, they fully shared Yang's experimental, gradualist approach to solutions and took a liberal approach to reforming Chinese society—they stressed educating people, in particular, cultivating their minds for national salvation. Mao declared, "The truth of the universe lies in each human being's mind. . . . Today, since we use the fundamental way of advocacy, how could human minds not be moved?"[89] Similarly, Cai noted: "If human minds and mental intelligence were interconnected and communicated with each other, humanity would not be exhausted. If a man were full of humanity, his thought would be connected to the universe. We should try hard to cultivate people's minds and educate people to become reasonable; this shows the utmost importance of education."[90]

It is thus hardly surprising that Mao once said about Yang, "Under his influence, I read a book on ethics translated by Cai Yuanpei and was inspired to write an essay which I entitled 'The Energy of the Mind.' I was then an idealist and my essay was highly praised by Professor Yang Changji, from his idealist viewpoint. He gave me a mark of 100 for it."[91]

Under Yang's influence, Mao formed an idealist outlook with an emphasis on willpower. Although Mao did embrace Marxism after 1920, there was not a complete cut off between his early and later way of thinking. For instance, the 1942 Yanan Rectification Campaign (*zheng-feng yundong*) was largely based on Mao's notion of "reforming the mind thoroughly" (*chedi gaizao sixiang*); the Cultural Revolution (1966–1976) revealed Mao's firm belief in the decisive role of mind and thought in governance; the Great Leap Forward (1958) was marked by Mao's exaggeration of man's willpower and his subjective initiative; the guiding principle for China's agricultural policy was Mao's well-known slogan *ren ding sheng tian* (man can conquer nature). The previous examples show that there was a linkage between Mao's early and later modes of thought.

Professor of Western Philosophy

When he was teaching ethics at First Normal, Yang used as a text-book a work by the German philosopher Friedrich Paulsen (1846–1908), translated into Chinese as *Lunlixue yuanli* (*The Principles of Ethics*),[92] a philosophically idealist Neo-Kantian work. Kant, who is best known for his view—called transcendental idealism—that we bring innate forms to our raw worldly experience, which would otherwise be unknowable, heavily influenced. We perceive the world by means of our senses and these innate categories, Kant argued, and therefore the thing-in-itself cannot be known. All our knowledge is necessarily synthetic, filtered by our senses. Kant's theory of knowledge was an attempt to solve the conflict between the rationalists, who said that knowledge without experience is possible, and the empiricists, who argued that nothing exists beyond experience. Thus he opens the introduction of his *Critique of Pure Reason*: "There can be no doubt that all our knowledge begins with experience. . . . But though all our knowledge begins with experience, it does not follow that it all arises out of experience"[93] In his belief that innate intuition is fundamental, Kant resembled the Neo-Confucians of the School of Li.

His ten years of study abroad had given Yang a solid grounding in Western philosophy. A disciple of Kant, Yang hoped to combine West-ern philosophy with a revitalized Chinese culture rather than replace the tradition with Western ideas in wholesale fashion, a stance that his students, including Mao found congenial. In 1916, Yang's article "Zhexue shang gezhong lilun zhi lüeshu" ("Exposition of Philosophical Theories")[94] was published in *Minsheng*. In this article, Yang gave a comprehensive introduction of Western philosophical theories and philosophical schools of thought. He also translated a book entitled the *Xiyang lunlixue shi* (*A History of Western Ethics*), which introduced Western philosophical theories and philosophical schools of thought to Chinese readers.[95] Mao borrowed the manuscript of this translation, which Yang had not yet published, and hand copied it into seven notebooks. This manuscript was widely circulated among the students of First Normal and had a profound influence on them.

Defining philosophy as "the sum of all scientific knowledge," Paulsen criticized the rationalists who "absolutely ignore experience and pay it no regard whatever,"[96] and opposed the empiricists who overlook the essential distinction between the psychical and the physical order of reality. Instead, he adopted a theory of metaphysical and psychological *parallelism* (which he called "pan-psychism"), insisting on the recognition of the demands of the mind and the supremacy of will over intellect. These philosophical concepts, expressed in *Lunlixue yuanli*, proved very attractive to Yang's students. The care with which Mao read this book during winter 1917–1918 is demonstrated by the thousands of words of marginal notes he made, which brought forward the theme "conservation of spirit, and conservation of matter."[97] These notes on Paulsen also reveal something of Mao's thought on the eve of the May Fourth movement of 1919 and his conversion to Marxism in 1920. As Meisner points out, the notes particularly provide insights into a powerful voluntarist strain. Next to a passage in the text where Paulsen asserts that "human beings are capable of changing their basic natures by using their wills," Mao approvingly wrote "the power of the will" and "the power of the mind."[98] And elsewhere Mao wrote:

> The great actions of the hero are his own, [they] are the expression of his motive power, lofty and cleansing, relying on no precedent. His force is like that of a powerful wind arising from a deep gorge, like the irresistible sexual drive for one's lover, a force that will not stop, that cannot be stopped. All obstacles dissolve before him.[99]

Paulsen further defined the self as "will, strengthened by resisting rather than accepting nature."[100] Apparently, Mao affirmed this idea of the greater the challenge, the greater the effect and the achievement. He noted in the margin of Paulsen, "Because there is the resistance of Monut Tai-hua, the river's strength inures its current."[101]

This notion of voluntarism remained an enduring characteristic of Mao's thought and profoundly influenced his reception and reinterpretation of Marxism.[102] In 1945, Mao recounted the Chinese fable "The Foolish Old Man Who Removed the Mountains," which reveals his belief that any task could be accomplished through sheer will.[103] In another article, "Report on the Investigation of the Peasant Movement in Hunan" written in 1927, Mao shows his great confidence in the power of the "harnessed" will of the people—especially the peasants. This voluntarist belief also gave Mao spiritual support in the battle against the old society and in his programs to modernize China by means of mass-mobilization campaigns such as the "Great Leap Forward" and the "Cultural Revolution." Schram describes the Great Leap Forward as "when Mao and his comrades indulged in the greatest orgy of voluntarist thinking in the history of the communist movement."[104]

In his classical work *History and Will*, Wakeman analyzes various Western and Chinese thinkers as the sources of Mao's thought. Western thought includes Paulsen and the Neo-Kantian's concept of reason creating social forms that liberate the self from customs and the power of the will; T. H. Green's glorification of the will and his depiction of society as the instrument of individual self-realization; and Darwin's notion of objective laws of evolutionary change, which led to Mao's "struggle for survival," and violent revolution, in which the strong overthrow the weak. "Those earlier reflections allowed Mao a commitment to continuous and unending historical change."[105] Therefore, Wakeman claims that Mao took the voluntarist idea out of Paulsen.[106] He suggests Green's contribution provided the keystone of the arch of Mao's philosophical outlook because of Mao's obvious exhilaration in the exercise of his own will, and in calling forth the will of the masses.[107]

When Yang Changji intensively exposed to Mao the Western intellectual tradition at First Normal during the 1917–1918 academic year, the Chinese classical thought, including Wang Yangming's doctrine of the innate knowing, the power of mind, and subjective initiative, was also passed on to him. Thus, both the Western thought and the Chinese classical thought were amalgamated in the mind of the young Mao. Perhaps Paulsen and Green merely reinforced what already existed in Mao.

Yang was especially interested in the Western ethical theory of self-realization, which he saw being advocated by "most modern ethical philosophers. . . . The self here meant the big self, which was united with the universe as an organic whole. Therefore, those who worked for the global public interest attained the ideal of self-realization."[108] He also declared: "To keep improving oneself and make oneself capable was the ideal of self-realization. And to take self-realization as one's highest goal in action was self-realization."[109] His students widely accepted his views of self-realization. For instance, in "Annotations and Commentaries on *Lunlixue yuanli*," Mao wrote: "The aim of human beings is to achieve self-realization. Self-realization is to fully explore our mental and physical abilities and develop them to the highest degree."[110]

Although he greatly admired such Western philosophers as Aristotle, Kant, F. H. Bradley, T. H. Green, Fichte, and Hegel, who also were supporters of the theory of self-realization, Yang criticized the weakness of their theories. He believed that these philosophers saw the goal of action as perfecting oneself and society through both pleasure and self-denial, and in doing so, they steered a middle course between hedonism and asceticism. Yang believed that a greater emphasis had to be put on man's responsibility to society.[111] "Man," Yang said, "could influence the development of the world, and to develop the world he developed himself."[112] Individual self-realization and responsibility to society were the two main themes in Yang's life and thought, and they strongly affected his students. Even though Yang was fascinated with Western self-realization, his acceptance of the notion underscored the dimensions of the Neo-Confucian idea of self-cultivation through education to serve society.

After he returned to China, Yang substantially changed his views on the relationship between desire and principle. Renouncing his earlier asceticism on the grounds that desire and reason could not be regarded simply as opposites, he advocated a unity of desire and reason. He thought that desire might be a source of both evil and good, and now viewed pleasure and desire as incentives to action: without them, men would cease to act and therefore cease to exist. Yang believed that moral conduct consisted in disciplining desire by reason in order to attain a goal. At the same time, desire and pleasure should be regarded only as facts of experience and not as moral principles, for they were fluctuating and unstable. The basis of society was not self-interest but altruism, which ensured the unity of the race. For all these reasons, Yang rejected both the "quantitative" hedonism of Jeremy Bentham and the "qualitative" hedonism of John Stuart Mill.[113]

The nature of Yang's individualism contradicts the need for social responsibility. The principle of the greatest good for the greatest number, Yang maintained, though it appeared universal, was in fact merely a multiplication of egoism. He felt, in any case, that the whole idea of a calculus of pleasure was meaningless, for the addition of pleasures and pains, unlike the addition of positive and negative numbers, could not yield zero.[114] Yang therefore resolved contradiction by advocating an individualism that stressed responsibility to the whole: "Education should cultivate the spirit of sacrificing one's own interest for right or for humanity, but not train people to be diffident or to produce unthinking individualists who had no sense of public responsibility to society."[115] This sense of responsibility felt by the Chinese intellectuals for their country and society can be traced back to the time of Qu Yuan (340–278 BC, an intellectual tradition that a scholar should put the fate of the country and the suffering of the common people above any individual desire and happiness. His students fully shared his views. Mao, in his "Annotations and Commentaries on *Lunlixue yuanli*," highly praised Yang's "individualism with public responsibility to society," which he called "spiritual individualism."[116]

As a man steeped in both Western and traditional Chinese scholarship, Yang sought to buttress ideas derived largely from Western thought with references to Chinese authorities. He compiled a small volume of extracts from the *Lunyu* (*Analects*), which he used to teach his students. Nevertheless, he vigorously rejected certain patterns of behavior that characterized Chinese society; for example, he strongly opposed studying simply to become an official. After selecting a number of passages from the *Lunyu*, a traditional teacher's task that he supplemented iconoclastically with passages from Darwin, he called the first section of his volume of extracts "*Lizhi*" ("Establishing Resolution"). He wrote: "If one established a determined resolution, one could realize the noble ideal, cultivate virtuous habits, and foster an upright personality."[117] By putting particularly emphasis on the term *lizhi*, he conveyed to his students the importance of the practice. Mao talked about *lizhi* in his "Annotations and Commentaries on *Lunlixue yuanli*." In a letter to his teacher Li Jinxi in August 1917, Mao wrote: "If a man did not learn the truth for ten years, he would lack resolution for ten years. If he failed to learn the truth for a lifetime, he would lack resolution for a lifetime."[118] Cai Hesen, Zhang Kundi, and Xiao San also recalled how, under the influence of Yang, they got together to discuss the *Lizhi*.

In addition to urging his students to acquire firm resolution, Yang also told them of his belief that intellectuals must be in touch with the masses; he worked to establish a handicraft course at First Normal to help students support their studies and, at the same time, to break down the barrier between worker and intellectual.[119] Here again, Yang's view inspired his students. In this area, Mao completely accepted Yang's ideas and himself advocated them. Mao said, "One shouldn't simply read books with words, one should also read books without." Mao felt that rather than being completely immersed in their studies, students should also learn from the working masses. Therefore, he often visited the nearby villages and factories with his friends during holidays to learn about the life of the common people. Yang's ideas had inspired Mao's essay on "Tiyu zhi yanjiu" ("A Study of Physical Education"), which was published in *New Youth* in 1917. This article combined an ardent Chinese national-ism with a no less ardent rejection of traditional Chinese culture—in this instance an attack on the Confucian separation between mental and manual labor, a prominent feature of the Maoist vision. Unlike other revolutionary leaders, Mao stressed the futility of "book learning" and the unity of theory and practice. During the Cultural Revolution, for instance, Mao was to call the urban educated youth to go to the coun-tryside to be reeducated by the poor and lower middle-class peasants.[120]

Mentor of Thought

It was through Yang that the First Normal students soon found themselves in touch with the mainstream of intellectual life in China. His personality and example attracted a circle of young men who had a desire to become just, moral, and virtuous. Yang was one of the early proponents of Chen Duxiu's magazine *Xin Qingnian* (*New Youth*), a radical, Westernized, and iconoclastic journal that emerged as the most important vehicle of the New Culture Movement before 1919. Not only was he an enthusiastic reader and partisan of *New Youth*, but he also urged his students to read it. He took out several subscriptions to it so that the journal might cir-culate among the students. As Angus McDonald has noted, "Even at the Beijing University, which was to emerge as the leader of the May Fourth Movement, very few had heard of the magazine before Chen was made dean of the College of Arts in 1917, but the magazine was known and read in Changsha well before that."[121] Yang published an essay on morals in the journal in December 1916 and January 1917.[122]

Because Yang had introduced and recommended *New Youth*, his students, especially the progressive ones, became very interested in reading the magazine. Zhou Shizhao recalled that for a long time, "besides going to classes and reading newspapers, we read only *New Youth*; for conversation, we talked only about *New Youth*. And for thinking, we thought only about the issues raised by *New Youth*."[123]

Although Yang was not a very good speaker, according to Xiao San, "His enthusiasm for learning drew around him a circle of thoughtful studious young men, among whom were Mao Zedong, Cai Hesen, and Chen Chang."[124] Yang's home thus became a meeting place for after-class discussions. The students made a habit of calling on Yang at his home on Sundays to discuss various problems, while Yang never tired of helping them or offering advice.[125] Xiao Yu also recalled: "Every Sunday morning my friends, Xiong Guangchu, Chen Chang, and I visited Mr. Yang's home to discuss our studies together. We read each other's notebooks, talked over our problems, and returned to school after lunch."[126] Xiao Yu said that every Sunday the three of them had lunch at Yang's house, joined by his wife and his daughter Kaihui, who became Mao's first wife. "Every week for two whole years we ate our meal rapidly and in silence, not one of us ever uttering a single word. . . . Mr. Yang himself never spoke a word and we all respected his silence and ate as rapidly as was possible. . . . Mr. Yang paid a great deal of attention to matters of hygiene but apparently he did not realize that it is better for one's health to talk and laugh normally during meals, that a happy atmosphere aids digestion."[127]

With Yang's encouragement, the group of students that had coalesced around him formed a society—*Xinmin xuehui*—"that was to have a widespread influence on the affairs and destiny of China."[128] Yang was the spiritual mentor of the members of this association. In discussing its founding in the first issue of *Xinmin xuehui huiwu baogao*, Mao first analyzed the historical environment that led to its birth and then wrote:

> Another reason [that contributed to the founding of the association] was that most of the members were students of Mr. Yang Huaizhong. The students were influenced by Yang's teaching, and became committed to the betterment or improvement of each individual, strengthening his moral and spiritual fiber and improving his education as their philosophy. [This was the environment in which] the *Xinmin xuehui* [New Citizens' Study Society] was founded.[129]

Of the twenty-one founding members—Cai Hesen, Mao Zedong, Xiao Yu, Chen Chang, Zhang Kundi, He Shuheng, and Luo Xuezan among them—twenty were students of Yang Changji from First Normal; the only outsider was Luo Zhanglung. *Xinmin xuehui* envisioned a renewal of Chinese society through the reeducation of its citizens, and a number of its members later designed the new institutions and policies of the PRC.[130]

Yang himself strongly criticized traditional Chinese society and culture. He launched an all-out frontal attack on the Confucian doctrine of the Three Bonds, which he thought was as cruel, in practice, as the religious autocracy of medieval Europe: "The doctrine of the Three Bonds led to the tyrannical and cruel practice of punishing the lowly with the utmost severity while forgiving the exalted."[131] The Chinese family system, in his view, was the primary institution on which the imperial ruling house relied for its existence. It was also the spiritual backbone of the clan authority, the authority of the husband, and patriarchy. In an article that appeared in *Jiayin zazhi* (Tiger Magazine) in 1915, Yang praised the Western family system for its marital relationship that allowed personal autonomy, the free choice of partners, and equal rights to women.[132]

Yang furiously denounced arranged marriages on both individual and social grounds and expressed great sympathy for women, whose status was the lowest of any individuals in Chinese society, and he saw changes in the laws as necessary: "Marriage is a lifelong, important matter; forcing a woman to marry without considering her opinions and feelings is the same as selling her. Women have to bear this, and there are no laws to protect them. This is indeed a terrible tragedy. It is a savage custom of China."[133] He further pointed out that Chinese women had no freedom in marriage because they were not financially independent. The financial independence of British widows gave them the rights of free marriage without being obstructed by family members on their fathers' or their husbands' sides. Such a practice accorded with humanitarianism, Yang believed; in contrast, the Chinese custom of insisting that a widow preserve her chastity after the death of her husband was inhumane and extremely uncivilized.[134]

Yang also opposed concubinage as immoral and destructive of basic family relationships. He thought concubines were slaves of a kind because "their personalities were deficient" (*renge bu wanquan*). Societies that practiced concubinage seriously compromised people's human rights, in his view. He thought it was unfair that women were allowed to have only one husband while men were allowed to have as many concubines as they were able to support. He therefore vigorously denounced the concubinage custom and firmly supported monogamy.[135]

Yang lived in a time of transition, during which the intellectuals went through a series of cultural crises as the penetration of Western ideas accelerated. They blamed traditional Chinese culture, especially the Confucian tradition, for China's backwardness. By comparing Yang and Liang Qichao[136]—the most influential intellectual of this transitional generation, who is mainly remembered as a radical reformer—we can see that the intellectuals of the day, as Hao Chang and Yu-sheng Lin point out, consciously attacked the Confucian tradition, especially the doctrine of the three bonds, but nevertheless retained certain Confucian values.[137]

Liang experienced a change in intellectual stance from traditional Chinese thinking to a perspective strongly influenced by Western ideas. But instead of totally repudiating the traditional Chinese culture and accepting Western concepts, Liang discovered the possibilities of combining Chinese and Western ideas. Following his exile to Japan in fall 1898 as the Hundred Days Reform was suppressed, Liang's ideas became more radical. Instead of condemning only Taoism, Liang now blamed the central Confucian ideal of *jen* for being the major source of Chinese meekness. No matter how his thinking developed, Liang remained intellectually committed to many Neo-Confucian ideals, which seemed to foster the dynamic, inner-directed personality necessary for the new citizen. Therefore, Hao Chang, in his *Liang Ch'i-ch'ao and Intellectual Transition in China, 1890–1907*, claims that Liang's personal and cultural ideals were the result of a selective synthesis of Chinese and Western values. Although Yang was well known as a man of Western learning, he was deeply rooted in the Neo-Confucianism of the School of *Li* (Principle), and he never discarded its core principles. However, there were some interesting similarities between Liang's ideas and Yang's.[138]

Bailey and Peterson and Hayhoe point out that the Chinese firmly believed in the transformative power of education, and "China's survival . . . depended on the quality of its people."[139] At the turn of the twentieth century, "saving the nation" was the most pressing issue in China. As the foremost reformer of the time, Liang Qichao firmly believed that in order to save China, a modern nation-state must be built that could survive in the modern order. And the fundamental means of building a modern nation-state was to cultivate an active and nationalistic corps of "new citizens" (*xinmin*). The term *xinmin* not only means "new citizens" but also carries a sense of "renovating the people." Liang was discouraged by his perception that Chinese in general lacked the character of citizens. He saw an urgent need to fundamentally change the Chinese conception of citizenship and of how to cultivate new citizens, a change that required educating a modern citizenry in the new civic virtues Liang believed were essential for creating a powerful and prosperous Chinese nation.

Liang's conception of "new citizenship" and a new republic was obviously linked to his deep Confucian convictions on private and public morality. He included individualism as one of the basic characters of a new citizen, but he stressed not so much individual liberty as individual virtue. Although Liang understood the need for laissez-faire and competition so that country could grow, he would not give up his demand on the state to take moral responsibility for collective achievement. In the end, he formulated something that more closely resembled the liberal welfare state than capitalism at its initial stage. Therefore, certain Confucian values continued to shape Liang's vision of a modern Chinese nation-state that would actually transcend the Western capitalism of his time.

Yang also believed that the only path to national salvation and to building a strong nation was to educate Chinese citizens, whom he believed generally lacked morality. Furthermore, Yang held himself to a stringent moral code, through the force of his own personality. He emphasized moral cultivation as the fundamental requirement for a good citizen. Liang, on the other hand, advocated character cultivation. Both men's views were profoundly shaped by Neo-Confucianism. Finally, the changing social and personal values evolving in Liang's ideal of the new citizen and Yang's ideal of a person useful to society were linked not only to a Confucian past but also to a communist present.

Such were the beliefs that Yang imparted to his students at the Hunan First Normal School. Although Yang's convictions were strongly rooted in Neo-Confucianism, he incorporated other concepts selected from Western philosophy and contemporary currents of the Chinese reform movement into an ethical framework very much oriented toward social change. The students who looked to him for intellectual guidance absorbed a strong sense of responsibility to society, with an emphasis on education and morality that took on a spiritual dimension. As this study of Yang's role as a classically trained mentor to young revolutionaries such as Mao makes clear, we must revise the common assumption that Confucian-trained educators were invariably stubborn obstacles to change. It also shows that the changes affecting the Chinese elite—Yang and other teachers—in turn greatly affected the young radical students at First Normal in their intellectual transformation and radicalization, as well as the development of the revolution. Moreover, the new school system—and the scholars like Yang who taught in it—played an important role in nurturing study societies such as the *Xinmin xuehui* that were of central importance to the formation and growth of the CCP. Such a role suggests another obvious connection between changes in elite society and the genesis of Chinese communism and the subsequent revolution.

Yang left to join the faculty of Beijing University in 1918 at the invitation of President Cai Yuanpei. He taught ethics there until his death two years later, but his influence lived on.

Illustration 4. Yang Changji

Illustration 5. Xu Teli

Illustration 6. Li Jinxi

Illustration 7. Wang Jifan

Illustration 8. Tan Yankai

Illustration 9. Fang Weixia

Illustration 10. Class Eight, 1918

Illustration 11. Mao Zedong at First Normal, 1918

Illustration 12. Cai Hesen

Illustration 13. Li Weihan

Illustration 14. He Shuheng

Illustration 15. Chen Zhangpu.

Illustration 16. Luo Xuezan.

Chapter 6

Provincial Scholars and
Young Radicals

The Student Body at First Normal

As Hunan's most distinguished academic institution in the early Republican years, First Normal School attracted and profoundly influenced the best students in the province. Many of those same students would become crucial in China's subsequent history, for they underwent an intellectual transformation and played a central role in transmitting new ideas and political movements.

First Normal did not limit its enrollment base to the surrounding area of Changsha, where the school was located. In fact, in 1912 and 1913, it admitted students from twenty of seventy-five counties in the province, reaching as far as Baoqing and Yuezhou districts. By 1914, it drew students from twenty-five counties, and later extended beyond that to include a certain number of students from all parts of the province.[1]

However, there was a distinctive geographical mark of the First Normal student body: Most of the students came from comparatively peripheral agrarian counties like Yongfeng, Xiangxiang, and Ningxiang. Often far from urban areas, these counties featured poor transportation and relatively sparse populations.

In addition to this geographical characteristic, the student body of First Normal also had a distinctive social background. As much by default as by choice, First Normal School came to have a special attraction for students from poorer families. They favored First Normal because of its free education, which included free room and board. Although their families were not well off, they were not the poorest either. Otherwise, those students would not be able to have enough education to pass the rigorous entrance examinations to get into the school. In return for a free education, First Normal students committed to teaching at elementary schools in the province. For students of families lacking independent means, elementary school teaching promised a respectable career, but one of stifled prospects.[2]

The sons of the provincial commercial and gentry elites sought a more liberal environment and better opportunities. They were preparing themselves for an advanced education in colleges and universities in major cities like Beijing and Shanghai. A Shanghai or Beijing college graduate had several options, including advanced studies abroad in Europe, America, or Japan. Students with such goals favored general secondary institutions in Changsha, such as the Provincial First Middle School. General secondary schools in Changsha usually required full payment of tuition and fees from their students in addition to the costs of living. They thus attracted mostly richer students.

The prearranged career as elementary school teachers was the major reason the provincial elites turned away from the school. It became obvious in the 1910s that school teaching in Hunan offered few possibilities either for upward mobility within the province or for outward mobility into other parts of the nation or the world. It also provided few opportunities for the Normal School students to continue their intellectual growth once they had completed their formal schooling.

Apart from their geographical and social backgrounds, First Normal students shared a solid preparation in traditional Chinese learning in their home villages. Like their fellow villagers, they were often conservative, comparatively isolated, and strongly committed to Confucian tradition. Yet, when these youths from the agrarian, backward, and conservative counties arrived in the capital city of Changsha, they faced a totally different world, both in space and time. They changed. New ideas, new thoughts, new concepts, and new knowledge challenged them. They formed a potent radical force and attacked all forms of tradition. However, they possessed a highly idiosyncratic intellectual bent. For instance, while radically attacking the Confucian tradition—particularly its emphasis on the Confucian *lijiao* (ritual, convention, and constraints), or *waifan daode* (outer molding virtues, ethics of social constraints)—the students unconsciously relied on Confucian values, the Confucian *neihua daode* (inner-transforming virtues, ethics of virtues).[3] While spreading new ideas, they often unconsciously regarded themselves as the Confucian "*xianzhi xianjue*"—the awakened elite, usually educated, who had the responsibility to waken the uneducated masses. These values played an important role in student intellectual transformation and their early communist activities. Schooling at Changsha thus opened their minds to a modernizing world and a different way of life, with profound political consequences for an entire generation of First Normal students in the 1910s.

New Citizens' Study Society

In 1918, a group of nationalistic youth formed a closely knit organization, the Xinmin xuehui dedicated primarily to "scholarly research, personality building, and moral development."[4] The group constituted the most steadfast pillar of the New Culture Movement and the May Fourth Movement. The members also were active in the work–study program that sent Hunanese students to France.

After a period of study and discussion, the founding members had realized that an organization that could unite progressives was a necessity, both in order to reform the country and in order to improve themselves. Therefore, they decided to form a student organization for the stated purpose of "strengthening China through strengthening Chinese youth."[5] On April 14, 1918,[6] the Xinmin xuehui was founded in Cai Hesen's home. The association's name echoed the writings of Liang Qichao advocating "the way of the new citizen."[7]

The founders were relatively independent, well read, and frustrated by the poverty of their individual resources. They had an urgent need to improve their lives. A pooling of resources and ideas provided an ideal way to solve these problems. Their scholarly and moral development, personal advancement, and social growth became the fundamental reasons for establishing the New Citizens' Study Society.[8] Like other intellectuals, they had become increasingly aware of the spreading New Culture Movement. Old ways of thinking, old ethics, and old culture seemed almost to be disappearing in the eyes of the young. They felt it wrong to continue to live a quiet and isolated life. Instead, they would seek to live a united life.[9] Because most of the founding members were students of Yang Changji, they were familiar with his teaching that they should become just, moral, virtuous men, useful to society.[10]

The association met weekly or biweekly to study together, discuss plans, and talk about current issues.[11] After the May Fourth Incident in 1919, the membership exceeded seventy. Individuals desiring to join had

to be recommended by five members, investigated by an advisory committee, and approved by half the members, with an announcement made
to the entire membership.[12] The moral requirements for members mixed
traditional values and behavioral norms of the new epoch. All members
had to lead a pure life, be utterly sincere, have a spirit of struggle, and
serve the truth. Specific rules prohibited untruthfulness, laziness, spend-
thrift ways, gambling, and visits to brothels.[13] "The significant thing
about the association," Xiao San recalled, "was that it united for the first
time all the progressive young men in Changsha into one organization."[14]
In fact, a substantial number of women joined the society later on.[15] Li
Weihan recalled that almost half of the forty new members who joined
the society during the May Fourth Movement were women.[16]

Although primarily dedicated to scholarly research, personal reformation, and moral development, the association quickly evolved into
a forum of political debate—how to reform China and the world. Xiao
Zisheng, the first director-general of the association, recalled:

> In the beginning, it was merely an association of carefully
> selected students of good moral character who had ideas and
> ideals similar to ours [Mao Zedong and Xiao himself]. The
> aims would be stated simply as the betterment or improve-
> ment of each individual, strengthening his moral and spiritual
> fiber and improving his education, as well as bringing about
> needed reforms in the country, but without expressing any
> political opinions nor affiliating with any party. Later, how-
> ever, Mao Tse-tung [Mao Zedong] and other members of the
> Association developed political ambitions and they accepted
> the Communist doctrine. At the present time [1961], a great
> many of the top rulers in Peking [Beijing] are former members
> of the old Hsin Min [Xinmin] Study Association; . . . Our
> Study Association must be regarded, therefore, as the embryo
> of Chinese Communism since, when the Communist doctrine
> began to awaken active interest, the nucleus of the movement
> was already in existence in our group.[17]

The Work–Study Program in France

In meetings of the association, members talked most about how to
develop outwardly. So, when they received a letter from Yang Changji
(then teaching at Beijing University) telling of a work–study program in

France, the program immediately caught the attention of the members of the New Citizens' Study Society.

In 1909, Li Shi founded a bean product company in Paris and employed more than thirty people from China. They worked during the day and studied at night. And they put forward the slogan of "work for study" and integrated work with study. In early 1912, Cai Yuan-pei, Li Shizeng,[18] Wu Zhihui,[19] and Wu Yuzhang[20] had established the work–study program in France, and clearly put forward a goal of "hard work and thrifty life, all for the study and for the increase of workers' knowledge." In spring 1916, some Chinese and French people founded the Sino-French Education Association in France, and Cai Yuanpei held the office of Chinese director and Li Shizeng held the office of secretary. The headquarters were in Beijing, China, and branches spread in Guangdong and Shanghai. They attracted idealistic young people to do part-time jobs to support their learning in France; meanwhile they founded a work–study association in France for promotion, which was aimed at studying Western advanced civilization and scientific technologies to enrich China and strengthen its military forces.[21] This work–study program attracted little notice at first.[22] After Cai Yuanpei became the chancellor of Beijing University in 1916, he gradually spread the idea that labor was an honorable and important pursuit for intellectuals who wanted to save their country.

Furthermore, France was viewed by intellectuals prior to the May Fourth period as a mythical place where one could pursue social equality to the time. Like many of his contemporaries, Chen Duxiu was attracted to the French Revolution, to its "Declaration of the Rights of Man," and to its motto, "Every man is equal before the law." In his pre-communist days, he looked to the "French civilization" as an inspirational model for the future of a better China.[23] Wu Yuzhang in his 1920 farewell speech to students departing for France, explained their purposes abroad: France was "the center of European civilization with new academic achievements and technological innovations."[24] This intellectual tradition partially led to the work–study program for Chinese students in France that began in 1912, which had had a deep impact on Chinese education. Between 1919 and 1920 alone, the Chinese students who studied in France totaled around 1,600.[25] The program developed into a strong movement when it gained ground in Hunan after the founding of the *Xinmin xuehui*.

Students from the First Normal School were very much interested in the work–study program in France because they lacked the funds to go abroad in any other way. Those young people who wanted to go to France also were influenced by the emergence of the New Culture Movement; it emphasized gaining knowledge and experiencing new ideas through work and study. They believed that these experiences would directly benefit China because the situation at home was so dire that Hunan had fallen under the rule of warlords. They hoped to come home with some knowledge that could save the nation.[26]

He Changgong, a student leader from Hunan and later a Red Army leader, recalled how he and others from Hunan tried to work and study in France:

> At that time, the government of Hunan was extremely corrupt and completely out of order. No one in the government was concerned with education anymore. A lot of young people thought that there was no clear road to the future. Mao Zedong and Cai Hesen were the main thrust for organizing the Xinmin xuehui in Changsha. This association played an important role in the Hunan student's attempt to go to France. . . . The main aim of the association was to reform traditional customs and the people's views. Apparently, they organized young people to research new ideas to reform and improve the social structure that was so prevalent in China. They also sought the path that would save the country and the Chinese race from what appeared to be impending doom, organized by nations wishing to colonize and exploit China and its people. In order to view the domestic situation and foreign ideas more clearly, the association also helped to organize young people wanting to go to France.[27]

Leaders of the Xinmin xuehui actively promoted the work–study program in France. The Xinmin xuehui came to a decision that "[Cai] Hesen and [Xiao] Zisheng were specially assigned to take charge of Hunan's Work-Study Program in France."[28] Of 1,080 Chinese who went to France, more than 430 were Hunanese, and one-third of the members of the Xinmin xuehui, eighteen people, departed as well.[29]

Cai Hesen's efforts were especially important. In June 1918, he was sent to Beijing as an advance guard to find out more about the work–study movement. When he first arrived, he lived at Yang Changji's home. Yang introduced Cai Hesen to Cai Yuanpei and Li Shizeng, the leaders of the Sino-French Education Association. Cai Hesen communicated to them the Hunan youths' request to participate in the work–study program and asked them to arrange for the Hunanese youth to travel to France. Cai Yuanpei explained to Cai Hesen his own plan to recruit capable people for the Ministry of Education and encouraged Cai Hesen to get more youth to come to Beijing in order to start building a "large and long-lasting foundation [for reform]."[30] Cai Yuanpei impressed Cai Hesen. In a letter to Xiao Zisheng, Cai Hesen wrote: "Mr. Jiemin [Cai Yuanpei] is, as it is said, especially trustworthy [youzu xinshi]."[31] After meeting with Cai Yuanpei, Cai Hesen also visited Li Dazhao in Beijing. He had read several articles by Li about Marxism. Afterward, he joined the Young China Association, which Li had founded.[32]

Because the work–study program was in its preparation stage, many problems needed to be solved. Uppermost was funding. Each person needed several hundred dollars in travel expenses and needed also to attend the preparatory school for French language. Cai sought sponsors to fund the Hunanese students' journey. He approached Cai Yuanpei and Li Shizeng. Yang Changji also helped considerably with fund raising.[33]

The problem of funds was quickly solved, but only twenty-five students from Hunan could go to France on this program. In order to secure an opportunity for more Hunanese youth to work and study in France, Cai Hesen wrote a letter to friends of the Xinmin xuehui: "This matter [the Hunan Work-Study Movement] assumes that if we get more people to go 'fishing,' we will have enough 'fish' to eat."[34] He told his correspondents,

> [We] absolutely cannot use the "quota" to restrain the desires of the youth and destroy their hopes. [We] should think of some intercessory method, and get as many people as possible [to come to Beijing] to form a large organization [and then go to France]. [This strategy] will accord with their cherished desires and avoid causing regrets.[35]

In August 1918, Mao Zedong, Xiao Zisheng, and twenty-two other Xinmin xuehui members went to Beijing to prepare for the work–study program in France. In 1919, the Xinmin xuehui membership had grown to about sixty, and almost one-third went to France. Both the French and Hunan branches were consumed by the same question: What was the best means for national salvation? The organization numbers reached seventy-two by 1920, and "nearly all of them later on became distinguished activists in the Communist movement in China."[36] They had great influence on subsequent events in Hunan and all of China.

Many Leaders, Many Martyrs, and a Moderate

Many members of the *Xinmin xuehui* made their mark on the CCP early and died young during the struggle for power. Many who survived continued to serve as leaders of their party and their country in diverse capacities. Some, including one of the brightest young radicals, declined to embrace communism and followed a different path.

Mao Zedong became the best known and historically the most important of the Chinese Communists. A native of Xiangtan, Hunan, Mao studied five-and-a-half years at First Normal (1913–1918). He excelled at Chinese classics, classical essay writing, and other social science subjects, but had more difficulty with drawing and natural science classes at First Normal. Because essay writing was considered the most important subject at that time, Mao was considered one of the school's outstanding students.

During the five-and-a half years Mao spent at First Normal, Yang Changji made the strongest impression. Under Yang's influence, Mao became an idealist. In fact, Yang highly praised one of Mao's essays entitled "Xinzhili" ("The Power of the Mind") from Yang's idealist viewpoint. Under Yang's encouragement, Mao attended the meetings of the Chuanshan Association: studying, discussing, and absorbing the most useful parts of traditional Chinese learning. Also directed by Yang, Mao became a serious reader of the most radical and Westernized journal, *New Youth*, after 1915. Mao's 1917 article "Tiyu zhi yanjiu" ("A Study of Physical Education") expressed a nationalist and military outlook.[37] At First Normal, Mao acquired the foundation of his worldly knowledge and for his political ideas. Also, Mao acquired his first significant experiences in social action.[38]

The Normal School also greatly influenced Cai Hesen. One of the first Chinese Marxists Cai was the first Chinese to advocate the establishment of the CCP, and became its most important early theorist. Mao has been extensively chronicled, but Cai's life story is less well known because he was killed by the Nationalist Party in 1931. Chapter 7 examines Cai's intellectual development in detail, as a prime example of the Hunan First Normal phenomenon.

Besides Cai Hesen and Mao Zedong, a whole group of radical youth from the Hunan First Normal School eventually became founding figures of the CCP. Among them were He Shuheng, Li Weihan, Zhang Kundi, Luo Xuezan, and Chen Chang. He Shuheng was the oldest of the founding members of the *Xinmin xuehui* and the oldest delegate present at the first CCP congress in July 1921. Of the twelve delegates representing Hunan at the founding congress of the CCP in Shanghai in 1921, two were Mao and He. Both of them graduated from First Normal. Li Weihan, Zhang Kundi, Luo Xuezan, and Chen Chang were all founding members of the *Xinmin xuehui*, all participated in the work–study program in France, and all became leading figures of early CCP. Li was also a founding member of the European Branch of the Chinese Communist Youth Corps (ECYC) and first organizational secretary of the ECYC. With so many founding figures, principal ideologists and activists from Hunan First Normal, the school's contribution to the students' ideological formation and transformation cannot be overlooked.

Among the radical youth from First Normal who also were the founding members of the *Xinmin xuehui*, many worked in education. For instance, Zhou Shizhao, a good friend and deskmate of Mao at the First Normal, was elected to head the literature department of the Student Friendship Society (*Xueyou hui*) and won the third place at the "mutual election of model students" at school in June 1917. He then taught at First Normal for many years after graduation. After 1949, he also served as director of the Education Department of Hunan Province, vice governor of Hunan Province, and the principal of Hunan First Normal School. He was also elected to the Standing Committee of the National People's Congress. Chen Shunong (1897–1968) was another one of the founders and one of the two secretaries (the other one was Mao) of the *Xinmin xuehui*. Chen spent his entire career teaching at Hunan University. Another classmate of Mao, Zou Wenzhen, had been teaching for many years until 1949 when he was sent to work in the Research Institute of the CCP's literary history.

Another founding member of the *Xinmin xuehui*, Xiao San, Xiao Zisheng's younger brother, also was a schoolmate and friend of Mao both at Dongsan primary school and the First Normal. He not only participated in the formation of the *Xinmin xuehui* in 1918 and the work–study program in France in 1920, but also in the founding of the Chinese Communist Youth Party in France.[39] Unlike his brother Xiao Zisheng who "later became a Kuomintang official in Nanking," Xiao San became Mao's close friend and comrade. In 1923, he went to study at the Sun Yat-sen University in Moscow and returned to China the following year. Then he became the secretary of Hunan Communist Youth League (CYL), the secretary of CYL North Bureau, the secretary of Zhangjiakou CCP, and the head of the organizational department of CYL, respectively. He attended the CCP's Fifth and Seventh congresses.

After 1949, he attended the First, Second, and Fifth congresses of the Chinese People's Political Consultative Conference (CPPCC) and was elected to the standing committee of the Fifth congress. He also attended the First and Second National People's congresses. An internationally known poet, he also was a biographer of Mao Zedong. Ironically, during the Cultural Revolution he and his German wife were put in prison for seven years on charges of espionage.

Hunan First Normal School, a seemingly ordinary school, produced many radical youth in the 1910s. First Normal graduates constituted the staunchest pillars in the New Culture Movement, the May Fourth Movement, and other social and political movements. By fostering so many young people's intellectual transformation and radicalization, the school began the process that ended in major transformations in Hunan and China. Most of the Hunan radicals became communists and went on to die for the party or to serve in its leadership, but Xiao Zisheng did not, providing an interesting contrast to the others.

Xiao Zisheng, 1894–1976

Xiao Zisheng (also called Xiao Yu or Xiao Xudong) was a native of Xiangxiang, Hunan. A schoolmate of Mao Zedong at Dongshan Primary School and First Normal, Xiao had been Mao's closest friend before 1921. He was a founder and the first director-general of the *Xinmin xuehui* and the most influential person in the work–study movement. As an advocate, organizer, and leader of the Hunanese students' work–study program in France, Xiao played a decisive role in this program. However, most accounts of early CCP history—particularly in the PRC—tend to ignore his important role in the *Xinmin xuehui* and the work–study movement because of his break with the radicals in early 1921, when he committed himself to moderate means for national salvation. He is an intriguing contrast to Mao and Cai, because he shared many of their experiences, accomplishments, and views up to the critical divergence over the issue of communism and violent revolution.

A brilliant student, Xiao was good at writing essays and outstanding at calligraphy. He could use both hands to write beautifully. Xiao was always the top student at First Normal. His essays were always exhibited as the best ones, though Mao's essays were also exhibited. From reading each other's essays, Xiao and Mao began to share ideas and opinions; thus, a bond of sympathy formed between them and they became close friends. They were together at First Normal for two-and-a-half years and "[their] evening talks became a regular habit. . . . [Their] greatest pleasure was in discussions, in hearing each other's opinions of things in general."[40] They also took a famous month-long trip together in summer 1917, traveling through Changsha, Ningxiang, Anhua, Yiyang, and Yuanjiang.[41]

Xiao became Yang Changji's favorite student. Yang Changji wrote in his diary and often repeated in public: "My three most notable students, of the several thousand I taught during my six years in Changsha, were first, Xiao Xudong (Zisheng); second, Cai Hesen; and third, Mao Zedong."[42]

After graduation from First Normal, Xiao taught at Chuyi Elementary School and maintained his friendships with schoolmates. They corresponded and often met at Chuyi School or Cai Hesen's house. Xiao and Mao formed the *Xinmin xuehui* after two years of discussion. According to Xiao, they first recruited Cai Hesen, their mutual friend who shared their ideas, and then Xiong Guangchu, Chen Chang, and Chen Shaoxiu.[43] Xiao was elected director-general of the association, while Mao and Chen Shunong were elected secretaries.

Xiao had a profound influence on his fellow Hunanese youth and played a decisive role in the work–study movement. Before he left for France in 1919, he accepted Cai Yuanpei and Li Shizeng's invitation to work for the Sino-French Educational Association, which allowed him to help his fellow students to work and study in France. Friends and acquaintances relied heavily on him for connections. A 1919 article in *Dagong bao* (Hunan) mentioned contacts who could help those who wanted to participate in the work-study movement: "There is Mr. Xiao Xudong (Zisheng). He is a Hunanese and has obtained the trust of Mr. Li [Shizeng], all public communication and pronouncements coming from his [Xiao's] pen."[44]

After he arrived in France, Xiao continued to work for the Sino-French Educational Association. He also played a leading role in the French branch of the *Xinmin xuehui*. However, he opposed the violent Russian type of revolution; he was committed to more moderate means for national salvation and sincerely believed that education was the best means for national reform.

Xiao debated with Cai and others about the best solution for China at a meeting of the *Xinmin xuehui* in Montargis, France, in summer 1920. After he returned to China, he continued the discussion and debate with his friends. Both Chen Chang and Mao Zedong told him that most of their friends had accepted Marxism and believed that Russian Communism was the most suitable system for China and the easiest to follow. Xiao recalled the days he spent in Changsha when he and Mao had many sincere talks and discussions about the problem. "Sometimes our talks made us very sad, even to the point of shedding tears, since we were unable to find a basis for mutual cooperation. I was unable to accept Mao's reasoning, but neither did my answers satisfy him. During the months consumed by these fruitless discussions, we never expressed a word of anger; rather it was a cause of genuine disappointment and sadness to both of us that we were unable to work out a common plan of action."[45] So, his old friend, Chen Chang said to Xiao:

> All our friends have secretly become members of CY and it would be very difficult to bring them back. You know that the association [the *Xinmin xuehui*] aimed at reforming China in a sort of abstract way. It had no political views and no fixed plan of action. They now think the only way to attain practical results is to follow Russia's lead and to go all out to propagate the Russian doctrine. No one is looking for any other way to bring about the reforms. Why? First, because they have Russia's model to follow. . . . I doubt if anything would induce them to turn back. I know that you have your own "anarchist" ideas of freedom, but everyone could not be expected to agree with Communism. I think you and Mao Runzhi (Mao Zedong) will follow different roads in the future.[46]

Soon Mao and his comrades began the formation of the CCP, while Xiao began to work in Beijing Guomindang Committee and served as professor and president of several universities. He also served as the vice-minister of agriculture and minerals in the Guomindang government.[47] In the years following 1949, he moved first to Taiwan and finally to Uruguay, where he died on November 21, 1976, at the age of 83. Mao died the same year.

An examination of the First Normal students' intellectual transformation in the 1910s reveals that their schooling there profoundly shaped them; the modernized Hunan First Normal School played a crucial role in transmitting new ideas and political movements, and the study society, the *Xinmin xuehui*, formed the essential interfaces through which these ideas and energies were "operationalized" and translated into concrete political action. The national moral crisis and the new knowledge and new ideas these students learned made them consciously and seriously question established ways. Many became cultural iconoclasts, transmitters of revolutionary ideas, and then communists as a result of the sharp differences between the two worlds, home and school, past and present. In particular, many of those students at the First Normal who took an active role in the May Fourth Movement as members of the Xinmin *xuehui* eventually became the founding figures of the CCP. Xiao Zisheng stands as an interesting contrast to Mao and Cai, as an example of the Xinmin members who traveled all but the final step of the journey to communism.

Chapter 7

Education of a Provincial Radical
Cai Hesen

In the 1910s, Cai Hesen, Mao Zedong, and many other important communist leaders were educated at the Hunan First Normal School. There, Cai acquired the foundation of his worldly knowledge and his political ideas. And, like Mao, Cai was prepared for his transformation by his training at First Normal and the May Fourth activities in the *Xinmin xuehui*. In fact, Cai personifies what Hunan First Normal School meant to those who attended, and to the China that they eventually crafted. His life provides a detailed example of the intellectual transformation of his fellow students and supplements the better-known example of Mao.

An examination of Cai Hesen's thought and mindset at First Normal, and his eventual ideological transformation, tells much about the era and those it shaped, and who, in turn, would shape modern China. One of the first Chinese Marxists and apparently the first Chinese to advocate in print the establishment of the CCP,[1] Cai helped found the CCP and became its most important early theorist. However, credit for shaping the CCP and for being its revolutionary theorist and strategist usually goes to Mao Zedong.[2] That characterization ignores much. Cai Hesen's firm belief that national salvation could be found in Russian Communism, which departed from the previous generation Yang Changji represented, influenced a generation of Chinese radical youths to join the communist cause.

Family Background

Cai Hesen, also known as Cai Linbin,[3] was a native of Xiangxiang, Yongfeng County (modern day Shuangfeng County), Hunan. Although

145

known as a Hunanese, he was actually born in Shanghai on March 30, 1895 and spent the first four years of his life in that city. His family had been famous for many generations for their production of "*Yongfeng lajiang*" (Yongfeng Thick Chili Sauce). Cai's paternal grandfather had taken the imperial examinations at the first level (*Xiucai*) in his early years, but had failed. Yet he served as a secretary to the famous Qing statesman Zeng Guofan for a while. Up to that time, the Cai family had been relatively prosperous. Cai's father, however, failed to manage the family business effectively, and the family had fallen on hard times. In 1890, he gave the business to others to handle and left for Shanghai with his wife and four children before Cai Hesen was born. He became a minor official in the Jiangnan Arsenal (*Jiangnan zhizaoju*) in Shanghai by using his father-in-law's relationship with Zeng Guofan.[4]

Cai Hesen's mother greatly influenced him. A modern-minded woman for her day, Ge Jianhao (1865–1943) was born into a well-to-do family in Xiangxiang, Hunan, in 1865. Her father served in Zeng Guofan's *Xiang jun* and died in a battle in Hubei province in 1868, at the age of 27. Ge's mother brought her and her elder brother up. From the age of 10 to 16, when she married Cai Hesen's father, Ge accompanied her brother and studied at a private tutorial school, where she became politically aware. In 1899, Ge left her husband in Shanghai and moved back to her mother's home in Hunan with her 4-year-old son Cai Hesen. Her husband followed her in the same year. The following year she bore her sixth and last child, Cai Chang.[5]

In spring 1914, at the age of 49, Ge entered a female teachers' school in Changsha.[6] She graduated the following year, and then returned to Yongfeng to open her own school, the Second Girls' School.[7] She functioned as both principal and teacher. In addition to academic studies, she encouraged her students to participate in activities such as singing, dancing, high jump, and long jump. She also encouraged her students to unbind their feet and cut their hair short. At that time, many women took the Second Girl's School as "Women's Abode" (*funü zhijia*) and said: "Once you enroll in the Second Girls' School, you will be living in a world of freedom."[8] Ge's radical methods of running the school infuriated the conservative elites. The resulting cessation of funding from the provincial government forced her to close the school.

As a modern woman who always gave education a priority, Ge Jianhao rebelled against her husband on several matters. She refused to bind her daughters' feet and she insisted that Cai Chang would go to school instead of accepting her husband's will to sell their daughter as a concubine.[9] Ge supported her son Cai Hesen's decision not to become a shop apprentice, a career he detested; she sold her personal possessions so that he could study. Although of limited means, Ge never failed to play host to the reform-inclined youth whenever they came to her house. The *Xinmin xuehui* was born in her home and founding members like Xiao San and Luo Zhanglong always recalled what tasty meals Mother Cai had prepared for them on particular days.

In 1919, when the work–study program in France (*liufa qingong jianxue*) sparked so much enthusiasm among Hunanese youth, Ge Jian-hao, at the age of 54, moved to France to study. Her son Cai Hesen, her daughter Cai Chang, and her would-be daughter-in-law, Xiang Jingyu[10] (1895–1928) accompanied her. Many contemporary publications praised her by name as an enlightened example of the older generation. On May 14, 1920, an article published in Hunan's *Dagong bao* said: "In recent times, there was a great tendency toward outward development in academic fields in our province. Many people have gone to France and South Asia to study. . . . Among them, I respect two the most. One was Xu Maoxun (Xu Teli), the other was Cai Hesen's mother. Both of them were nearly fifty years old and went as far away as France to work and to study, which was really admirable. . . . As young people, what should we do? We don't want to be laughed at by those two elders."[11]

Ge remained in France for four years and, on her return in 1923, could speak and read French fluently. She moved several times because of the danger to her as a result of her children's political activities. She finally settled in Yongfeng, Hunan, in 1928, and never saw her sons again. The deaths of both (Cai Hesen in 1931, the second son in 1927) were concealed from her. Her husband died in 1932, and she passed away in 1943 at the age of 78.

Cai Hesen's family life, thus, did not represent a traditional one in which the father ruled. Apparently, Cai Hesen's father did not play a major positive role in his children's lives and did not have a close personal relationship with them. Cai Hesen's mother inspired him to look beyond his own situation to the needs of the society around him. She supported her children's participation in the work–study movement by joining it herself. She also encouraged her children to choose their marriage partners freely, and fully supported her family's political activities. On her deathbed, she asked her oldest daughter to write to her other children: "Mother could not see the final victory of their cause, but the revolution was bound to be a success."[12]

Because of family's financial difficulties, Cai Hesen did not go to school regularly as a small child. In 1908, at the age of 13, he became an apprentice in his cousin's *Cai Guangxiang* shop where he spent three years.[13] Although he had asthma and was not very strong physically, Cai had to do heavy physical labor. His supervisors often cursed and beat him. Understandably, he disliked the work intensely and left as soon as the three-year apprenticeship ended. In 1911, at the age of 16, Cai entered the third grade of Yongfeng Guomin Elementary School.[14] Ridiculed by some pupils as an older student, Cai paid little attention to the scorn and applied himself industriously. Because of his academic excellence, he skipped to the Shuofeng Higher Elementary School after only one semester.[15] During his school days in Shuofeng, the hard-working student wrote essays that won high praise from his teachers. During this period, he became aware of the activities of the *Tong meng hui* (Revolutionary Alliance). He especially admired Sun Yat-sen. He was the first at his school to cut off his pigtail when the Nanjing Provisional Government encouraged Chinese to do so. Cai encouraged his mother to cut hers as well. The radical actions of the Cai family attracted attention and had a far-reaching influence in the conservative local area.[16] Although his nontraditional family background may have influenced Cai's radicalization, the environment he encountered at First Normal, and the political activities he participated in there, played a much larger role in his intellectual transformation.

School Days in Changsha

In early 1913, Cai was admitted to the Hunan Railroad School and moved to Changsha. He studied there for only one semester before he was accepted into the Hunan First Normal School. There he became acquainted with Mao Zedong, and studied under the direction of Yang Changji, Xu Teli, Li Jinxi, and Fang Weixia.

At First Normal, Cai grew interested in the study of literature, philosophy, and history, and pursued these subjects with great enthusiasm. Hard-working as ever, he liked to pursue his own studies. He kept a reading plan of his own, which was largely one for private studying. After classes, he often could be found in the library reading. Cai, as well as Mao, was good at essay writing. His literary essays were considered great events in the school.[17] At that time, "life in the First Normal School was highly exciting. Exhibitions of the work of the students, athletic meets, debates, and meetings of research groups on special topics, followed each other in dazzling succession."[18] Cai's essays were often exhibited. His literary efforts and the contents of his compositions attracted considerable interests.[19] His friend, Luo Zhanglong (1896–1995) recalled, "One day, our teacher took us to the tourist site, *Aiwan ting* at the foot of Mount Yuelu. After coming back to school in the evening, the teacher asked us to write an essay on our tour to *Aiwan ting*. All the other students used flowery language to praise the beauty of the site, except Cai Hesen who wrote that he never liked *Aiwan ting*. The topography of *Aiwan ting* was low, he continued, and its visual field was narrow. The teacher said, Cai Hesen's essays were always out of the ordinary."[20] "Like Mao," Liu Ang (1910–2005) recalled, "Cai's essays were good in wording and unique in viewpoints/ideas. Both [Cai and Mao] were concerned with the current social problems and salvation of China. . . . They did not bother about small matters, such as appearance or clothing. Sometimes, they even forgot to eat. Long before the May Fourth Movement, Mao and Cai became well-known and well-liked among the Hunanese youth."[21]

Yang thought highly of Cai Hesen and considered him one of the top three students. Cai and other students also highly respected Yang and greatly influenced by Yang. They made a habit of visiting Yang Changji's house on Sundays to consult with him on various questions.[22] Sometimes they would visit him in the evenings. If their discussion lasted in to the late hours, they would stay at Yang's house for the night.[23]

Under the encouragement of Yang Changji, Cai often visited the Chuanshan Association. The association offered lectures every Sunday in Changsha on various aspects of Wang's teachings. Members of the the association sought insight for the present in the traditional Chinese learning, especially in Wang's teachings. Cai, Mao, and their associates absorbed that point of view as well.

Yang greatly admired Wang Chuanshan and showed his high regard for Wang's advocacy of nationalism and patriotism, which greatly influenced Cai Hesen. Luo Zhanglong recalled, "Once Hesen said, 'Wang Chuanshan was a well-known scholar from Hunan. He refused to be an official, but concentrated on scholarly writings. In his books, he wrote about resistance against alien aggression, alien ruling, and recovery of China. Those ideas were very influential at the time. However, Wang was influenced by Confucianism too much. We should discard the dross and select the essential [of his writings].'"[24]

Cai grew concerned with social problems. As he and his friends talked about how to reform China, they realized that they must not only develop scholarly and morally, but also physically and mentally. As a result, Cai, Mao, and many other students followed Yang Changji in his way of living. Yang opposed the old and corrupt type of living and advocated living in a new and scientific manner. "He advocated doing away with breakfast, but said people should go in for quiet sitting (*jing zuo fa*, similar to Chan meditation) and cold baths year-round, winter included, to build firmness of will." Saio San (Emi Saio) recalled, "Mao Zedong, Cai Hesen and others took imitating him with all their youthful enthusiasm. For almost two years they went without breakfast."[25]

> One year, during the summer vacation, Mao, Tsai [Cai], and a student named Chang Kun-ti [Zhang Kundi] (1894–1932) shared a pavilion on top of the Yuehlu [Yuelu] Mountain, on the riverbank opposite Changsha. They went without breakfast and supper as well. Their diet consisted largely of fresh broad beans. Of course, there was an idea of economizing since none of them had much money. They went to the hilltop to meditate in the morning and then came down to bathe in a cold pond or in the river. This went on until the end of the vacation. They believed in the steady practicing of this "austerity training" programme.[26]

While imitating Yang's practices of "quiet sitting" and cold baths, Cai and his friends "also enlarged what the term 'bathing' usually connotes, often stripping and exposing their bodies to the elements: sun, wind, and downpours, . . . [and] referred to these practices facetiously as 'sunbath,' 'windbath,' and 'rainbath.' They often frequented a little isle in the Xiang River (*Xiang jiang*) where swimming was good. All this was intended to help build up a strong constitution. . . . Another hobby of theirs was 'voice-training.' They would go to the hills and shout or recite the poets of the Tang dynasty; or climb up the city walls and there inflate their lungs and yell to the roaring winds."[27] Because of financial difficulties, Cai did not have enough warm clothes for the winter season. "At cold winter nights, Cai sometimes intensified his exercises, sometimes worked on his 'voice-training'—loudly singing or reciting the poems, in order to keep himself warm."[28]

Because he was concerned with social problems, Cai was interested in social investigations and wanted to know more of the life of the people. Xiao San recalled Cai's experience as a wandering scholar:

> In the summer of 1918, together with Mao, he traveled via *Liuyang*, *Xiangyin*, and *Yiyang* all around the Dongting Lake. They started from Hesen's house at the foot of the Yuelu Mountain outside Changsha, . . . each armed only with an

umbrella, a towel wrapped around it, and a pair of sandals. They did not have a penny with them. Before they left, Cai Hesen told his mother and his sister, Cai Chang (1900–1990), "We'll be back in two or three days." They did not return until almost two months later.[29]

Xiao continued, "They earned their way around the counties by writing scrolls and letters for the peasants. Sometimes they also slept out in the open and subsisted on a diet of hill haws and berries."[30] He also noted that during their journey, "they inquired into the customs and manners of the various villages along their way, investigated the life of the peasants, rent conditions, and relations between landlords and peasants, and the want and destitution of the poor peasants. . . . We really admired Mao and Cai's ambition, firmness of will, and endurance of hardship."[31]

Cai also was interested in the study of philosophy. He had many contacts with and was heavily influenced by another teacher, Li Jinxi. In 1914 and 1915, Cai joined the Study Group of Philosophy"organized by Li Jinxi, Yang Changji, and other teachers. Yang and Li thought very highly of Cai. Not long before his death in 1920, Yang sent a letter to his old friend, Zhang Shizhao, in which he said: "I sincerely inform you that two students of mine [Cai Hesen and Mao Zedong] are real comers in China who have the prospect of very successful careers. If you are not working on national salvation, that's fine. [But] if you are, you must pay great attention to these two students of mine."[32] As Li Lisan (1899–1967) later recalled: "Long before the May Fourth Movement, Mao and Cai already had great fame among the reformist-minded Hunanese youth who regarded the two as their examples to follow."[33]

At First Normal, Cai's favorite teacher, Yang Changji, encouraged his students to study the useful parts of China's traditional knowledge. He objected to the wholesale rejection of Chinese institutions and culture. Yang also urged his students to study Western thought and institutions in all their aspects, as he believed they would prove essential to the revitalization of Chinese society. His teacher's experimental, gradualist approach to solutions appealed to Cai. Before he engaged in more radical Western ideas in 1919, Cai had sought only to reform Chinese society in accordance with certain Western principles and institutions.[34]

Soon after the Xinmin xuehui was founded in spring 1918, Cai and Mao planned to establish a "New Village," an ideal world in which the new families, new schools, and new society would unite as one.[35] Cai and Mao added Mozi's[36] ideas of "equality" and "universal love." Because of the civil wars in 1918, their New Village never existed. However, during this period, Cai's ideal society came to be a "small country with a small population" with equality and love for others. Owen's utopian socialism combined with Mohism to influence Cai's view of the world.

Xie Binghuai, Cai's classmate, maintains that Cai was a utopian socialist of the petty bourgeois with Mohism as his core idea.[37] If so, it should not be a surprise that Cai Hesen, later known as a militant Marxist-Leninist, passed through a stage in his political career that veered far from extremism; in fact, such idealism appealed to the educated youth of China at this time. Actually it represented the most important source of intellectual inspiration in China before Marxism caught the attention of Chinese intellectuals during the May Fourth Movement of 1919. Mao Zedong had also been a liberal of sorts.[38]

Yi Baisha (1886–1921), who taught Chinese classics and history at First Normal in 1916 and 1917, possibly influenced Cai's study of Mozi. Yi had intimate knowledge of the Confucian classics, especially the works of late Ming and early Qing Confucian scholars, Huang Zongxi (1610–1695), Gu Yanwu, and Wang Fuzhi. However, Yi had become especially interested in the teachings of Mozi. Before he came to First Normal, Yi taught at Anhui province where he knew Sun Yat-sen (1866–1925), Zhang Taiyan (1869–1936), and Chen Duxiu (1879–1942) and was heavily influenced by their ideas. Therefore, Yi tried to combine the teachings of Mozi, such as "appointing people on their merits regardless of their social backgrounds," "denouncing offensive warfare," "universal love," "every individual without distinction between the noble and base has his obligation to serve the people and to abolish what is harmful to the society," with those of Sun Yat-sen, such as, "freedom," "equality," and "universal love," into one.

Cai particularly adored Mozi and thought him a great philosopher. From Mozi's teaching, Cai considered Mozi much more concerned about common people's life and sufferings than other philosophers. He thought highly of Mozi's teaching of "universal love," and interpreted Mozi's saying, "To promote what is beneficial universally, and to abolish what is harmful universally" (xing tianxia zhi li, chu tianxia zhi hai) as "Let all people under Heaven have enough food to eat, warm clothes to wear, and live peacefully and happily."[39] He interpreted another phrase from Mozi: "Consider only what is in the general interest, regardless of personal advantages and disadvantages" (zhiji dati zhi gongli, buji xiaoti zhi lihai) as "In order to have all the people under Heaven benefit, one should not hesitate to sacrifice one's all, including forfeiting one's honor and bringing disgrace to oneself."[40] Cai thus advocated using Mozi's ideal of "universal love" and "equality" to replace orthodox Confucianism and establish an ideal, equal society. Tang Duo recalled, "According to Hesen, Mozi was not only a scientist and an engineer, but also a hard-working and practical philosopher. He wore plain clothing, had simple food, and lived a simple life, but he always thought of doing what was beneficial to all the people under Heaven. That was why people should follow Mozi's example. . . . Hesen continued, Mozi advocated 'xingli chu-hai' [To promote the beneficial and to abolish the harmful] for all the people under Heaven. In order to reach this goal, Mozi had to choose what was the utmost priority to do. He had to be practical and get away with some old unfit rules. . . . Therefore, Mozi opposed to Confucius's complicated rites and his complex funeral ceremony. Mozi advocated simplifying these ritual ceremonies."[41]

Cai believed that the central thought of Mozism was yi (righteous-ness), for Mozi held that yi was above everything (wanshi mo gui yu yi). Therefore, yi was a standard to test right and wrong in dealing with people. Tang Duo recalled how Cai said that Mozi taught that if some went to other people's orchard to steal fruits, or to other people's stable to steal horses and cows, or to kill other people to take their clothing, then all those were reaping without sowing, and that was immoral. Tang noted that Hesen accepted Mozi's words that the wars between king-doms always caused the commoners to suffer the most. That was why he opposed those unrighteous fighting, denounced offensive warfare, and advocated universal love, and equality between the rich and the poor, as well as men and women. Hesen thought that if everybody could reach the manhood of Mozi, the society would become ideal.[42]

Shen Yijia recalled, "[At that time] both Hesen and I believed in all of Mozi's teachings, such as 'universal love,' 'denouncing offensive warfare,' and 'xingli chuhai.' However, Mozi believed in ghosts and did not pursue pleasure [feile]. Hesen did not believe in ghosts and did not pursue pleasure either, so he was a 99% Mozist follower. I did not believe in ghosts, but enjoyed pleasure, so I was a 98% Mozist follower. Both of us were opposed to Confucianism. . . . We were against the Confucian teaching of studying for the purpose to become a government official and thus bring honor to one's ancestors. . . . We were also against Confu-cian despising labor, for both of us came from working families. . . . We felt autocratic Confucianism centralized people's thinking and controlled China for about two thousand years. The harmful result was that none of the cultures nowadays could reach that of the Hundred Schools in the Spring and Autumn period."[43]

Among the modern thinkers, Tan Sitong influenced Cai Hesen the most. Cai grew very interested in Tan's 1896 philosophical work, *Renxue* (*On Benevolence*). He learned to recite many paragraphs from the *Renxue* and fully supported Tan's proposition of "ripping apart and bursting all the ropes" of the Confucian doctrine. He even developed Tan's proposition further into "ripping apart and bursting all kinds of ropes around the people in the world."[44] In this, Yang Changji likely heavily influenced Cai. Yang greatly admired Tan Sitong and Tan's universalistic conception of *ren* (benevolence) and sense of cosmic dynamism. Yang praised Tan's philosophical and political views, especially the "energy of the mind," and approved Tan's criticism of the Confucian three bonds.[45] Cai also applauded Tan for his constant search after the truth and the effort Tan had put into national salvation. In turn, Cai also advocated attacks on Confucianism.

Yang especially emphasized subjective initiative, human minds, and the function of education, which greatly influenced his students. For instance, before 1919, Cai had fully shared Yang's views and had sought only to reform China by educating people, especially cultivating their minds, which he believed was the utmost importance of education.[46] At Hunan, Cai passed through one stage on this way to becoming a militant Marxist-Leninist extremist.

Cai studied very hard at school and especially liked reading. Sometimes he became so absorbed in reading a book that he missed his classes. For instance, because of his absences from classes, Cai would have been expelled from the Higher Normal School at the end of the school year, had Yang Changji, who also was teaching there then, not vigorously interceded for him.

Under Yang's direction, Cai became an ardent reader of Chen Duxiu's iconoclastic magazine, *New Youth*, which began publication in 1915, and he seriously studied its most important articles. The role of the new media, Averill asserts, proved very important in raising students' consciousness about politically significant issues facing China.[47] After reading the radical magazine, Cai became more concerned about national salvation.[48]

As a new school, First Normal played a vital role in the networks as places that both brought together and promoted interaction among capable, motivated students, and nurtured and facilitated their politicization.[49] Cai and his friends not only talked in classrooms every school day, but they also met outside of class as well.[50] During his school days in Changsha, Cai had made close friends with several other politically minded youth such as Mao Zedong, Xiao Yu, Xiao San, He Shuheng, Zhang Kundi, Chen Chang, and Luo Xuezan, at First Normal. They often studied together, discussed affairs of state and issues of the day, and traveled around the province. Nationalistic, highly motivated, and drawn together by the common interest of serving their country, they remained close. Cai continued to correspond with them after he left the school. His home often became the place for those friends to meet as well. Liu Ang recalled:

> Our [rented] house located at the foot of Yuelu Mountain, across the Xiang River, became the meeting place of Hesen and his friends where they talked about their studies, exchanged their views, and discussed about the current national affairs. Our family had half *mu* land where we planted vegetables. Whenever Mao Zedong and other friends came, they always felt they came home. They always went to the vegetable garden to pull out weeds and water the vegetables, and had meals with us. When they came, they always talked deep into the night. . . . Sometimes when more friends came and there were not enough places for them to sleep, they would talk through the night. Zhang Kundi recorded his conversation with Hesen in his diary on 23 August 1917 . . . that Hesen decided to write a history book himself, one that would mainly reflect the lives of commoners. . . . Mao Zedong's mother was once ill who came to Changsha to see a doctor and stayed with us for a few months. . . . My maternal grandmother was very hospitable. She was very fond of my uncle's friends. Although we had very little income, she always saved on food and expense of our own and treated those friends when they came.[51]

Zhang Kundi wrote in his diary that about his visit to Hesen on August 23, 1917. "I planned to stay one night, but ended up staying there for three days. In the past few years, I rarely stayed with a friend or a relative for three nights. However, [Hesen] was a good and helpful friend. The longer I stayed with him, the more benefit I received. . . . Next semester, I plan to come across the river more, so that I can be benefited more."[52]

Cai could not find a teaching position immediately after his graduation in June 1917 because all teaching openings were announced in the spring rather than in the fall. At that point, he moved to Changsha, together with his mother, two remaining sisters (Cai Qingxi and Cai Chang) and niece (Liu Ang). His younger sister, Cai Chang, who taught at Zhounan Girl's School, provided the main financial support for the family.[53]

As time passed, the already poor household came under severe financial stress during this period. Xiao Yu, a good friend, said that Cai lived with him at Chuyi elementary school (*Chuyi xiaoxue*) during this period because he did not have a job. According to Xiao Yu, Cai's lack of initiative coupled with his unwillingness to ask for help from others left him jobless after graduation.[54] However, it seemed that Cai would rather starve, sleeping with his books in an open-air pavilion, than ask a friend for assistance, which turned his life trajectory into the perfect arc of a revolutionary martyr.[55] Xiao Yu remembered that one day [in 1917] Mao Zedong hurriedly came to see him in the school and told him that the Cai family had no rice and Hesen had taken a basket of books and gone to live in *Aiwan Ting*, an open-air pavilion. Xiao Yu went to Hesen's pavilion, where Hesen sat on a stone, book held in one hand, and was reading earnestly. Xiao Yu invited Cai to live with him at *Chuyi* by convincing Cai that he felt lonely there, and this way, they could study and talk together.[56]

Although life proved extremely hard during this period, Cai continued to study. In August 1917, after he had read the important sections of *Ershi si shi* (*The Twenty-Four Histories*; dynastic histories from remote antiquity to the Ming Dynasty) and *Zizhi tongjian* (*Annals of History*; dynastic histories from the Zhou Dynasty to the Song Dynasty), Cai voiced his sadness that China did not have a complete history book. In a conversation with Zhang Kundi, he said that history books like *Ershi si shi* and *Zizhi tongjian* had only recorded the histories of emperors, ministers, and high-ranking officials.[57] He noted that "[history] should mainly record the lives of commoners and the society in which commoners were living."[58] At the time, those who advocated the New Culture Movement usually abandoned traditional learning, whereas those who supported the traditional learning usually refused to read new books. Cai instead claimed: "Regarding the Chinese culture and system, we don't need to adopt it completely, and referring to the Western culture and institutions, they should be used by us selectively, and we should not accept everything from the West. We should keep the good parts of our ancient institutions and change the bad parts under consideration of the situation of the nation. The same thing can be said of the Western institutions. That which we can use to serve our purpose, we should adopt, otherwise, we should ignore it. . . . This is what we should remember while we are reading, no matter whether the books are new or old."[59]

The rapid diffusion of new ideas and political movements from China's major cities into the countryside was facilitated by the multi-tiered networks of educational and personal interaction put in place by the new school system.[60] And the students played a mediating role of transmitting new ideas.[61] Cai realized the importance of getting to know the common people and their social realities, so, together with Mao and Zhang Kundi, Cai often made walking trips in the countryside during his vacations. In spring 1918, Cai and Mao took a trip around the Dongting Lake region of northern Hunan.[62] They learned a great deal from this experience of social investigation and spread new ideas along the way.

Students in the modern schools centered their work in study societies.[63] Such organizations were vital for the genesis and long-term propagation of political parties and programs. Both the functional malleability and the organizational particularity of these groups, then, played a significant part in their evident political utility.[64] Cai was a founding member of the Xinmin xuehui, Luo Zhanglong recalled, "Hesen proposed many constructive suggestions, such as the requirements for membership should be strict, and members should have a broad range of knowledge. . . . He also stressed that if only an effective study association was organized that could break the current oppressive atmosphere in the educational and academic fields."[65] The group constituted the most steadfast pillar of the New Culture Movement and the May Fourth Movement. The members were also active in the work–study program that sent Hunanese students to France.

Although primarily dedicated to scholarly research, personal reformation, and moral development, the association quickly evolved into the pursuit of a political issue—how to reform China. "Later Mao Zedong and other members of the Association," Xiao Yu recalled, "developed political ambitions and they accepted the Communist doctrine."[66]

Beijing, France, and Radicalism

Cai participated in the organization of the Xinmin xuehui in April 1918, and by June had become deeply engaged in the work–study program in France. During his stay in Beijing for this purpose, Cai not only labored very hard on the work–study preparations, but became ever more enthusiastic about acquiring fresh new ideas and knowledge. Following the success of the October Revolution in Russia, Cai seriously began to explore the doctrines of Marx and Lenin and eagerly devoured "the latest theories."[67] In a letter to Mao Zedong before Mao arrived in Beijing, Cai wrote: "Our ultimate goal is to rip apart and sever all the restraints that the [old] world created around us, to create a free personality, a free position, and free enterprises, and doubly to enlarge the undertakings of Lenin."[68] Cai believed a "red thread" linked Mozi to Tan Sitong and then to Lenin. The red thread involved "saving the people," and "working for the people." "What Mozi advocated [in ancient times], Lenin from Russia in recent time was quite capable of putting into practice. I, therefore, am willing to follow them."[69]

Not yet a Marxist, Cai was still groping for answers. He mixed the teachings of the ancient thinker Mozi with the doctrines of the modern-day Lenin. His mature ideology, like those of most other revolutionaries, took time to develop. However, it should be noted that, among his *Xin-min xuehui* comrades, Cai Hesen first advocated "following the example of Lenin" before the May Fourth Incident.[70]

The May Fourth Incident occurred in 1919 in Beijing, and it radicalized Chinese politics. Living in such an intense environment, Cai Hesen, an impressionable and enthusiastic young man at the age of 24, paid close attention to the development of the situation in Beijing. He vigorously organized youth from Hunan to participate in the movement. One day in late June, when he learned that the Chinese delegation at the Paris Peace Conference had agreed to sign the Versailles Peace Treaty, Cai Hesen immediately organized a protest against it. One of the protesters, Tang Duo, recalled, "On that day the protest lasted a whole day and a whole night."[71]

As the May Fourth Incident developed into a full-fledged movement, Cai's patriotic passion grew; this in turn pushed him to speed up preparations for the work–study program in France. In late June 1919, he returned to Changsha from Beijing, bringing the latest news from the capital. He enthusiastically publicized the political situation of the May Fourth Movement, and urged the Hunanese youth to participate in this movement. He also encouraged them, particularly women, to participate in the work–study program in France. In order to "let the Hunanese women evolve [politically] at the same time,"[72] Cai asked his sister, Cai Chang, and her school friend Xiang Jingyu (who would become his wife) to help organize Hunanese women to go to France. Cai Chang and Xiang Jingyu soon set up the *Zhounan nüzi liufa qingongjianxue xuehui*

(Association of Zhounan Woman's Work-Study Program in France) in Changsha. The number of Hunanese who would subsequently go to France increased steadily. Eventually, Hunan sent the largest number of people to France among all the provinces of China.

On December 25, 1919, Cai Hesen left for France, accompanied by his sister, Cai Chang, his mother, Ge Jianhao, his future wife, Xiang Jingyu (1895–1928), and thirty or so other people from Hunan. Mao Zedong came from Hunan to see them off, but did not wait for them to depart. On the docks of Shanghai, Mao bade the first group of Hunanese students farewell and left for Beijing for his second visit in order to organize the movement to oust Zhang Jingyao.

The long journey to France for the worker-students was especially uncomfortable. They often traveled in fourth class: overcrowded, inadequate accommodations, with little lighting or fresh air. Cai Chang, Cai Hesen's sister recalled: "Most of the more than thirty worker-students boarded in fourth class, which was said to have been used to carry domestic animals. It was at the bottom of the ship. Hesen lived there, too. Only six of us females who were physically weak boarded in the third class."[73] Li Weihan also recalled:

We traveled in the so-called fourth-class cabin, which actually was steerage at the bottom of the ship. We tossed about almost forty days on the sea, and many people felt dizzy, threw up, and lost their appetite. We were especially bothered by the numerous bedbugs and we couldn't get a sound sleep at night. [At night] some people had to use socks to cover their hands, tie the bottom ends of their trousers, use towels to cover their faces and necks, and only leave nostrils and eyes uncovered, all in order to have a undisturbed sleep.[74]

Despite the difficult trip, Cai Hesen did not lose his high spirits. He retained the ability to inspire his friends when they grew discouraged. A steadfast friend, he also had a gentleness underneath. As Xiao Zisheng recalled: "He was strong-willed and, though one rarely saw him smile, he was very kind to his friends."[75] Also, on the voyage to France, Cai Hesen fell in love with Xiang Jingyu. They progressed both in their quest for a free relationship and in their commitment to their political ideals. Liu Ang, Cai's niece, who had been living with Cai until he left for Beijing in 1918 and had written to the couple during this period, recalled:

On the long journey [to France], Comrade Jingyu and Comrade Hesen often discussed theories and political problems. They discussed ideals to their heart's content. Their ambitions were the same, and there was mutual adoration. In the China of that period, a free romance was looked upon as an offense against public decency. But Comrade Jingyu did not concern herself with this and made their romance public. They wrote a poem, "The Alliance of Advancement" (*Xiangshang tongmeng*), to express that they wanted mutually to progress forward on the road to revolution. In June 1920, Comrade Jingyu and Comrade Hesen were married in Montargis, France. I can see in their wedding picture that they are sitting together, shoulder to shoulder, both holding open a copy of *Das Kapital*, which was one of Comrade Jingyu's favorite Marxist works. This picture means that their union was established on a mutual belief in Marxism.[76]

Cai Hesen and the group arrived in Marseilles, France, on January 30, 1920. In early February, the Sino-French Educational Association sent them to the Montargis Middle School. In Montargis, they spent their time studying French while waiting for suitable jobs. Cai had a recurrence of asthma, but a month later, he recovered and entered the Montargis Middle School for Men.[77] At first, Cai planned "to stay in France for about five years. The first year [he would] not participate in activities, but focused on the study of French and tried to gain a full understanding of each country's socialist party and labor body, as well as of the international communist party."[78] He soon found that "the school work was too easy for him, which could not satisfy his strong thirst for knowledge, so he decided not to go school anymore. Instead, he kept reading two pages of newspapers each day, with the help of a dictionary."[79]

Cai studied very diligently, reading and translating many French radical tracts. Three months later, Cai "could gradually read the newspapers, [so, I] knew a couple of news [stories] of each country's socialist movement every day."[80] After six months, he had read about one hundred booklets on socialism. He translated *The Communist Manifesto* (by Marx and Engels, 1848), "Socialism from Fantasy to Scientific Development," "Nation and Revolution" (by Lenin), "The Proletarian Revolution and the Traitor Kautsky" (by Lenin), and " 'Left-wing' Infantilism in the Communist Movement" (by Lenin).[81] He also collected about a hundred important booklets about the Russian October Revolution and prepared to edit a series of books to introduce Marxism and the Russian October Revolution to the Chinese.

Cai's experience in France proved fateful for his ideological transformation. In France, with other Hunanese students, Cai formed a branch of the *Xinmin xuehui*, which remained in close touch with developments at home.[82] The French group led by Cai soon drew closer to Marxism. In France, for the first time, Cai observed at close range the actual working of the Western principles and institutions that he previously knew about only from book learning. What he saw disappointed him and changed his intellectual predisposition. Observing the degradation of the French workers by a bourgeois, capitalist government,[83] he discarded the idea of seeking solutions to China's problems in the West. He also examined the anarchist movement in France and found it inadequate.

Cai had come to admire Western political systems and institutions from his study with Yang Changji at the Hunan First Normal School. As one of the chief Western doctrines, anarchism enjoyed immense popularity among Chinese intellectuals after the turn of the twentieth century. Cai, like many other young men and women of his generation, was drawn to anarchism immediately.

In the beginning, Cai had felt that anarchism and Leninism had similar goals. "The ultimate ideal of the anarchist party I believe is the same as that of Lenin," Cai wrote to his friend Mao Zedong from France, "but to arrive at anarchism I think we must adopt the methods presently used in the Soviet Union . . ."[84] Cai, like many other work–study students who had acquired these beliefs and brought them with them to France,[85] also supported anarchism when he arrived in France.[86] However, in Cai Hesen's case, the weaknesses he perceived in anarchism led him to embrace Marxism. After much serious thinking and deliberation, Cai chose to become a Marxist.

As he studied the labor movement in France, Cai found that the French syndicalists, followers of the anarchist Pierre Joseph Proudhon (1809–1865), could not even protect themselves against government suppression.[87] Proudhon, a French socialist-anarchist, is most famous for asserting "Property is theft!" in his missive *What is Property?* He called for a complete reorganization of modern society to abolish most of its trappings—including money and the state itself. Proudhon advocated communitarianism as the form of reorganization of society and argued that "goodwill" would emerge naturally once "social constructs" ended. Moreover, Cai felt the narrow economic focus of syndicalism "not only is not beneficial to the workers, but on the contrary, strengthens the organization of production in the capitalist state, and thus the workers will find it even harder to liberate themselves."[88] Therefore, Cai felt anarchism not appropriate for China.

In a letter to Mao Zedong from France, Cai wrote:

> Without authority, [we] can neither collectivize nor nation-alize the industries. In other words, [we] cannot change the economic system. Without authority, [we] can neither protect the revolution nor prevent counter-revolution. . . . Therefore, I think the current world as yet cannot practice anarchism.[89]

After six months of massive immersion in reading and translating French radical tracts, Cai had had a synthetical study of all schools of socialism and the recent developments of Russia. In a letter to Mao, Cai told of his transformation:

> Recently I have done a comprehensive study of all the "isms." I feel that socialism is the real remedy for the reformation of the world, and China is no exception. The methods indis-pensable to socialism are class struggle and the dictatorship of the proletariat.[90]

After earnest study of all sorts of ideologies and of the Russian Revolu-tion, Cai found his previous intellectual beliefs deficient and consciously veered towards Marxism. By summer 1920, he identified himself as a Marxist and had begun to convert others. In a letter to Chen Duxiu, later published in the August 1, 1921 issue of *New Youth* under the title "Marxist Theory and the Chinese Proletariat" (*Makesi zhuyi yu zhong-guo wuchan jieji*) Cai stated that as "an extreme Marxist," he advocated "extremism: dialectical materialism, class struggle, and the dictatorship of the proletariat."[91] Cai became so captivated by this new ideology that he devoted the rest of his stay in France and the rest of his life to his political education and activities as a Marxist.

Increasingly, Cai became known as a leading theoretician due to his speeches and letters to members of the *Xinmin xuehui*. He told about socialism, Marxism, the "salvation of China," the Russian revolu-tion, and the creation of CCP.[92] Even before the founding of the CCP, a common saying among the Hunanese students went: "Hesen is the theorist, and Runzhi [Mao Zedong] the realist."[93] While in France, Cai not only provided sophisticated analysis for the worker-students there but also wrote several important articles for home consumption, letters to politically active friends in China, and articles to Chinese journals, all of which contained analysis of the European working situation and the application of Marxism to the Chinese situation. For instance, he published several important articles in the journals of Youth world (*Shaonian shijie*) and New Youth.[94] In his letter to Mao Zedong on August 13, 1920, Cai detailed his understanding of Marxist and Leninist doctrines and urged that a Communist Party similar to that of the Soviet Union be set up in China. He also became increasingly known for his speeches at meetings of the *Xinmin xuehui* and the Work–Study Students Society (*Gongxue shijie she*).[95]

Cai revealed his political commitment to Marxism and faith in Soviet Communism at the Montargis Meeting in July 1920. Thirteen members of the *Xinmin xuehui* [96] attended the meeting in Montargis. They passed Cai's proposal to set the *Xinmin xuehui*'s goal as "reforming China and the world." However, there appeared to be disagreement on the issue of how a socialist revolution could best be brought about in China. One group, represented by Cai, advocated "setting up a Communist Party [in China] and exercising the dictatorship of the proletariat, whose principles and scheme are similar to that of Russia."[97] They argued that only a violent revolution led by a Communist Party, like that in Russia, would solve China's national problems.

The other group, represented by Xiao Zisheng, did "not think the Russian type revolution—the Marxist type—suitable for China."[98] Xiao wanted a moderate reform approach to national salvation. He suggested "a moderate revolution—a revolution using education as its tool"[99] as most suitable for China. Both sides vigorously expressed their ideas and opinions. An intense debate developed about whether or not China should adopt Russian Communism as its political system. Although Cai's eloquence converted some anarchist members to Marxism, eventually eight of the thirteen members at Montargis joined the European branches of the Chinese Communist organizations. Yet the fundamental problem remained unsolved. Li Weihan recalled,

> Finally, it was decided that [the French branch] should write to Mao Zedong, giving him full details of the two opinions, so he could circulate it, have members in China discuss them, and give their responses to the French branch. In his letter to Mao, [Cai] Hesen detailed his understanding of Marxism and the importance of forming a Communist Party.[100]

Xiao Zisheng also wrote a long letter to Mao Zedong, giving him the details of the five-day meeting. Mao Zedong published both Cai's and Xiao's letters in the *Xinmin xuehui Journal*. Cai became the first spokesman to accept Marxism among the work-study students in France and the first to advocate forming a Communist Party in China.

After the Montargis Meeting in July 1920, Cai began to reform the Work–Study Students' Society and convert its members, most of whom were anarchists, to Marxism. Li Weihan, one of the founders of this society, recalled:

> I had the opportunity to concentrate on reading [Cai] Hesen's translation from French of the *Communist Manifesto*, "Socialism from Fantasy to Scientific Development," "Nation and Revolution," "The Proletarian Revolution and the Traitor Kautsky," " 'Left-wing' Infantilism in Communist Movement," and many booklets about the Russian October Revolution. Besides, I had several long talks with Hesen, which covered a wide range of topics, including the European revolutionary situation, the experience of the Russian October Revolution, the difference between the Bolsheviks and Mensheviks, the nature and mission of the Comintern, and how the Third International[101] (1919–1943) broke from the Second International[102] (1889–1914). After reading and talking [with Cai], I realized that the only way to achieve our goal of "reforming China and the world" was to follow the Russian October Revolution.[103]

By August 1921, the Work-Study Students' Society had more than thirty members, mostly Marxists. The aim of the society became very similar to that of the *Xinmin xuehui*. Afterward, the society gradually evolved into the French branch of the CCP.

Cai's personal and political growth was enhanced by his marriage in summer 1920 to Xiang Jingyu, also a member of the *Xinmin xuehui*. Like Xiao Zisheng, Mao Zedong, and Cai Hesen—the three favorite male students of Yang Changji—Xiang Jingyu was one of the three favorite female students of Yang Changji.[104] Friends praised their marriage not only as an example of "freedom to choose one's spouse" but also as an anti-traditional political alliance, since Xiang was very attracted to Cai's ideas and became a staunch Marxist herself. In a letter to her parents, Xiang wrote: "Hesen is Jiuer's [Xiang's nickname] true love. There is no difference in our aspirations and interests, . . . He and I are new-born persons of the 1920s and can be called children of the twentieth century."[105]

During this period in summer 1920, in addition to his campaign to convert others to Marxism, Cai contributed to the growth of Chinese Communism in other ways. Together with Zhou Enlai and Zhao Shiyan, Cai helped establish the early European branch of the CCP and became one of the founders of the French branch of the CCP.[106] His special contribution to the establishment of the CCP came in his description of the theory involved, as expressed in his letters to Mao Zedong and Chen Duxiu.[107] Because he was one of the first Chinese to study Lenin and the most advanced Chinese Marxist-Leninist [among his friends] at the time,[108] Cai expressed a more sophisticated understanding of Marxism and Russian Communism than his comrades. He expounded cogently and systematically on the theory, the course, the policy, and the principle of the establishment of the CCP. [109]

First, he argued that socialism could save China and reform the world. He wrote to Mao in France that "socialism is the real remedy for the world, China included. . . . I feel that the socialist principles and plans are completely suitable for China's future reform."[110] By cogently analyzing the materialist conception of history, the development of capitalism, class struggle, and China's social and economic situation, Cai refuted those who contested the adequacy of Marx's materialist conception of history in China because they argued that China had no classes and did not have the objective preconditions for carrying out socialism. He concluded that a social revolution would inevitably break out in China.

Leninist success also attracted Cai. Originally, Marxism was a doctrine of salvation for the working class in Western Europe and depended for its fulfillment on the presence of certain political, social, and economic preconditions. These preconditions consisted of a capitalistic economy and its byproduct, the proletariat, whose revolutionary consciousness had been awakened by collective discontent. Therefore, in the original Marxian sense, China was an underdeveloped country, with neither capitalism nor an unhappy working class, and seemed irrelevant to the problems Marx had considered. However, Lenin revised Marxism and made it adaptable to underdeveloped countries like Russia and China. He created the concept of a proletarian party led by intellectual elite, thus making it possible for other elements of society, aside from the working class, to start the revolution. Lenin also introduced the theory of imperialism, which showed that as imperialist expansion drew the underdeveloped countries into the worldwide capitalist system and made them into colonies and semi-colonies, those underdeveloped countries had more than a passive role to play in the world revolution. This Leninized Marxism seemed to be confirmed by the success of a Russian Revolution led by a Communist Party constituted of bourgeois intellectuals; significantly also, it had occurred in a situation similar to that of China. Cai thus was attracted to the Leninized Marxism, and argued that China would definitely carry out a socialist revolution. In a letter to Chen Duxiu, Cai wrote:

> I have the courage to say that nowadays among the total population of 400,000,000 Chinese, 350,000,000 of them don't have a means of livelihood. Since the situation has reached this state, . . . we probably cannot avoid the fate of socialist revolution. At this time, the eruption of revolution becomes an inevitable tendency, which is similar to the happening of the thunder in the natural world; all is inevitable. When the revolution comes, it will not consider success or failure, advantage or disadvantage, and no reformed philosophers or great scholars can control it either.[111]

Cai also wrote earnestly to Mao Zedong:

> I predict that a Kerensky government will definitely appear in China within three to five years. That means a Russian February Revolution must erupt [in China]. Its leaders must be the old warlords, political magnates, and plutocrats, who suddenly changed their old identities. The result is that a neither "ass nor horse" German-Austrian type of revolutionary government will come into being [in China]. I predict that some youth will participate, but I don't want you to partici-pate in this. I encourage you to get ready for the Russian November Revolution [in China]. I'm very confident that my prediction is 90 percent correct. Therefore, you must make early preparations for this at home.[112]

Second, Cai argued that a proletarian dictatorship should be the fundamental path for realizing socialism. In another letter to Mao, Cai wrote: "The only way to carry out socialism successfully is to have 'class struggle'—the dictatorship of the proletariat."[113]

> The important mission [of socialism] is to break the capitalist system; its method is the dictatorship of the proletariat, using the state's political power to reform the social-economic system. Therefore, class struggle is in fact a political conflict; it will break the old institutions (congress and government) and establish a [new] proletarian institution—the Soviet.[114]

He pointed out that without the dictatorship of the proletariat, the society could not be reformed, because without receiving political power, the proletariat definitely could not achieve economic liberation. He also maintained:

> The world revolutionary movement, since the success of the Russian Revolution, has already gone through an important turning point, which is that the proletariat has seized political power so as to reform society.[115]

With the success of the Russian Revolution, Cai believed that with proper guidance, the Chinese working class could seize political power too, as part of the world revolutionary movement.

Third, like Lenin, Cai accepted the concept of a revolutionary vanguard and believed that the key to revolutionary victory lay in the formation of a tightly organized political party.[116] He urged that a CCP be set up to take the leadership of the revolution. In a letter to Mao, Cai wrote: "I think a party—a Communist Party—should be established first."[117] In comprehensive terms, he expressed what the nature and policy of the party should be. He emphasized the need for total discipline, outlined the specific steps necessary for the establishment of the party, and suggested that the CCP must be a political party of the proletariat, a "vanguard, and battle headquarters [of the proletariat]."[118] He was the first formally to name the party "the Chinese Communist Party," and the first to advocate the establishment of a party modeled on the Russian Communist Party. He firmly believed that only after the establishment of the CCP, "could the revolutionary movement and labor movement have a nerve center."[119]

At that time, not many people had discussed the necessity of the establishment of a proletarian party. In spring 1921, Li Dazhao, one of the founders of the CCP, had said: "[In order to] have a fundamental reform in China, [we should set up] a political party for the common people of the laboring class."[120] But Cai's proposal for the establishment of a CCP came five months earlier than the *Communist Manifesto* formulated by the Shanghai branch of the party.[121]

Cai also advocated a party directed by Marxist doctrines. Only after the party totally accepted Marxist principles could it keep the political direction of the proletariat. He called on the party to adopt revolutionary methods to oppose those reformists who objected to the methods of the Russian October Revolution and promoted nonviolence and education as the preferred tools of revolution. Cai stated that the fundamental goal of a thorough revolution must be to mobilize workers and peasants to seize the state power, to destroy the old state apparatus, and to carry out the dictatorship of the proletariat.[122]

Cai insisted that the party must maintain close ties with the masses. Party members should go to the factories, to the rural areas, and to the schools and become the organizers and leaders of all the mass movements.[123] He argued that the party must be a highly centralized organization with iron discipline. Supreme authority would be the Central Committee of the CCP.[124]

Cai further insisted, "The policy must include several other elements. All newspapers, parliaments, organizations, and all kinds of movements must be under the leadership and supervision of the Central Committee of the Party and never be set free."[125] Cai shared Lenin's idea that party leaders who gained revolutionary consciousness and then instilled it in the workers so as to prepare them for the task of revolution. That concept resembled the age-old Confucian teaching "*xianzhi xianjue*": The awakened elite, usually educated, had the responsibility to waken the uneducated masses.

Cai also was dedicated to the internationalist commitment of Marxism. Despite its German origins, Marxist doctrine transcended national boundaries, seeking to speak for all working men and women. Therefore, the followers of Marx should be internationalists. However, many of the Chinese Marxists were staunch nationalists, a problem for Chinese Marxism. Unlike his comrades, Cai had broken free of most nationalist emotions. In a letter to Chen Duxiu, who shared the same idea, Cai wrote:

> The liberation of the working class is positively not the problem of one place, one nation, or one people, but is a universal social problem. Marxist socialism is international socialism, and we certainly do not want to bear the taint of territory and race. China's class struggle is the international class struggle.[126]

Cai's ideas finally became so pervasive that many other members of the *Xinmin xuehui* changed their opinions and adopted Marxism. He also had a profound impact on his friends back in China. Cai's theorizing from France intensified Hunan's theoretical debates. The members remaining in China held several meetings, in which they debated the same issues as the members in France.

Mao Zedong, who remained in continuous contact with the group from Changsha while they were overseas, supported Cai's opinions. In a reply to Cai's September 16 letter, Mao wrote: "Your last letter was extremely insightful. I don't have any disagreement with even one word of yours."[127] Mao and He Shuheng also organized the three-day New Year's meeting of the *Xinmin xuehui* in Changsha. The members discussed Cai Hesen's opinions—his sophisticated analysis of the materialistic vision of history, the development of capitalism, the class struggle, the importance of the dictatorship of the proletariat, the spirit of internationalism, the theoretical foundations of Marxism, the structure of the Soviet Communist Party, the urgency of establishing a Communist Party in China, the need for propaganda and training, the need for total discipline to the party, the theory of establishing a Communist Party in China, and the theory of the communist way of developing the revolutionary consciousness of the masses. Robert Scalapino concluded that Cai had a great impact on his comrades:

> Mao at this point had unmistakenly taken his stand with Marxism, not because of any profound understanding of Marxist or Marxist-Leninist theory (except as derived from Cai's descriptions) but because he had been convinced by Cai and possibly others that the Russian route was the only successful road to revolution, and that revolution was necessary for China and the world.[128]

The French experience had molded Cai into a Marxist. During the first period of his stay in France, he spent most of his time studying and translating; his marriage to Xiang Jingyu reinforced his political identification with Marxism. He gained status as the most sophisticated and most advanced Chinese Marxist. As Cai increasingly engaged in political agitation activities, his leadership profile rose during 1921.[129]

Deported from France on account of the Lyons Incident, in which Chinese students occupied a college building, Cai returned to China in late 1921[130] as a confirmed Marxist-Leninist with a broadened outlook and sophisticated Marxist theoretical perspective. Quickly elected to the Central Committee of the CCP, he served on the party's Second Congress from July 1922 to the Sixth Congress in summer 1928, and also sat on the Politburo from 1927 to 1928. At the Second Party Congress, Cai became the chief editor of *Xiangdao* (*Weekly Guide*),[131] one of the party's most influential journals. He published some 130 articles under the name of "Hesen" and many more as "our colleague" and "reporter."[132] In 1925, he was one of the chief organizers of the trade union demonstrations known as the May 30 Movement of 1925. In April 1927, he was appointed minister of the CCP's Propaganda Department at the Fifth CCP Congress in Wuhan.[133] Four months later, he became secretary of the CCP's North China Regional Bureau. But on June 5, 1931, British colonialists arrested him in Hong Kong and extradited him to Guangzhou. There, he died a martyr's death at the age of 36, after refusing to renounce his beliefs in the midst of torture. He had been spread-eagled on a wall, with his hands and feet nailed into the wall, and beaten to death, his breast torn by bayonet wounds.[134]

A detailed examination of Cai Hesen's intellectual development reveals the too-often neglected importance of the Hunan First Normal experience in transmitting new ideas and spreading the revolutionary movement. Such a study supplements the better-known example of Mao. As one of the founders of and one of the most important theoreticians for the CCP, Cai contributed the theory, strategy, and propaganda that proved especially important in early CCP history. In his evolution from an idealist to a radical Marxist, Cai began his ideological transformation while at the Hunan First Normal School, which itself underwent a series of educational reforms in the early decades of the twentieth century. While facing the national moral crisis, Cai learned the new Western ideas for the first time at the school, and started consciously and seriously to question established ways. At the school, Cai became greatly influenced by the elite—his teachers who were well known as men of both Chinese and Western learning. They also advocated the educational reforms of the late Qing and early Republic.

The new school system significantly intensified student interaction and facilitated the growth of radicalism. At the First Normal Cai made friendships with those classmates, including Mao, who became very significant in his life. Highly motivated and encouraged by Yang, Cai and his friends shared a common interest in reforming China and formed the *Xinmin xuehui*,[135] which would "have a widespread influence on the affairs and destiny of China."[136]

Hunan First Normal and the *Xinmin xuehui* became portals for radical students' transnational travel and political activism outside their local area of origin. Cai's involvement with the association completely changed his course of life. Soon after, the association sent Cai to Beijing to work on the work–study program in France for the Hunanese students. His stay in the capital, especially his participation in the May Fourth Movement, represented another important stage in his intellectual transformation, for he acquired a new intellectual identity by exposing himself to Marxism and Leninism. However, his French experience consolidated his identity with Marxism and actually converted him into a more militant Marxist-Leninist. In fact, Cai exemplifies what Hunan First Normal School meant to those who attended, and to the China that they crafted. His life provides a detailed example of the intellectual transformation of his fellow students, and stresses again how much more there was to Chinese Communism than just Mao.

Chapter 8

Conclusion

Study of the Hunan First Normal School in the second decade of the twentieth century reveals its importance in transmitting new ideas and spreading the revolutionary movement. The First Normal was one of many reformist schools established in China in the early twentieth century in response to the challenge of modernizing the nation. It produced a large group of radical students, including Mao Zedong and Cai Hesen, many of whom became the founders, thinkers, and activists in the CCP. Some became major leaders of the nation.

Why was the Hunan First Normal School able to produce so many radical intellectuals in the second decade of the twentieth century but not repeat the process after 1920? At one level, China passed through a transitional era. Conditions changed, with the threat of China's dismemberment by foreign powers, the changing ideas among the educated classes after 1895, the shift from reform thinking toward revolution, the more vocal advocacy by the educated classes, and the simple fact that many of those teaching in the 1910s at First Normal had left the school before 1920. Educational reforms continued, and the tradition of the First Normal School remained, but the social and political issues were now different.

Several characteristics made First Normal distinct and facilitated the radicalization of its students. For instance, its unique faculty body, its curriculum, its reform-minded principals, its local historical circumstances, its Hunan intellectual tradition, its geographical setting, and its place in educational reforms in China, Hunan, and the school all changed. Therefore, it provided a venue that nurtured and spread ideas that fed into the May Fourth Movement and the spread of revolution,

173

ideas that produced the first generation of communist leadership in the
1910s.

A group of liberal, open-minded teachers at First Normal fostered
the students' intellectual transformation. They were deeply grounded in
both Chinese and Western learning, and they worried about the fate of
their country and its people. They believed that education offered the
best means for saving their country. The First Normal teachers exemplified the shift of the goals of Chinese educators during this period, from
training an official elite to transforming their students into agents of
social and political change. Progressive and knowledgeable, with high
moral standards, they gained the respect of their students and had a
profound influence on them, not only in academic studies but in the way
the students lived their lives. Reform-minded principals, such as Kong
Zhaoshou and Zhang Gan, advanced the free atmosphere of academic
research at First Normal. These men promoted a series of educational
reforms integrating Western educational practices and ideals into domestic educational traditions and local values. Their effort was to train
students not only academically, but also socially and politically.

Challenges to the existing culture can lead to changes to and
reforms of local society, to adjustments of traditional culture to the
new culture, and to a war against tradition. During the second half of
the nineteenth century and the early decades of the twentieth century,
politically tumultuous China was deeply affected by Western culture,
resulting in China's social and cultural reforms, the rise of radicalization, denouncement of Confucian traditions, the organization of political
nationalism, and the breakout of revolution. The best means to national
salvation was to realize that modernization depended on learning from
the West. Educational reforms in Hunan thus provided a moment for
revolution in early twentieth-century China. However, radicalization
arose only when those education reforms interacted with the specific
local, social, cultural, and historical conditions.

Historical changes inspired the radicalization of the student generation at First Normal. Most were born between 1890 and 1905 when
their generation confronted a series of national crises. The humiliation
of the defeat by Japan in the Sino–Japanese War remained with them
from their early childhood. As children and teenagers, they witnessed
the abortive Qing reforms, the corruption of the Qing government, the
impact of the imperialist powers on China, and the sufferings of the
common people. The Wuchang Uprising of 1911 also affected them.
Although they did not play a role in the Republican Revolution, they

experienced the event. As youngsters, they witnessed its failure and the turmoil of the warlord era. The rule of despotic warlords such as Zhang Jingyao added to their radicalization, as did the humiliating unequal treaties, the Twenty-One Demands, and the Versailles Peace Treaty. By then they were mature enough to participate in political activities that began the May Fourth Movement.

In addition to political and social conditions, the intellectual atmosphere in Hunan also helped radicalize the students. Famous Hunan scholars from the second half of the nineteenth century had generated interest in learning from the West: Wei Yuan, the famous reform-minded scholar-official of the Qing dynasty, Zeng Guofan and Zuo Zongtang, the leading figures of the Self-Strengthening Movement, and Tan Sitong, the reformer and legendary martyr of the Hundred Days Reform Movement of 1898. Hunan's special *Huxiang* culture emphasized moral cultivation, "investigating fundamental principles," *jingshi zhiyong* (bureaucratic statecraft), "the unity of knowledge and action," and searching for truth that could contribute to national salvation, matched many of the characteristics of the May Fourth Movement, and those contributed to students' intellectual transformation as well. Immersed in such an atmosphere, the students often discussed current issues and how to save the country. During the early twentieth century, Hunan developed important educational reforms. There was local autonomy for educational reforms. During the New Culture and the May Fourth movements, a new nationalism brought attacks on traditional culture, especially on Confucian tradition. The emergence of new values, and a new kind of literature all demonstrated the new intellectual ferment. *Xinmin xuehui*, the student study organization at First Normal became very influential.

The May Fourth Movement represented the first attempt by a generation of students to reform Chinese society. Imbued with the theory of "the unity of knowledge and action," those students eagerly put into practice all kinds of theories they had learned, and they used practice as a standard to test whether the theories should survive. If a theory did not work, they immediately abandoned it and began to pursue a new one. That is why this generation of students exhibited rapidly changing ideals during the May Fourth period and why most of them embraced communism after Russian Communism seemed to them successful.

This generation of students also experienced the abolition of the civil service examinations in 1905, which disrupted their educational training in a Confucian tradition. Still, they had solid training in traditional Chinese learning and were the last generation to memorize the

Chinese classics for career preparation. Although they later consciously attacked traditional culture, especially the Confucian tradition, they unconsciously remained intellectually committed to many Confucian ideals. They saw themselves as the enlightened and called themselves the *xianzhi xianjue*, or the awakened. They often expressed their views and concerns in a style reminiscent of their Confucian forebears. They still felt the weight of Confucian living in the sense of personal destiny. Thus, they continued to be influenced by the concept of the role of the intellectual as a moral example.

This generation was also the first to be educated in the new Western learning, and Western education was essential in their intellectual transformation. From moderately poor families, the students chose First Normal because of its free education, board, and lodging. From conservative rural backwaters with strong Confucian tradition to the industrial center, with its entirely new intellectual stimulus, the First Normal students were astonished by the bustling urban world in the 1910s Changsha. This movement from rural to urban helped to radicalize educated youths. In Changsha they saw foreigners, foreign steamships, and foreign products for the first time. The New Culture Movement, spread through its newspapers and journals, had an impact. So did the differences they saw between the two worlds—home and school, old and new—which made them consciously rethink their previous views about the national crisis and their own responsibilities. They sensed that they had a unique mission: to save their country. Many of the members of the *Xinmin xuehui* participated in the work–study program in France, and the experience gave them a still broader worldview, one more understanding of advanced technology and the West. The French experience brought an ideological conversion to many of them, and contributed to the formation of the CCP.

After searching among the values, ideologies and concepts that might solve their country's problems, they finally turned to communism as the most effective solution. They joined in the formation and activities of the CCP, which they believed offered a new moral leadership. The notions of the party-state and its political leadership recalled those favored by their Confucian literati precursors, and were fashioned by their education at First Normal. The earnest search for solutions to personal and national crises derived from their feverish interest in modern ideologies and traditional thought, an interest fed by their schooling. Although their Western education did not in itself determine their radicalism, it did lead them to rethink traditional ideas and values. The combination of traditional thought and Western influences facilitated their intellectual transformation into radicals and later into communists.

As they turned to communism, students from First Normal changed their world. Today, well into the twenty-first century, the revolution is long over. The historical circumstances have changed and the social and political issues are different. But China still faces the challenges of educational reform and learning from the West as it modernizes itself. The process of changing values and institutions goes on. In 2009, a minister of education at the "60 nian jiaoyu gaige fazhan" conference (sixty years of educational reform and development) said that in order to build a strong and modernized China, the fundamental approach was still to make education a priority and to continuously promote educational reforms. As First Normal's recruiting advertisements proclaimed in the 1910s, it was education that would determine the rise and fall of the country.

The First Normal School fostered the intellectual transformation of its students during the decade of the 1910s. It encouraged the values such as equality, freedom, and humanism that became part of the May Fourth Movement. It was able to do so because the central government was weak throughout the period of First Normal's existence. Ironically, many of its students joined the CCP and advanced the cause of revolution because the school functioned as a major transmission route for new concepts and political movements. China has always been an authoritarian state, and in modern times schools have been under government control. Even today the communists have assigned party secretaries to all the schools as a way to enforce government control. But we may hope that the legacy of liberal education taught at Hunan First Normal may yet prevail as China marches toward modernity.

Notes

Notes to Introduction

1. Sun Hailin, telephone interview by author, April 15, 2011. Sun was the former principal of Hunan First Normal School and is the author of *Hunan diyi shifan xiaoshi—1903–1949* (*The History of Hunan First Normal School—1903–1949*).

2. Maurice J. Meisner, *Li Ta-chao and the Origins of Chinese Marxism* (Cambridge: Harvard University Press, 1967); Benjamin Isadore Schwartz, *Chinese Communism and the Rise of Mao* (Cambridge: Harvard University Press, 1951); Arif Dirlik, *The Origins of Chinese Communism* (New York: Oxford University Press, 1989); idem, *Anarchism in the Chinese Revolution* (Berkeley: University of California Press, 1991); Peter Gue Zarrow, *Anarchism and Chinese Political Culture* (New York: Columbia University Press, 1990). Hans van de Ven traced the origin of Chinese communism to a much later time. Hans J. van de Ven, *From Friend to Comrade: The Founding of the Chinese Communist Party, 1920–1927* (Berkeley: University of California Press, 1991).

3. Peng Dacheng, *Huxiang wenhua yu Mao Zedong* (Huxiang Culture and Mao Zedong) (Changsha: Hunan chubanshe, 1991); Jin Guantao, "Rujia wenhua de shenceng jiegou dui Makesi zhuyi Zhongguo hua de yingxiang" (The effect of Confucian culture's deep structure upon sinicized Marxism), *Xin guancha wenzhai* (New Examination Digest), September 1988. Jin claims that Marxism and Leninism were totally Confucianized by Maoist communists.

4. For instance, each of the works examines a crucial aspect of educational reform in the early twentieth century: the strength and weakness of both the traditional schools and the new ones, the modern gentry's contribution to educational reform, the impact of the new schools on Chinese society, and the development of popular education. Ruth Hayhoe and Marianne Bastid (eds.), *China's Education and the Industrialized World: Studies in Cultural Transfer* (Armonk, NY, and London: M. E. Sharpe, 1987), vii; Paul John Bailey, *Reform the People: Changing Attitudes towards Popular Education in Early Twentieth-century China* (Vancouver: University of British Columbia Press, 1990); Sarah C. McElroy, "Transforming China through Education: Yan Xiu, Zhang Bolin, and the Effort to Build a New School System, 1901–1927" (PhD dissertation, Yale

University, 1996); Glen Peterson, Ruth Hayhoe, and Yongling Lu, ed. *Education, Culture, and Identity in Twentieth-Century China* (Ann Arbor: University of Michigan Press, 2001); Barry C. Keenan, *Imperial China's Last Classical Academies: Social Change in the Lower Yangzi, 1864–1911* (Berkeley: Institute of East Asian Studies and University of California Press, 1994); Stephen C. Averill, "The Transition from Urban to Rural in the Chinese Revolution," *China Journal* 48 (July 2002); Xiaoping Cong, *Teachers' Schools and the Making of the Modern Chinese Nation-State, 1897–1937* (Vancouver: The University of British Columbia Press, 2007).

5. Charlton M. Lewis, *Prologue to the Chinese Revolution: The Transformation of Ideas and Institutions in Hunan Province, 1891–1907* (Cambridge: East Asian Research Center and Harvard University Press, 1976). Joseph W. Esherick, *Reform and Revolution in China: The 1911 Revolution in Hunan and Hubei* (Berkeley: University of California Press, 1976); Stephen R. Platt, *Provincial Patriots: The Hunanese and Modern China* (Cambridge: Harvard University Press, 2007); Stephen C. Averill, "The Cultural Politics of Local Education in Early Twentieth Century China," *Twentieth Century China* 32, no. 2 (April 2007), 6.

6. Wen-hsin Yeh, *Provincial Passages: Culture, Space, and the Origins of Chinese Communism* (Berkeley: University of California Press, 1996).

7. Ibid.

8. Ibid., 1–5, 193–96.

9. There were three regional styles of Confucianism: Huxiang (Hunan) scholars emphasized *jingshi zhiyong* (bureaucratic statecraft); Jiangnan (Zhejiang) scholars stressed *gewu* (the investigation of things, or diligent study); Lingnan (Guangdong) scholars focused on the importance of *xinzhi* (cultivation of the mind). See Yang Nianqun, *Ruxue diyuhua de jindai xingtai: sanda zhishiqunti hudong de bijiao yanjiu* (The Modern Forms of Regional Confucianism: A Comparative Study of the Interactions among Three Intellectual Groups) (Beijing: Sanlian shudian, 1997), 113–59.

10. Averill, "Cultural Politics," 32.

11. Annals of Hunan First Normal School Committee, *Hunan shengli diyi shifan xuexiao xiaozhi* (Annals of Hunan Provincial First Normal School) (Changsha: Hunan Provincial Archives, [1918]: 59–5–37), Section 2.

12. Lewis, *Prologue to the Chinese Revolution:* 40.

13. Huxiang culture was deeply influenced by the Confucian school of *li* (principle) and the idea of *jingshi zhiyong*, or "bureaucratic statecraft." Hao Chang points out while *jingshi* is conventionally translated as "bureaucratic statecraft," its literal translation is "setting the world in order." In the Neo-Confucian tradition, bureaucratic statecraft was only one of three parts of a general renovation. See Hao Chang, "The Intellectual Heritage of the Confucian Ideal of *Ching-shih*," in *Confucian Traditions in East Asian Modernity: Moral Education and Economic Culture in Japan and the Four Mini-dragons,* ed. Tu Wei-ming (Cambridge: Harvard University Press, 1996), 72–91.

14. Hunanese scholarship (*xiangxue*) as a distinctive school started with Hu Anguo (1074–1138), son Hu Hong (1106–1161), and disciple Zhang Shi (1133–1180), and several of their disciples in the Song. However, Zhou Dunyi (1017–1073) has been acknowledged by Hunanese scholars as one of the most important sources of the Hunanese intellectual heritage.

15. Wang Xingguo, *Yang Changji de shengping ji sixiang* (Life and Thought of Yang Changji) (Changsha: Hunan renmin chubanshe, 1981).

16. "Xinmin xuehui huiwu baogao" (Report of the affairs of the New Citizen Study Society) (1920), *Xinmin xuehui ziliao* (Documents Collection and Memories of the New Citizen Association) (Hunan Provincial Archive, 1920), No. 1; Zhou Shizhao's memoir "Xiangjiang de nuhou" (Soar of the Xiang river) in *Xinmin xuehui ziliao*; reprinted 1979), 391–444.

17. In the Lyons Incident, 125 Chinese students, led by Cai Hesen, occupied a dormitory at Lyons University on September 21, 1921 requesting that the Sino-French Institute at the University keep their promise by accepting them with scholarships. This is discussed further in Chapter 7.

18. Zhonggong zhongyang dangshi yanjiushi, *Zhongguo gongchandang de qishinian* (The History of the Chinese Communist Party in the Past Seventy Years) (Beijing: Zhonggong dangshi chubanshe, 1991).

19. Chow Tse-tsung viewed the movement as a patriotic awakening. See Chow Tse-tsung, *The May Fourth Movement: Intellectual Revolution in Modern China* (Cambridge: Harvard University Press, 1960). Leo Ou-fan Lee concluded that the movement was analogous to the European Romantic movement. See Leo Ou-fan Lee, *The Romantic Generation of Modern Chinese Writers* (Cambridge: Harvard University Press, 1973). Vera Schwarcz maintained that the movement was analogous with the European Enlightenment. See Vera Schwarcz, *The Chinese Enlightenment: Intellectuals and the Legacy of the May Fourth Movement of 1919* (Berkeley: University of California Press, 1986). Lin Yu-sheng argued that the totalistic anti-traditionalism of the May Fourth period was typical of traditional Chinese thought, a "monistic and intellectualistic mode of thinking." See Lin Yu-sheng, *The Crisis of Chinese Consciousness: Radical Antitraditionalism in the May Fourth Era* (Madison: University of Wisconsin Press, 1979). Hao Chang, by contrast, saw it as the interaction of various cultural discourses that transcended the themes of democracy, science, nationalism, and anti-traditionalism. See Hao Chang, "Xingxiang yu shizhi: zairen wusi sixiang" (Image and Reality: a Re-examination of May Fourth Thought), in *Ziyou minzhu de sixiang yu wenhua* (Liberal Democratic Thought and Culture), ed. Wei Zhengtong (Taibei: Zili wanbaoshe, 1990), 23–57; Benjamin I. Schwartz, *In Search of Wealth and Power: Yen Fu and the West* (Cambridge: Harvard University Press, 1964); Hao Chang, *Liang Ch'i-ch'ao and Intellectual Transition in China, 1890–1907* (Cambridge: Harvard University Press, 1971).

20. Zhongguo shehui kexueyuan jindaishi yanjiusuo (China Social Sciences Institute Modern Chinese History Department), *Wu si aiguo yundong* (The

May Fourth Patriotic Movement), 2 vols. (Beijing: Zhongguo shehui kexue yuan, 1979); Song Feifu, *Xinmin xuehui* (The New Citizen Association) (Changsha: Hunan renmin chubanshe, 1980); Zhongguo shehui kexueyuan jindaishi yanjiushuo, *Wusi yundong huiyilu* (Reflections of the May Fourth Movement), 2 vols. (Beijing: Zhongguo shehui kexueyuan, 1979); Zhou Yanyu, *Mao Zedong yu Zhou Shizhao* (Mao Zedong and Zhou Shizhao) (Changchun: Jilin renmin chubanshe, 1993).

21. Zhonggong zhongyang dangshi yanjiushi, *Zhongguo gongchandang de qishinian* (The History of the Chinese Communist Party in the Past Seventy Years) (Beijing: Zhonggong dangshi chubanshe, 1991), 16–19, 25–27, 78, 83–97, 118–23, 543–44.

22. Some advocated educational reform and the programs endorsed by the Second International.

23. Averill, "Cultural Politics," 6.

Notes to Chapter 1

1. Liyan Liu, *Yixue boshi Hume zhai Zhongguo* (Edward H. Hume M.D. in China) (Hong Kong: Hong Kong Yinhe Press, 2000), 6–8.

2. Esherick, *Reform and Revolution in China*; Lewis, *Prologue to the Chinese Revolution*.

3. *Hunan Shengzhi: Hunan jinbainian dashijishu* (Hunan Provincial Annals: Chronological record of major events in Hunan during the past one hundred years) (Changsha: Hunan renmin chubanshe, 1959), 1: 126–29.

4. Ibid., 138–39.

5. Ibid.

6. Michael Dillon, ed., *China: A Historical and Cultural Dictionary* (Richmond, Surrey, GB: Curzon Press, 1998), 376.

7. Shao Yanmiao, *Xinhai yilai renwu nianli lu* (Who's Who from the Republican Period to Present) (Nanjing: Jiangsu renmin chubanshe, 1993), 84.

8. Wang Xianqian was successful in commercial affairs. For instance, he had a gold mine in Pingjiang. Fei Xingjian, *Jindai mingren xiaozhuan* (Biographical Sketches of Famous Men in the Modern Period) (Taibei reprint, n.d.), 180–81.

9. Marianne Bastid, Paul J. Bailey trans., *Educational Reform in Early Twentieth-Century China*; Paul J. Bailey, *Reform the People*.

10. *Hunan Shengzhi*, 139–40; Sun Hailin claims that the Current Affairs School was established by Tan Sitong, Tang Caichang, and Xiong Xiling, with the support of Gov. Chen Baozhen and judicial commissioner Huang Zunxian. The Editing Committee of the History of Hunan First Normal School, *Hunan diyi shifan xiaoshi—1903–1949* (The History of Hunan First Normal School—1903–1949) (Shanghai: Shanghai Educational Press, 1983), 2.

11. Lewis, *Prologue to the Chinese Revolution*, 47. For more information on Huang's activities in Hunan, see Richard C. Howard, "Japan's Role in the Reform Program of Kang Youwei," in Lo Lung-pang, ed. and tr., *Kang Youwei: A Biography and a Symposium* (Tucson: University of Arizona Press, 1967).

12. Hao Chang, *Liang Ch'i-ch'ao and Intellectual Transition in China: 1890–1907*, 125.

13. Li Weige was a native of Jiangsu. In later years he became a manager of the Hanyeping industrial complex at Wuhan. Tian Fulong, ed. *Hunan jin 150 nian shishi rizhi, 1840–1990* (The Daily Records of Hunan's Historical Events in the Latest 150 years, 1840–1990) (Beijing: Zhongguo wenshi chubanshe, 1993), 40.

14. Ibid., 40.

15. *Hunan Shengzhi*, 140.

16. For more information on Xiong Xiling, see Zhou Qiuguang, *Xiong Xiling zhuan* (Biography of Xiong Xiling) (Changsha: Hunan Normal University Press, 1996); Howard L. Boorman, ed., *Biographical Dictionary of Republican China* (New York: Columbia University Press, 1971), 4: 108–10.

17. Michael Dillon, ed., *China: A Historical and Cultural Dictionary*, 308.

18. Hao Chang, *Chinese Intellectuals in Crisis: Search for Order and Meaning, 1890–1911* (Berkeley: University of California Press, 1987), 66–67.

19. Lewis, *Prologue to the Chinese Revolution*, 48.

20. For more details of New Text, see John K. Fairbank, *China: Tradition and Transition* (Boston: Houghton Mifflin Company, 1989), 267–69; 373–76.

21. Michael Dillon, ed., *China: A Historical and Cultural Dictionary*, 308.

22. The term *radical* and its cognates refer to some new types of political activities, such as strikes and demonstrations and new modes of beliefs, such as new structures of political power, not recognized as legitimate by the authorities of the state. Thus, advocacy of parliamentary government was "radical" in 1897–1898, but it was not radical after 1906, when the Qing court announced its own preparations for constitutional government.

23. Lewis, 49–50.

24. See the letter in *Wuxu bianfa* (The Reform Movement of 1898), ed., Chinese Academy of Historical Studies. 4 vols (Shanghai: People's Publishing House, 1957), 2: 533–35.

25. Charlton M. Lewis maintains that this proposal of Liang Qichao was not particularly radical, because in Hunan the provincial elite had sometimes defied the central government over the issue of foreign encroachment. Lewis, 50.

26. Angus W. McDonald, Jr. *The Urban Origins of Rural Revolution: Elites and the Masses in Hunan Province, China 1911–1927* (Berkeley: University of California Press, 1978), 14–15.

27. *Hunan Shengzhi*, 139–40.

28. Ibid., 146–52.

29. Liang Qichao, *Wuxu zhengbian ji* (An Account of the 1898 Coup) (Taibei: Reprinted, 1964), 8: 10b.

30. *Xiang bao leizuan* (Topical collection from the *Xiang bao*)(Shanghai, 1902; Taibei: Reprinted, 1968), 1: 157.

31. *Xiang bao leizuan*, passim; Esherick, 15–16.

32. Hunan shengzhi bianzuan weiyuanhui (Committee for the Hunan provincial gazetteer), ed., *Hunan jinbainian dashijishu* (Chronological record of major events in Hunan during the past one hundred years), 150.

33. The Editing Committee of the History of Hunan First Normal School, *Hunan diyi shifan xiaoshi*, 2.

34. Liang Qichao, *Intellectual Trends in the Qing Period*, trans. Immanuel C. Y. Hsü (Cambridge, Mass: Harvard University Press, 1959), 123.

35. Liang Qichao, *Wuxu zhengbian ji*, 3:130–37.

36. Liang Qichao, *Intellectual Trends in the Qing Period*.

37. This was the main hall of Xiaolian Academy, one of Changsha's leading literary academies.

38. Tian Fulong, ed. *Hunan jin 150 nian shishi rizhi, 1840–1990* (The Daily Records of Hunan's Historical Events in the Latest 150 years, 1840–1990), 41.

39. *Hunan xianzhi: Hunan jinbainian dashijishu*, 157.

40. Shao Yanmiao, *Xinhai yilai renwu nianli lu*, 152.

41. *Hunan xianzhi: Hunan jinbainian dashijishu*, 147.

42. Su Yu, ed. *Yijiao congbian* (A General Collection to Protect the Faith) (Taibei: reprinted, 1970), 242.

43. Wang Xianqian's letter in Su Yu, 397.

44. *Hunan xianzhi: Hunan jinbainian dashijishu*, 142–46; also see Zhongguo renmin zhengzhi xieshang huiyi, Hunan sheng weiyuanhui wenshi weiyuan huibian, *Hunan jin 150 nian shishi rizhi, 1840–1990* (The Daily Records of Hunan's Historical Events in the Last 150 Years, 1840–1990), 40–42.

45. *Hunan xianzhi: Hunan jinbainian dashijishu*, 151–52.

46. Ibid., 143.

47. The imperial court ordered both Tan Sitong and Huang Zunxian (Huang was appointed minister to Japan) to go to Beijing and to participate in the National Reform Movement. Tan was ill and did not reach Beijing until early September. Huang also was ill and only arrived in Shanghai after the Hundred Day Reform was crushed by the Empress Dowager Cixi on September 21, 1898.

48. Tian Fulong, ed. *Hunan jin 150 nian shishi rizhi, 1840–1990* (The Daily Records of Hunan's Historical Events in the Last 150 Years, 1840–1990), 42.

49. Joseph W. Esherick argues that the motive of Zhang Zhidong's order to destroy all the records of the South China Study Society was undoubtedly to protect many gentry participants. Joseph W. Esherick, *Reform and Revolution in China: The 1911 Revolution in Hunan and Hubei* (Berkeley: University of California Press, 1976), 18.

50. *Hunan xianzhi.*

51. Tang Caichang was reunited with Liang Qichao in Japan in 1898. Liang established Great Harmony High School (*Gaodeng datong xuexiao*) in Tokyo the following year and eleven former students from the Changsha Current Affairs School came to Japan to continue their studies with him.

52. Lewis, 69.

53. Li Shoukong, "Tang Caichang yu Zilihui" (Tang Caichang and the Independence Society) in Wu Xiangxiang, ed., *Zhongguo xiandaishi tongkan*, 6: 41–159.

54. *Hunan xianzhi*, 170–98.

Notes to Chapter 2

1. Yang Nianqun, *Ruxue diyuhua de jindai xingtai* (The Modern Forms of Regional Confucianism).

2. Daniel McMahon, "The Yuelu Academy and Hunan's Nineteenth–Century Turn Toward Statecraft" in *Late Imperial China*—26, 1 (Baltimore: The Johns Hopkins University Press, 2005), 72–109.

3. *Hunan xianzhi*, 160–97.

4. Hunan Shengzhi shengzhi bianzuan weiyuanhui (Editorial Committee for the Hunan Provincial Gazetteer), ed. *Hunan Shengzhi: Hunan jinbainian dashijishu* (Hunan Provincial Annals: Chronological record of major events in Hunan during the past one hundred years) (Changsha: Hunan renmin chubanshe, 1959), 1: 166–67.

5. Esherick argues that the imperial court turned toward reform because the conservative anti-foreignism of the Boxers had brought such massive defeat and humiliation. Joseph W. Esherick, *Reform and Revolution in China*, 41.

6. *Hunan xianzhi.*

7. The decree was called *Renyin xuezhi* in 1902 and *guimao xuezhi* in 1903.

8. Zhang Shi (1133–1180 AD) was a well-known Confucian in the Southern Song Dynasty and enjoyed equal popularity with two other contemporary famous Confucians, Zhu Xi and Lü Zuqian. They had the reputation of being "The three sages of the southeast" (*dongnan sanxian*).

9. *Hunan shengli diyi shifan xuexiao xiaozhi* (Annals of Hunan Provincial First Normal School) (Changsha: Hunan Provincial Archives, [1918]: 59–5–37), Section 2, 5.

10. *Hunan xianzhi.*

11. Ibid., 176–77.

12. Hunan shengzhi bianzuan weiyuanhui (Editorial Committee for the Hunan Provincial Gazetteer), *Hunan jinbainian dashi jishu* (Chronological record of major events in Hunan during the last hundred years), 1: 177–78.

13. *Hunan shengli diyi shifan xuexiao xiaozhi* (Annals of Hunan Provincial First Normal School), Section 2, 1–2.

14. Editing Committee of the History of Hunan First Normal School, *Hunan diyi shifan xiaoshi*, 4.

15. *Dongfang zazhi* 1.1:22 (Feb. 1904) emphasized the urgency of the text-book problem and suggested the Hunan authorities translate Japanese books for use in the province. Tian Fulong, ed., *Hunan jin 150 nian shishi rizhi, 1840–1990*, 45.

16. Wang Xianqian, *Xushou tang wenji* (Collected writings from the studio of pure reception) (16 juan in 2 han. N.p., 1921), I, 15a–b.

17. Ibid., I, 15b–16.

18. Wang Xianqian, *Wang Xianqian ziding nianpu* (A chronological auto-biography of Wang Xianqian) (3 juan in 3 che. N.p., n.d.), II, 90b, date might be between late eighteenth and early nineteenth centuries.

19. In 1904, the combined Hunan Normal School and Hunan Provincial Normal School was renamed the Central Route Normal School. In 1912, the name became Hunan Public First Normal School. The school was renamed the Hunan Provincial First Normal School in 1914. In 2008, the name became the Hunan First Normal College.

20. Tian Fulong, ed. *Hunan jin 150 nian shishi rizhi, 1840–1990*, 46–48.

21. Hunan Shengzhi shengzhi bianzuan weiyuanhui (Editorial Commit-tee for the Hunan Provincial Gazetteer), ed. *Hunan Shengzhi: Hunan jinbainian dashijishu* (Hunan Provincial Annals: Chronological record of major events in Hunan during the past one hundred years), 1: 221.

22. *Hunan shengli diyi shifan xuexiao xiaozhi* (Annals of Hunan Provincial First Normal School), Section 2, 15.

23. Ibid., Section 3, 101–03.

24. In 1909, for example, First Normal only had twenty-nine faculty and administrative staff for 225 students in four classes. The Editing Committee of the History of Hunan First Normal School, *Hunan diyi shifan xiaoshi*, 8.

25. In 1910, the school burned and was rebuilt by 1912, becoming the first modern buildings in Changsha. In 1938, First Normal was once again burned in the Changsha Fire. Today's First Normal was reconstructed in 1968 accord-ing to the original feature of the school. *Hunan diyi shifan xiaoshi*, 2, 9; *Hunan shengzhi*, 259–60, 704–05.

26. Ibid.

27. *Zhongguo quanshi* (The Complete History of China), Shi Zhongwen, ed. (Beijing: Renmin chubanshe, 1994), 91. 29.

28. Ibid., 28–31.

29. *Hunan xianzhi*, 335–36.

30. Ibid., 337–39.

31. The national leader of the Peace Planning Society in Beijing was Yang Du, a native of Xiangtan, Hunan. His associates in Changsha included Ye Dehui, educator Fu Dingyi, and the powerful merchant Zuo Yizhai.

32. Li Rui, *Mao Zedong tongzi di chuqi geming yundong*, 49–50.

33. *Hunan xianzhi*, 69.

34. For more information on Cai Yuanpei, see Timothy B. Weston, *Beijing University and Chinese Political Culture, 1898–1920* (dissertation, University of California, Berkeley, 1995); Howard L. Boorman, ed., *Biographical Dictionary of Republican China*, 3: 295–96.

35. For more information on Cai Yuanpei, see Wen-Hsin Yeh, *Provincial Passages: Culture, Space, and Origins of Chinese Communism*, 76–83; Timothy B. Weston, *Beijing University and Chinese Political Culture, 1898–1920* (dissertation, University of California, Berkeley, 1995), 86–101.

36. William Duicker, Cai's American biographer, maintains that Cai's study in Germany "provided him with the philosophical basis for a new world view." However, he was still drawn to the moral strain in Confucianism. Therefore, Kant, who tried to mediate materialism with the transcendent moral force, and the neo-Kantian philosopher Friedrich Paulsen, who emphasized morality, held great appeal for Cai Yuanpei. For more on Cai's years in Germany, see William Duicker, *Ts'ai Yuan-p'ei: Educator of Modern China* (University Park: Pennsylvania State University Press, 1977), chapter 3.

37. There were separate curriculum guidelines for universities passed by the Ministry of Education in 1912 that reflected some of Cai's ideals in the article. The article was published serially in *Linli bao* from February 8–10, under the title "*Duiyu xin jiaoyu zhi-yijian* (Opinions concerning new education). See Gao Pingshu, ed., *Cai Yuanpei quanji* (Collected works of Cai Yuanpei) (Beijing: Zhonghua shuju chuban she, 1988), 2: 130–37; for an English-language translation, see Ssu-yu Teng and John K. Fairbank, eds., *China's Response to the West: A Documentary Survey, 1839–1923* (Cambridge: Harvard University Press, 1982), 235–38.

38. Timothy Weston points out that Cai Yuanpei's education for citizens' morality (*gongmin daode*) represented a clear break from the moral education of the past, in that it was explicitly grounded in the French Revolution ideals of "liberty, fraternity, and equality." See his *Beijing University and Chinese Political Culture, 1898–1920* (diss.), 88.

39. For a fuller discussion of Cai's views on aesthetics, see Duicker, op. cit., 28–30. See Ssu-yu Teng and John K. Fairbank, eds., op. cit., 237.

40. The principles were embodied in documents called "Principles for Education" (*jiaoyu zongzhi*), "The School System" (*xuexiao xitong*), "Decree on Elementary Schools" (*xiaoxue xiaoling*), "Decree on Middle Schools" (*zhongxue xiaoling*)," Decree on Universities" (*daxueling*), "Regulations for Students" (*xun gexiaosheng ling*), "Emphasis on the Military Spirit" (*zhuzhong shangwu jingshen ling*), "Decree on Education of Normal Schools" (*shifan jiaoyu ling*), and "Regulations for Normal Schools" (*shifan xuexiao guicheng*).

41. Cai resigned as Minister of Education in July 1912, along with premier Tang Shaoyi and three other cabinet members. After that, Cai went back to Europe to study again.

42. Tang Qianyi, *Xiang shiji*, 2: 4b.

43. *Hunan shengli diyi shifan xuexiao xiaozhi* (Annals of Hunan Provincial First Normal School), Section 3, 1–27.

44. The New Culture Movement started in 1915 with Chen Duxiu's founding of the "New Youth." Intellectuals fiercely attacked Chinese traditions, especially Confucianism, and turned to science and democracy, the essence of modern Western culture. The movement split into leftist and liberal wings. The latter advocated gradual cultural reform as exemplified by Hu Shi while leftists like Chen Duxiu and Li Dazhao introduced Marxism and advocated political action. Ibid., Section 1, 1–5.

Notes to Chapter 3

1. Siao Yu (Xiao Zisheng), *Mao Tse-tung and I were Beggars* (London: Hutchinson & Co. Ltd., 1961), 34. See note 95 for the buildings of the school.

2. Ibid., 34.

3. Ibid.

4. The editing committee of Hunan diyi shifan xiaoshi, *Hunan diyi shifan xiaoshi—1903–1949*, 5–6.

5. Tan Yankai (1879–1930), a native of Hunan, was a Hanlin scholar. He earned the highest *jinshi* degree at age 24. Tan was president of the Hunan provincial assembly and served several times as governor of Hunan from 1912 to 1920. He was the principal of the Hunan First Normal School from 1905 to 1906. Tan was regarded as the leader of gentry reformers in Hunan. For more information on Tan Yankai, see Sun Hailin, ed., *Hunan diyi shifan mingren pu* (Who's Who from Hunan First Normal School) (Changsha: Hunan First Normal School, 2003), 17–18; Howard L. Boorman, ed., *Biographical Dictionary of Republican China*, 4: 220–23.

6. *Hunan shengli diyi shifan xuexiao xiaozhi* (Annals of Hunan Provincial First Normal School), Section 2, 97.

7. For details of "Decree on Principles for Education," see *Hunan shengli diyi shifan xuexiao xiaozhi*, Section 2, 9–10.

8. Ibid., Section 2, 10–25.

9. Ibid., Section 2, 19–21 & 106.

10. See illustration 5.

11. Ibid.

12. *Hunan diyi shifan xiaoshi*, 15.

13. Ibid., 17–18.

14. First Normal only accepted male students before 1927. The candidates for *yuke* had to be older than age 14 years and had to have graduated from a higher elememtary school or equivalent; for *benke*, students had to be older than age 15 and had to have graduated from the *yuke* or equivalent; for *shifan*

benke, students had to be older than age 17 and had to have graduated from secondary school or equivalent.

15. *Hunan diyi shifan xiaoshi*—1903–1949, 20.

16. Ibid.

17. The detailed content of the moral cultivation course included: 1) To educate students to live according to the specifications of moral cultivation listed in the textbooks and to train students to practice lofty moral values in daily life, so students could cultivate a noble moral character (*gaoshang renge*); 2) With quotations and remarks from the Confucian classics, moral principles should be set clearly for the students to follow; 3) With citations of fine conduct and remarks about moral cultivation of well-known scholars from both China and the West, the Great Unity of moral cultivation would be made clear to all; 4) To commend model figures (to demonstrate the exemplary deeds and words of the model figures); . . . *Hunan shengli diyi shifan xuexiao xiaozhi* (Annals of Hunan Provincial First Normal School), Section 4, 30.

18. Yang Changji, *Riji*, entry of the 7th day of the ninth month, 1896" in Wenji, 7.

19. Zhou Shizhao, *Women de shibiao*, 54.

20. *Hunan diyi shifan xiaoshi*—1903–1949, 86.

21. "*Jiangtanglu*" was the class notes Mao took at First Normal from November to December 1913. The notes of ethics class were taken from Yang Changji's lectures, while notes of Chinese classics were from Yuan Zhongqian's class. Yuan urged Mao to study Han Yu's works and to learn the classical style of writing.

22. For details of Chinese literature course, see *xiaozhi*, Section 4, 31–33.

23. The specific requirements for teaching the selected readings included: 1) The students should prepare the reading before going to class. 2) They should review each selected reading. 3) They were expected to think about the material. The professor would ask questions whenever necessary, so as to train the students' ability in reasoning. 4) The gist of the reading material should be made clear. The outline of the whole essay should be given to the students. . . . *Hunan shengli diyi shifan xuexiao xiaozhi* (Annals of Hunan Provincial First Normal School), Section 4, 40.

24. Ibid.

25. Ibid.

26. Ibid.

27. Ibid.

28. Siao Yu (Xiao Zisheng), *Mao Tse-tung and I were Beggars*, 32.

29. Xiao San, one of the founding members of the "*Xinmin xuehui*," did not mention his brother, Xiao Zisheng, when discussing the best essays exhibited at the First Normal in his book *Mao Tse-tung: His Childhood and Youth*, due to the rupture between Mao Zedong and Xiao Zisheng.

30. *Hunan shengli diyi shifan xuexiao xiaozhi*.

31. Xiao San, *Mao Tse-tung: His Childhood and Youth*, 39.

32. *Hunan shengli diyi shifan xuexiao xiaozhi* (Annals of Hunan Provincial First Normal School), Section 2, 20–21.

33. Ibid., Section 2, 20–21.

34. Ibid., Section 2, 20–21.

35. Ibid., Section 2, 18–19.

36. In the extant archives of the First Normal School, there are sixty-seven specific regulations in six categories that were used for student management. These regulations demonstrate the administrative work of the school in the 1910s. For details of the content of the regulations, see *Hunan shengli diyi shifan xuexiao xiaozhi* (Annals of Hunan Provincial First Normal School), Section 2, 44–110.

37. Ibid., Section 2, 9.

38. Ibid., Section 2, 21–22.

39. Ibid., Section. 2, 22.

40. Siao Yu (Xiao Zisheng), *Mao Tse-tung and I were Beggars*, 56.

41. In First Normal's disciplinary code, there were twenty-eight rules. Each rule stated that the students could not do a particular thing. For example, rule 1: students were not allowed to engage in managing any kind of nonacademic enterprises. For detailed information on the clauses, see *Hunan shengli diyi shifan xuexiao xiaozhi* (Annals of Hunan Provincial First Normal School), Section 2, 45–46.

42. For detailed information on the clauses of regulations, see Ibid., Section 2.

43. Ibid., Section 2, 47–49.

44. Paul J. Bailey, Reform the People, 83.

Notes to Chapter 4

1. Edgar Snow, Dong Leshan trans. *Xixing manji* (Beijing: Xinhua chupanhe, 1984), 125; Edgar Snow, *Red Star Over China* (New York: Random House, 1938), 128.

2. He Shuheng was 37 years old in 1913 when the school admitted him. He was seventeen years older than Mao Zedong.

3. "Three-inch golden-lily" was a metaphorical name for woman's bound foot.

4. Qing Yang, *He Shuheng* (Shijiazhuang: Hebei renmin chubanshe, 1997), 22–23.

5. Paul J. Bailey, *Reform the People*.

6. Sarah C. McElroy, *Transforming China through Education* (dissertation).

7. Sun Hailin, ed., *Hunan diyi shifan mingren lu, 1903–1949* (Who Is Who of Hunan First Normal School, 1903–1949) (Hunan diyi shifan bian, 2003), 62.

8. *Hunan diyi shifan xiaoshi, 1903–1949*, 71.

9. Li Rui, *Sanshisui yiqian de Mao Zedong* (Mao Zedong before Thirty Years Old) (Guangzhou: Guangdong renmin chubanshe, 1994), 197–200.

10. *Hunan diyi shifan xiaoshi, 1903–1949*, 71.

11. Sun Hailin, ed., *Hunan diyi shifan mingren lu*, 63.

12. *Hunan diyi shifan xiaoshi, 1903–1949*, 72.

13. Ibid., 72.

14. On May 9, 1915, Yuan Shikai accepted Japan's "Twenty-One Demands," which infuriated the whole nation and provoked an anti-Japanese movement in China. After that, May 9 was termed "National Humiliation Day." Some places took May 7 as "National Humiliation Day." May 7, 1915 was the date of Japan's ultimatum to China.

15. Quotation from Kong's speech on "National Humiliation Day" in 1917. For details of Kong's speech, see *Hunan shengli diyi shifan xuexiao xiaozhi* (Annals of Hunan Provincial First Normal School), Section 4, 16–31.

16. Ibid., Section 4, 16–31.

17. Quotation from Kong's 1916 proposal to Governor Tan (concerning the establishment of a student voluntary army) by the editing committee of the Hunan diyi shifan xiaoshi, *Hunan diyi shifan xiaoshi, 1903–1949*, 74–76; For details of student voluntary army, see *Hunan shengli diyi shifan xuexiao xiaozhi*, Section 2, 71–73.

18. Li Rui, *Mao Zedong*, 192.

19. Zhou Shizhao, *Women de shibiao* (Our Teacher and Model) (Beijing: Beijing chubanshe, 1958), 7.

20. Fan Zhe, *Zhongguo gujin jiaoyujia* (Chinese Educators from Antiquity to Today) (Shanghai: Shanghai jiaoyu chupanshe, 1982), 223.

21. Zhang Xing, "Xu Teli weida de wuchanjieji jiaoyujia," ed. Fan Yujie, *Shifan qunying guangyao zhonghua* (Outstanding figures from Normal Schools Glorify China) (Xian: Shanxi renmin jiaoyu chubanshe, 1992), 49.

22. Ibid., 224.

23. *Hunan diyi shifan xiaoshi—1903–1949*, 84–85.

24. Ibid., 85.

25. Xu's article, "The Study of the Pedagogy of Chinese" was published in the *Gongyan* journal (1914), 1, no. 3.

26. Sun Hailin, "Yihu xunchang de guanhuai he aihu: Xu Teli zhai Hunan yishi" in *Xu Teli yanjiu* (The study of Xu Teli), 1996, 4: 29.

27. Xu's student, Zhou Shizhao, wrote about what Xu said in *Women de shipiao*, 30.

28. Sun Hailin, "Yihu xunchang de guanhuai he aihu: Xu Teli zai Hunan yishi," 29.

29. *Hunan diyi shifan xiaoshi—1903–1949*, 86.

30. Zhang Xing, "Xu Teli weida de wuchanjieji jiaoyujia," 51.

31. Zhou Shizhao, *Wo men de shibiao*, 51–52.

32. Sun Hailin, "Yihu xunchang de guanhuai he aihu: Xu Teli zhai Hunan yishi," 30.

33. Zhang Jinyao issued 2 million lottery tickets. Each ticket was sold at five silver dollars. *Hunan jin 150 nian shishi rizhi, 1840–1990*, 73; also see Zhou Shizhao, *Wo men de shibiao*, 34–35.

34. Li Rui, *Mao Zedong tongzhi de chuqi geming huodong*, 114.

35. Sun Hailin, "Yihu xunchang de guanhuai he aihu: Xu Teli zhai Hunan yishi," 30.

36. *Hunan diyi shifan xiaoshi—1903–1949*, 87.

37. Zhou Shi-zhao, *Wo men de shibiao*, 58.

38. Ibid., 82.

39. Sun Hailin, ed., *Hunan diyi shifan mingren lu*, 25.

40. Ibid., 25.

41. *Hunan diyi shifan xiaoshi*, 80–83.

42. The Nanchang Uprising was led by CCP leaders, Zhu De, Zhou Enlai, He Long, and Ye Ting on August 1, 1927, and joined by another insurrectionary army of the Autumn Harvest Uprising led by Mao Zedong on September 9, 1927. The two insurrectionary armies organized into the Chinese 4 Worker-Peasant Red Army.

43. The Long March (1934–1935) was a major strategic movement of the Chinese Red Army. It started from Jiangxi province and reached northern Shanxi province. It traversed eleven provinces and covered 25,000 li, or 12,500 kilometers.

44. Xiu Juan, ed., *Mao Zedong yu qinjuan* (Mao Zedong with his relatives) (Beijing: Zhongguo renmin daxue chubanshe, 1993), 52.

45. Sun Hailin, ed., *Hunan diyi shifan mingren lu*, 61.

46. Ibid., 54.

47. Xiu Juan, ed., *Mao Zedong yu qinjuan*, 58.

48. Yan Ru, "Chundu de xuezhe" (Li Jinxi—The studious scholar), ed. Ma Xingfu, *Shifan qunying guangyao zhonghua* (Xian: Shanxi renmin chubanshe, 1991), 2: 92.

49. Ibid., 2: 93.

50. *Hunan deyi shifan Xiaoshi*, 103.

51. Wang Xingguo, *Yang Changji de shengping ji sixiang* (Changsha: Hunan renmin chubanshe, 1981), 92; *Hunan deyi shifan Xiaoshi*, 103.

52. During summer vacation 1915, Mao Zedong, Chen Zhangfu, and Xiong Guangchu stayed at the Hongwen Publishing House located at Lishi Yuyuan and worked on after class readings under the auspices of Li Jinxi and Yang Changji.

53. *Hunan deyi shifan Xiaoshi*, 103–05.

54. Ibid., 93.

55. Yan Ru, "Chundu de xuezhe" (Li Jinxi—The studious scholar), ed. by Ma Xingfu, *Shifan qunying guangyao zhonghua*, 2: 102.

56. Mao Zedong, *Mao Zedong zaoqi wengao*, 31.

57. Yan Ru, "Chundu de xuezhe" (Li Jinxi—The studious scholar), ed. Ma Xingfu, *Shifan qunying guangyao zhonghua*, 2: 102.

58. Zhou Yanyu, *Mao Zedong yu Zhou Shizhao*, 24.

59. Ma Yuqing, *Mao Zedong de chengzhang daolu* (The Way Mao Zedong Grew) (Xian: Shanxi renmin chubanshe, 1986), 68.

60. Sun Hailin, ed., *Hunan diyi shifan mingren pu*, 113–14.

61. Snow, *Red Star Over China*, 129.

62. The Second Revolution, led by Sun Yat-sen, was a military uprising of the Guomindang against Yuan Shikai in the summer of 1913. Its direct cause was the assassination of Song Jiaoren. Jiangxi, Jiangsu, Anhui, Hunan, Guangdong, and Fujian provinces as well as Shanghai and Chongqing declared independence from Yuan's government and joined the anti-Yuan force. However, Yuan crushed this uprising in September 1913.

63. Sun Hailin, ed., *Hunan diyi shifan mingren pu*, 100–01.

64. Wang Xingguo, unpublished manuscript about the May Fourth Period, 19–20.

65. Wang Xingguo quoted this event in his manuscript, 20.

66. The school of Mozi was a school of thought in the Spring and Autumn and Warring States Periods, 770–221 BC. Mozi, the founder of the school, emphasized the "universal love," pacifism, awareness of the otherworldly, and interest in problems of logic. His interest in logic gave rise to the school of Logicians.

67. Cai Yuanpei, "Zhonghua zhiye jiaoyu she xuanyan shu" (Manifesto of the Chinese Society of Professional Educators), Gao Pingshu ed., *Cai Yuanpei quanji* (Collected works of Cai Yuanpei) (Beijing: Zhonghua shuju chubanshe, 1971), 3: 12.

Notes to Chapter 5

1. Hao Chang, *Chinese Intellectuals in Crisis*, 4.

2. Yang Changji, *Dahuazhai riji* (Diaries from the Dahua studio) (Changsha: Hunan renmin chubanshe, 1980), 56.

3. Wang Xingguo, *Yang Changji de shengping ji sixiang*, 7–8.

4. In this work, Zhou expounded the Daoist *Taiji tu* (The Diagram of the Great Ultimate) through using the *Book of Changes*, a Confucian classic, to elaborate a metaphysical cosmology, in which the universe on inates from the Great ultimate (*taiji*) and the Ultimate of Non-being (*wuji*). See Tu Weiming's *Centrality and commonality: An essay on Confucian Religiousness* (New York: State University of New York Press, 1989), 16–72; Bounghown Kim, *A study of Chou Tun-i's (1017–1073) thought* (PhD dissertation, The University of Arizona, 1996), chapter 5; Ming Zhang, *A Journey between East and West: Yang Changji (1871–1920) and his thought* (PhD dissertation, University of Edinburgh, 2002), chapter 1.

5. Zhou Dunyi, *Tongshu* (Penetrating the Book of Changes) in *Zhouzi quanshu* (The complete works of Zhou Dunyi), chapter 2; Chan, Wing-tsit, *A source book in Chinese philosophy* (Princeton: Princeton University Press, 1963), 461.

6. Ibid.

7. Zhang, "A Journey between East and West, chapter 1.

8. Ibid.; Zhou Dunyi, *Tongshu*; Chan, *A source book*, 463.

9. Zhou Dunyi, *Tongshu*; Chan, *A source book*, 469–77.

10. For detailed discussion, see Conrad Schirokauer, "Chu His and Hu Hung," in Wing-tsit Chan, ed., *Chu Hsi and Neo-Confucianism* (Honolulu: University of Hawaii Press, 1986), 480–502; Hoyt Cleveland Tillman, *Confucian Discourse and Chu His's ascendancy* (Honolulu: University of Hawaii Press, 1992), chapter 1, 2.

11. Li Xiaodan, *Xiangxue lüe* (An outline of history of Hunan scholarship) (Changsha: Yuelu shushe, 1985), 143.

12. Yan-shuan Lao, "Junshi heyi yu Cheng-Zhu zhengzhi sixiang" (Ruler–teacher unity and Cheng-Zhu's political thoughts) in (*Lao Zhenyi xiansheng jiuzhi rongqing lunwenji* (Collection of essays for the Celebration of Mr. Lao Zhenyi's Ninetieth Birthday) (Taipei: Lantai, 1997), 579–91.

13. Zeng was a voluminous writer whose memorials to the throne and his literary disquisitions were held in high esteem by Yang and his contemporaries; they revered Zeng's collected works in 156 *juan*, which were edited by Li Hongzhang (1823–1901) in 1876.

14. Zeng's diaries show the detailed records of his daily digging up the secret thought and motivation that lay behind his mistakes and shortcomings in order to improve himself. Teng Ssu-yu, "Tseng Kuo-fan" in Reading in Modern Chinese history (New York: Oxford University Press, 1971) 183; *Zeng Guofan quanji*, "jiashu" (Family letters), 130, in Chiu Wei-chun, 220. For detailed discussion of "character-building programme," see Chiu Wei-chun, 149–61.

15. Luo Ergang, *Xiangjun xinzhi* (A new treatise on the Hunan Army) (Changsha: Shangwu chubanshe, 1939), 23–24.

16. "Quanxue pian" (On encouraging learning). *Gongyan Zhazhi* (Public Opinion), Changsha, 1: 1, October 1914. Reprinted in *Yang Changji wenji*, 1983, 198–204.

17. Ibid.

18. Li Peicheng, *Yang Changji jiaoyu sixiang jianlun* (Yang Changji's Educational Philosophy) (Changsha: Hunan Educational Press, 1983), 7.

19. Yang Changji, *Dahuazhai riji* (Diaries from the Dahua studio), 40.

20. Susan M. Jones and Philip A. Kuhn, "Origin of decline of the Ch'ing dynasty and rebellion," in *Cambridge History of China*, 10: 158. For detailed discussion of Wang Fuzhi's influence on Tan Sitong, see Hao Chang, *Chinese Intellectuals in Crisis*, 43, 72–3, 81–4, 87–94.

21. For Wang's distinctive idea of history, see He Lin "Wang Chuanshan de lishi zhexue" (Wang Fuzhi's philosophy of history), in *Zhexue pinglun*

(Philosophical review), 10 (1935): 23–29; Ji Wenfu, *Wang Chuanshan xueshu luncong* (Collected essays on the scholarship and thought of Wang Fuzhi) (Beijing: sanlian shudian, 1978), 122–163; Teng Ssu-yu, "Wang Fu-chih's views on History and Historical Writing" in *Journal of Asian Studies* 28.1 (1968), 111–123.

22. Xiao Gongquan, *Zhongguo zhengzhi sixiangshi* (History of Chinese Political Thought) (Taibei: Lianjing, 1982), 670–71; Hou Wailu. *Zhongguo sixiang tongshi* (History of Chinese Philosophy) (Beijing: Renmin chubanshe, 1956), vol. 5: 69, 114.

23. Ian McMorran, "Wang Fu-chih and the Neo-Confucian tradition" *The Unfolding of Neo-Confucianism* (N. Y. & London: Columbia University Press, 1975), 413–14. de Bary (ed.) *Sources of Chinese tradition* (1963), 597.

24. Wang Fuzhi, *Du sishu daquan shuo* (Commentary on and notes of Complete Four Books) (Beijing: Zhonghua), 519.

25. When asked what the heavenly principle was, Zhu Xi answered: "When being raised it becomes Three Bonds, and when being spread, it becomes the Five Constant Virtues." (See Zhu Zi yulei daquan, chapter 24.) Thus, Three Bonds became the basis of Neo-Confucian values, which was promoted as the official orthodoxy from the Song dynasty on. The Four Books singled out by Zhu Xi and his commentaries became the standard curriculum for the imperial civil service examination system in 1313 and continued until the whole system was abolished in 1905. Yan-shuan Lao, "Junshi heyi yu Cheng-Zhu *zhengzhi sixiang*" (Ruler–teacher unity and Cheng-Zhu's political thoughts), 580.

26. For detailed discussion of Wang Fuzhi study in Hunan, see Li Xiao-dan, *Xiangxue lüe* (An outline of history of Hunanese scholarship) (Changsha: 1985), 151.

27. Shi guwei mulu shuhou" (Notes after writing the content of *the subtle ancient meaning hidden in the `Book of Poetry'*) in *Wei Yuan ji*, pt. 2, 940–41.

28. Hao Chang, *Chinese Intellectual in Crisis*, 66–103.

29. Ian McMorran, "Wang Fu-chih and the Neo-Confucian tradition," *The Unfolding of NeoConfucianism*, 413.

30. Ibid.

31. Wang Fuzhi, *Du Tongjian lun*, vol. 6, in *Chuanshan quanli* (Complete Works of Wang Fuzhi) (Taibei: Dayuan wenhua fuwushe, 1965).

32. Ming Zhang, 32.

33. Hao Chang, *Chinese Intellectual in Crisis*, 26.

34. For discussion on the directors of the Yuelu Academy, see Zhu Hanmin, *Huxiang xuepai yuanliu* (The Origin of Huxiang School) (Changsha: Hunan Education Press, 1992), 202–20. For more details on statecraft, see Hao Chang, *Chinese Intellectuals in Crisis*, 16.

35. His father died in 1884 when he was 13. He counted his age 14 according to the traditional Chinese way of counting age—as soon as the baby was born, he or she was 1 year old. After the baby had his or her first birthday, he or she was 2 years old.

36. Yang Changji, *riji*, 1894; Wang Xingguo, *Yang Changji*, 18.

37. Ibid., 1893; Ibid., 18.

38. Yang Changji, *Riji*, entry of the 7th day of the ninth month, 1896" in Wenji, 7.

39. Ibid., 1895; Ibid., 19–20.

40. The five constant elements of virtues are benevolence (*ren*), righteousness (*yi*), propriety or ritual propriety (*li*), wisdom (*zhi*), and trustworthiness or faithfulness (*xin*).

41. Yang Changji, *riji*, 1891; Wang Xingguo, *Yang Changji*, 21.

42. Ibid., 1891; Ibid., 21–22.

43. Ibid., 1919.

44. Ming Zhang, chapter 1.

45. Li Peicheng, *Yang Changji jiaoyu sixiang jianlun* (Yang Changji's Educational Philosophy), 8.

46. Ming Zhang, chapter 9.

47. Mao Zedong, "Lunlixue yuanli pizhu" (Marginal Notes to Freidrich Paulsen, A *System of Ethics*) in Mao *Zedong zaoqi wengao* 1912.6–1920.11 (Early Writings of Mao Zedong June 1912–November 1920) (Changsha: Hunan Chubanshe, 1990), 203. For the English translation, see Schram ed. Mao's Road to Power, vol. 1, 251.

48. Liyan Liu, *Reflections across the Yellow Sea: Essays of Chinese and Japanese Studies* (Hong Kong: Milky Way Press, 2001), 119 & 126.

49. Ibid., 113–14.

50. This event was known as the famous *gongche shangshu*.

51. For detailed discussion on this article, see Wang Xingguo, *Yang Changji de shengping ji sixiang*, 33–38.

52. Yang Changji, *Luyu leichao* (Changsha: Changsha hongwei tushushe, 1914), 20.

53. Yang Changji, *Dahuazhai riji*, 48.

54. Yang Changji, *Luyu leichao*, 35.

55. Ibid., 37.

56. Wang Xingguo, *Yang Changji de shengping*, 64–65.

57. For more on his motives for overseas study, see Yang, 1913.

58. Zhu Deshang, "Guimao riji" (Diaries in the Guimao Year of 1903) in *Hunan lishi ziliao* (The Historical Documents of Hunan, 1979), vol. 1.

59. Wang Xingguo, *Yang Changji de shengping ji sixiang*, 49–60.

60. Yang Chang, "Zhexue shang gezhong lilun zhi lueshu" (Brief review of the different philosophical theories) in *Dongfang zhazhi*, 1916, vol. 2.

61. Yang Chang, "quanxue pian" (On encouraging learning) in *Gongyan Zhazhi*, 1914, vol. 1.

62. Li Xiaodan, "Ban xiao gu jiaoshou Yang Huaizhong xiansheng shiji" (Memories of late Mr. Yang Huaizhong of our school) in *Daily journal of Beijing University*, January 28, 1920.

63. For instance, taking cold bath year-round.

64. Yoshida's lecture notes were translated later by Yang to be used as teaching material for his ethics class at First Normal. Mao's "Marginal notes to: Friedrich Paulsen, A *System of Ethics* revealed that he copied Yang's translation of Yoshida's "Xiyang lunlixue shi" (Lecture notes of a history of Western ethics) by hand. Wang Xingguo, ed. *Mao Zedong zaoqi wengao*. Stuart Schram, ed. *Mao's Road to Power: Revolutionary Writings 1912–1949: The Rise and Fall of the Chinese Soviet Republic 1931–1934 (Mao's Road to Power: Revolutionary Writings, 1912–1949)* (Armonk NY: M. E. Sharpe, 1997), 585 n 11.

65. Yang Changji, "Zhisheng pian" (A study of managing livelihood), New Youth, 2.4 (1916): 353–60; 2.5 (1917): 451–58. Reprinted in Wenji (1983), 229–46.

66. Bain's work was in Yang's required reading list for his "Education" course taught by William Davidson who was profoundly influenced by Bain. In 1915, Yang re-read Bain's psychology for use of his teaching at First Normal. Ming Zhang, 219; Yang, *Riji* (1915), March 19, 23, and April 20.

67. "Sugelan xiaoxuexiao guiyu" (Primary school regulations in Scotland) published in *Hunan Journal of Education* 2.7 (31 April 1913) and "Ji Yingguo zhi jiaoyu qingxing" (A narration of the British education) in *Hunan Journal of Education* 2. 14/5 (31 August 1913), 2.17 (30 Nove 1013), 3.3 (31 March 1914) and 3.4 (30 April 1914); and in Hangzhou Jiaoyu zhoubao or Hangzhou Education Weekly, no. 30–33 (30 Jan., 8, 15, 22 February 1914) Shortly after Yang's return home in the spring.

68. Li Peicheng, *Yang Changji jiaoyu sixiang jianlun*, 12; Wang Xingguo, *Yang Changji de shengping ji sixiang*, 66.

69. In a letter to Zhou Shizhao in 1915 Yang wrote, "The works I am translating include Spencer's *Ethics, Sociology and System of Synthetic Philosophy*, Kant's *Critique of pure reason* and *Critique of practical reason*, etc. The letter was published in *The Tiger*, 1.8 (August 10, 1915).

70. Yang Changji, "Jiaoyuxue jiangyi" (Lecture notes of education), *Wenji*, 100–197.

71. There are different versions regarding the year of Yang's return to China. However, Yang wrote, "I came back to China this spring" in his article "Yu guiguo hou duiyu jiaoyu zhi suogan" (My thought on education after my return to China), in *Hunan jiaoyu zazhi* (Hunan educational journal) (November 1913), vol. 17.

72. Li Xiaodan, "Benxiao gu jiaoshou Yang Huaizhong xiansheng shiji" (The brief biography of the late professor Yang Huaizhong," originally published in *Beijing daxue rikan* (Beijing University Daily), January 28, 1920. Now the article has been collected in *Yang Changji wenji*, 375.

73. Li Xiaodan, "Benxiao gu jiaoshou Yang Huaizhong xiansheng shiji," in *Beijing daxue rikan*, Janjuary 28, 1920.

74. Siao-Yu (Xiao Yu), *Mao Tse-tung qingnian shidai*, 38.

75. Emi Siao (Xiao San), *Mao Tse-tung, His Childhood and Youth* (Bombay: People's Publishing House Ltd., 1953), 39.

76. Ibid., 39.

77. Siao Yu (Xiao Yu), *Mao Tse-tung qingnian shidai*, 39.

78. Ibid. 40.

79. Wang Xingguo, ed., *Yang Changji wenji*, 199. This article, "*Quanxue-pian*" (An exhortation to study) was originally published on *Gongyan*, vol. 1, no. 1 in November 1914. *Gongyan* was a journal published in Changsha at that time.

80. Cao Dianqiu wrote in his *Biography of Yang Changji*: "After the experience of the Hundred Days Reform Movement of 1898, Yang retreated to the mountains as a hermit and rarely went to cities. He totally gave up the idea of taking the civil service examinations but was only interested in reading *Tongjian* and Wang Fuzhi's *Du Tongjian Lun*. He used the past as a mirror for criticizing current corrupt practices; he studied statecraft and prepared for its future use." Cao Dianqiu, "Yang Changji xiansheng zhuan" (Biography of Mr. Yang Changji) in Wang Xingguo, ed., *Yang Changji wenji*, 383–87.

81. Peng Dacheng, *Huxiang wenhao yu Mao Zedong* (*Huxiang* Culture and Mao Zedong) (Changsha: Hunan Press, 1991), 61.

82. Yang Changji, *Dahuazhai riji*, 46; Wang Xingguo, "Yang Changji and the xinmin xuehui" in Zhonggong Hunan shengwei dangshi ziliaozhengji yanjiu weiyuanhui bian, ed., *Hunan dangshi luncong* (On the history of the Communist Party of Hunan Branch) (Changsha: Hunan renmin chubanshe, 1986), 24.

83. Yang Changji, *Dahuazhai riji*, 46.

84. Yang Changji, *Dahuazhai riji*, 47.

85. Harrison Salisbury, *Changzhen xinji* (The Long March: An Untold Story), ed. and trans. by Xinhuashe cankaoziliao bianjibu (Department of reference material editing, Xinhua News Agency) (Beijing: Xinhuashe cankaoziliao bianjibu, 1990), 67; Peng Dacheng, *Huxiang wenhao yu Mao Zedong*, 82.

86. Wang Xingguo, *Yang Changji de shengping*, 156.

87. Edgar Snow, *Red Star Over China*, 129.

88. *Yang Changji wenji*, 45.

89. Wang Xingguo, "Yang Changji and the xinmin xuehui" in *Hunan dangshi luncong*, 25.

90. Ibid., 25.

91. Snow, *Red Star Over China*, 129.

92. *Lunlixue yuanli* was part of Friedrich Paulsen's major work *System der Ethik*. In 1900, the Japanese scholar Kanie Hidemaru translated the preface and the second volume of *System der Ethik* into Japanese and published it under the title *Rinrigaku genri*, divided into "Joron" (preface) and "Honron" (Principal argument). In 1909, Cai Yuanpei translated the work from Japanese into Chinese and it was published by Shanghai Commercial Press.

93. Immanuel Kant, *Critique of Pure Reason*, Trans. Norman Kemp Smith (New York: St. Martin's 1929 [1965]), 41.

94. This article was first published in vol. 1, no. 1, 2, and 3, of the journal of *Minsheng* in Changsha, in November 1916. After Yang's death in 1920,

Li Shiqin republished this article in vol. 2, no. 2, 3, and 4 of the journal of *Mingduo* in Shanghai in 1920. The article was collected in Wang Xingguo, ed., *Yang Changji wenji*, 247–73.

95. Wang Xingguo, ed., "Yang Changji and the xinmin xuehui" in *Hunan dangshi luncong*, 26.

96. Friedrich Paulsen, *Lunlixue yuanli* (The principles of ethics), trans. Cai Yuanpei. Reprinted, Zhonggong zhongyang wenxian yanjiushi (The Department of Research on Party literature, Central Committee of the Chinese Communist Party) (Beijing: zhongyang wenxian yanjiushi, 1990 [1909], n. 1, 276.

97. The copy with Mao's annotations and comments was borrowed by one of his classmates, Yang Shaohua, who returned it to Mao in 1950 after the founding of the PRC. Zhou Shizhao later recalled that Yang Shaohua asked him to return the book to Mao when he went to Beijing in 1950. When handed the book, Mao said: "What I wrote in this book was not all correct. It concerned not materialism but dualism. What we learned at that time was idealist philosophy. So, once we came into contact with something on materialism, I felt it was fresh and reasonable, and the more I read it the more I became interested in it. It gave me new inspiration and helped me critique the book I had read and analyze the questions I once raised." Zhou Shizhao, *Mao zhuxi qingnian shiqi de jige gushi* (Early Writings of Mao Zedong 1912.6—1920.11) (Beijing: Zhongguo shaonian ertong chubanshe, 1977), 14; also see *Mao Zedong zaoqi wengao 1912.6—1920.11*, 276.

98. Mao, *Mao Zedong zaoqi wengao*, 274–75; Maurice Meisner, *Mao Zedong: A Political and Intellectual Portrait* (Cambridge, UK: Polity Press, 2007), 12.

99. Mao, *Mao Zedong zaoqi wengao*, 219; Meisner, *Mao Zedong*, 12.

100. Frederic Wakeman, *History and Will: Philosophical Perspectives of Mao Tse-Tung's Thought* (Berkeley: University of California Press, 1973), 202.

101. Mao, *Mao Zedong zaoqi wengao*, 180–81; Meisner, *Mao Zedong*, 203.

102. For more discussion on this topic, see Wakeman, *History and Will*; Meisner, *Mao Zedong: A Political and Intellectual Portrait*.

103. Wakeman, *History and Will*, 47.

104. Stuart Schram, "A review article: Mao Tse-tung as Marxist dialectician" in *China Quarterly*, 29 (January–March, 1967): 160.

105. Wakeman, *History and Will*, 294.

106. Ibid., chapter 18.

107. Ibid., 291.

108. Quoted by Wang Xingguo, "Yang Changji and the xinmin xuehui" in *Hunan dangshi luncong*, 49.

109. Ibid., 268.

110. *Mao Zedong zaoqi wengao 1912.6—1920.11*, 116–275.

111. Wang Xingguo, ed., *Yang Changji wenji*, 82; Howard L. Boorman, *Biographical Dictionary of Republican China*. 4: 2.

112. Wang Xingguo, ed., *Yang Changji wenji*, 84.

113. Wang Xingguo, *Yang Changji de shengping*, 111–20.

114. Ibid., 247–273; also see Boorman, *Biographical Dictionary of Republican China*. 4: 1.

115. Wang Xingguo, ed., *Yang Changji wenji*, 124.

116. *Mao Zedong zaoqi wengao 1912.6—1920.11.*

117. Wang Xingguo, ed., *Yang Changji wenji*, 69.

118. *Mao Zedong zaoqi wengao 1912.6—1920.11*, 87.

119. Li Rui, *Mao Zedong tongzhi di chuqi geming yundong* (Early revolutionary activities of Comrade Mao Zedong), 19–21.

120. The theme on "the unity of learning and practice" is a complicated issue that cannot be fully addressed here. For those interested in the topic, see Arif Dirlik and Ming Chan, *Schools into Fields and Factories: Anarchists, the Guomindang, and the National Labor University in Shanghai, 1927–1932* (Durham: Duke University Press. 1991). Zhixin Su, "Teaching, Learning, and Reflective Acting: A Dewey Experiment in Chinese Teacher Education" in *Teachers College Record*, 98 (1996), no. 1, 126–152; Tao Xingzhi, *Complete Works of Tao Xingzhi* (Chengdu: Sichuan Education Press, 1991), vol. 1 of 12 vols., and *Collected essays on the unity of teaching, learning and doing* (Shanghai: Shanghai ertong shuju, 1932).

121. McDonald, *The Urban Origins of Rural Revolution*, 92.

122. Mao also published his first article "A Study of Physical Education" in the April 1917 issue of the magazine. In this article, Mao expressed his nationalist outlook and point of view on military matters.

123. Zhou Shizhao, "Xiangjiang de nuhou," in *Xinmin xuehui ziliao* (Beijing: Renmin chubanshe, 1980), 392.

124. Emi Siao, *Mao Tse-tung, His Childhood and Youth* (Bombay: People's Publishing House LTD, 1953), 39.

125. Ibid., 40.

126. Siao Yu, Mao Tse-tung and I were Beggars, 40.

127. Ibid., 41–43.

128. Snow, *Red Star Over China*, 130.

129. *Xinmin xuehui ziliao*, 2.

130. Ibid.

131. Wang Xingguo, ed., *Lunyu leizhao*, 88.

132. Yang Changji, *Dahuazhai riji*, 57–64.

133. Ibid., 130.

134. Ibid., 57–64.

135. Ibid., 65–66.

136. For more information about Liang Qichao, see Hao Chang, *Liang Ch'i-ch'ao and Intellectual Transition in China*; Philip Huang, *Liang Ch'i-ch'ao and Modern Chinese Liberalism* (University of Washington Press, 1972).

137. Hao Chang, *Liang Ch'i-ch'ao and Intellectual Transition in China*; Yusheng Lin, *The Crisis of Chinese Consciousness*.

138. Ibid.

139. Paul J. Bailey, *Reform the People*; Glen Peterson, Ruth Hayhoe and Yongling Lu, ed., *Education Culture, and Identity in Twentieth Century China*, 83.

Notes to Chapter 6

1. *Hunan diyi shifan xiaoshi—1903–1949*, 17–18.

2. Ibid.

3. For detailed discussion on *waifan daode* and *neihua daode*, see Hao Chang, *Youan yishi yu minzhu chuantong* (The Democratic Tradition and the Consciousness of the Dark Side of Life) (Taiwan: Lianjing chuban shiye gongsi, 1989), 33–78.

4. Xinmin xuehui huiwu baogao" (Report of the affairs of the New Citizens' Study Society) (1920), in *Xinmin xuehui ziliao*, no. 1, 3. Also see "Xinmin xuehui huiwu baogao" (1920) in *Xinmin xuehui wenxian huibian* (Documents Collection of the New Citizen Association) (Changsha: Hunan renmin chubanshe, 1980), no. 1, 119.

5. Song Feifu, *Xinmin xuehui* (New Citizens' Study Society) (Changsha: Hunan renmin chubanshe, 1980), 1–13; Boorman, *Biographical Dictionary of Republican China*, 4: 284.

6. The *Xinmin xuehui* was formed on April 14, 1918, according to Xiao San's dairy (March to April 1918), Zhou Shizhao's memoir "Xiangjiang de nuhou" in *Xinmin xuehui ziliao* (1979), 394, and Luo Shaozhui's article "Cai Hesen," in Hu Hua, ed., *Zhonggong dangshi renwu zhuan*, 6: 7. However, it was recorded that the Xinmin xuehui was formed on April 17, 1918, "Xinmin xuehui huiwu baogao," 1920.

7. "*Xinmin*" is both an adjective–noun (new citizen) and verb–noun (renew the people). The society's name therefore is reflexive: The new citizen will renew the whole un-renewed people. Wang Jianyu, "Xiao Zisheng yu Xinmin xuehui," Zhonggong Hunan shengwei dangshi ziliaozhengji yanjiu weiyuanhuibian, ed., *Hunan dangshi luncong* (On the history of the Communist Party of Hunan Branch), 105; also see Xiao San, "Mao Zedong tongzhi zhai wusi shiqi" in *Xinmin xuehui ziliao* (Archives of the New Citizens' Study Society), no. 1, 367.

8. "Xinmin xuehui huiwu baogao" (Report of the affairs of the New Citizens' Study Society) (1920), in *Xinmin xuehui wenxian huibian* (Documents Collection of the New Citizen Association), no. 1, 120.

9. Ibid., no. 1, 120.

10. Ibid., no. 1, 120.

11. Zhou Shizhao, "Xiangjiang de nütao" in *Xinmin xuehui ziliao* (Archives of the New Citizens' Study Society), 394–95.

12. Song Feifu, *Xinmin xuehui* (New Citizens' Study Society), 11.

13. "Xinmin xuehui huiwu baogao" (Report of the affairs of the New Citizens' Study Society), in *Xinmin xuehui wenxian huibian* (Documents Collection of the New Citizens' Study Society), no. 1, 119–21.

14. Emi Siao (Xiao San), *Mao Tse-tung, His Childhood and Youth*, 57.

15. Hunan First Normal remained a male school until 1927. The women who participated in the New Citizens' Study Society were from other girls' schools in Changsha.

16. Li Weihan, "Huiyi Xinmin xuehui," in *Xinmin xuehui ziliao* (Archives of the New Citizens' Study Society), 462–63.

17. Siao-Yu (Xiao Zisheng), *Mao Tse-Tung and I Were Beggars*, 60–61.

18. Li Shizeng (1881–1973), a native of Hebei Province, was a founder of the Work–Study Movement. He studied biology in France. As a believer in anarchism, he was an editor of an anarchist journal, *Xin shiji*. He also founded a bean curd product factory and a publishing enterprise. In early 1920s, Li became more conservative. Later, he became a high-ranking official of the Nationalist government. After 1949, Li lived in Uruguay and Taiwan.

19. Wu Zhihui (1865–1953) was a native of Jiangsu province. Wu joined the "Aiguo xueshe" founded by Cai Yuanpei and Zhang Taiyan in the late Qing. Later, he joined the Tongmenghui in France. He studied and lived in Britain for several years. He edited the *Xin shiji* with Li Shizeng and was one of the founders of the Work–Study Program in France. He served as the president of Tangshan University, the chief editor of *Zhonghua xinbao* in Shanghai, and the president of Lyons Sino-French Institute. Becoming more conservative in the early 1920s, he was one of the most famous intellectual officials of the Nationalist government. After 1949, Wu lived in Taiwan.

20. Wu Yuzhang (1878–1966) was a native of Sichuan province. In his early years, he joined Tongmenghui and the 1911 Revolution. An important educator and promoter of the Work–Study Movement, he joined the CCP in 1925. He served as the president of several universities, and the secretary of Sichuan Provincial Party Committee, He also was elected as a member of the standing committee of the Chinese Congress.

21. Shi Xiaoming, "An Outlook of the Work–Study Program for Chinese College Students from the Perspective of Times," *Canadian Social Science* 5 (2009): 47–53.

22. Song Feifu, *Xinmin xuehui*, 13–14.

23. Peng Ming, *Wusi yundong shi* (A history of the May Fourth Movement) revised ed. (Beijing: Remin chubanshe, 1998), 139–44.

24. Ibid., 548.

25. Xiaomei Chen, *Occidentalism: A Theory of Counter-discourse in Post-Mao China* (2nd ed.) (Lanham, MD: Rowman and Littlefield, 2002), 17. For more discussion on the work–study program in France, see Marilyn A. Levine, *The Found Generation: Chinese Communists in Europe during the Twenties* (Seattle: University of Washington Press, 1993).

26. Xiao San, "Mao Zedong tongzhi zhai wusi shiqi," in *Xinmin xuehui ziliao*, no. 1, 369.

27. Li Moqing, "The Overseas Chinese Work and Study Movement," unpublished lecture (1994) quoted and translated by Dean Andrew Polizzotto,

"*Young Chinese Revolutionaries in France: How They Contributed to the Success of the Chinese Communist Revolution*" (PhD diss., University of Washinton, 1996), 34–35.

28. "Xinmin xuehui huiwu baogao" (Report of the affairs of the New Citizens' Study Society) (1920), no. 1, 122.

29. The total member of the *Xinmin xuehui* was 54 in 1919. Both Li Weihan and Song Feifu stated that eighteen people, one-third of the members of the *Xinmin xuehui*, left for France. Li Weihan, "Huiyi Xinmin xuehui," in *Huiyi yu yanjiu*, 12; Song Feifu, *Xinmin xuehui*, 13–14.

30. Cai Linbin (Cai Hesen) letter to Chen Shaoxiu, Xiao Zizhang (Xiao San), Xiao Zisheng, and Mao Zedong, August 27, 1918, in *Xinmin xuehui huiyuan tongxin lu*, 1: 10.

31. Cai Hesen Letter to Xiao Xudong (Xiao Zisheng), July 1918, in *Xinmin xuehui huiyuan tongxin lu*, 1: 4.

32. Li Dazhao, 1888–1927, professor of history and librarian at Beijing University, one of the founders of the CCP. He was the first important Chinese intellectual to support the Bolshevik Revolution in Russia. A leader in the May Fourth Movement. Although the early party did not favor his populist, nationalistic view of the peasant role in the revolution, it deeply influenced Mao Zedong. Manchurian general Chang Tso-lin executed him. *The Columbia Electronic Encyclopedia*, 6th ed. Columbia University Press, 2005. For more information, see M. J. Meisner, *Li Ta-chao and the Origins of Chinese Marxism* (1967).

33. Zhou Shizhao, "Xiangjiang de nuhou" in *Xinmin xuehui ziliao*, 395–96; also Li weihan, "Huiyi Xinmin xuehui" in *Xinmin xuehui ziliao*, 458–60.

34. Cai Linbin (Cai Hesen) letter to Chen Shaoxiu, Xiao Zizhang (Xiao San), Xiao Zisheng, and Mao Zedong, August 27, 1918, in *Xinmin xuehui huiyuan tongxin lu*, 1: 10.

35. Ibid., 6.

36. Emi Siao (Xiao San), *Mao Tse-tung, His Childhood and Youth*, 57.

37. For more imformation on this article see Li Rui, *Sanshisui yiqian de Mao Zedong* (Mao Zedong before Thirty Years Old), 162–63; also see The Editing Committee of the History of Hunan First Normal School, *Hunan diyi shifan xiaoshi—1903–1949* (The History of Hunan First Normal School—1903–1949), 111–13.

38. Mao's activities are only considered here in passing because a number of studies have already been done on Mao, including Li Rui, *Mao Zedong tongzhi di chuqi geming huodong* (Early Revolutionary activities of Comrade Mao Zedong); Ma Yu-qing, *Mao Zedong de chengzhang daolu* (The Way Mao Zedong Grew) (Xian: Shanxi renmin chubanshe, 1986); Stuart Schram, *Mao Tse-tung* (New York: Simon and Schuster, 1966); and Benjamin I. Schwartz, *Chinese Communism and the Rise of Mao* (Cambridge: Harvard University Press, 1964).

39. Hu Qiaomu, "Huainian Xiao San tongzhi" (In Memory of Comrade Xiao San), Wang Zhengming, *Xiao San zhuan* (Biography of Xiao San) (Chengdu: Sichuan wenyi chubanshe, 1992), 1.

40. Siao Yu (xiao Zisheng), *Mao Tse-tung and I were Beggars*, 35.

41. Zhonggong Hunan shengwei dangshi ziliaozhengji yanjiu weiyuanhuibian, *Hunan dangshi luncong* (On the history of the Communist Party of Hunan Branch), 104; also see Siao Yu (xiao Zisheng), *Mao Tse-tung and I were Beggars*.

42. Yang Changji, *Dahuaozhai riji* (Diaries of Dahua Studio); also Siao Yu (xiao Zisheng), *Mao Tse-tung and I were Beggars*, 41.

43. Ibid., 58–59.

44. *Dagong bao* (Hunan), July 19, 1919. Also see Marilyn A. Levine, *The Founding Generation: Chinese Communists in Europe, 1919–1925* (Seattle: University of Washington Press, 1993), 52.

45. Siao Yu (xiao Zisheng), *Mao Tse-tung and I were Beggars*, 191.

46. Ibid., 189–90.

47. Mao accused Xiao of selling some of the most valuable national treasures and of absconding with the funds in 1934, when Xiao served as the director of Beijing Palace Museum. See Snow, *Red Star Over China*, 146.

Notes to Chapter 7

1. Cai Linbin (Cai Hesen) letter to Mao Zedong, August 13, 1920, *Xinmin xuehui wenxian huibian* (Documents Collection of the New Citizens Study Society) (Hunan Provincial Archive, 1920), 87.

2. Zhonggong zhongyang dangshi yanjiushi, *Zhongguo gongchandang de qishinian* (The History of the Chinese Communist Party in the Past Seventy Years) (Beijing: Zhonggong dangshi chubanshe, 1991), 16–19, 25–27, 78, 83–97, 118–23, 543–44.

3. According to *Xiangxiang Cailinshi zupu*, the surname of the ninth generation ancestor of Cai Hesen was Lin, and he lived in Fujian province. In 1672, an uncle from his mother's side whose surname was Cai adopted him. Then that ancestor moved to Xiangxiang, Hunan and changed his surname to Cai-Lin, a compound surname. Luo Shaozhi and others, "Cai Hesen" in Hu Hua, ed., *Zhonggong dangshi renwu zhuan* (Xian: Shanxi renmin chubanshe, 1982), 6: 1.

4. According to *Geshi sixiu zupu* (The fourth edition of the Ge family pedigree) and *Dajie Zengshi wuxiu zupu* (The fifth edition of the Zeng family pedigree), the sixth daughter of Zeng Guofan was married to the fourth brother of Cai Hesen's maternal grandfather. Quoted by Luo, "Cai Hesen" in Hu, ed., *Zhonggong dangshi renwu zhuan*, 6: 1.

5. The six children included three girls and three boys. The oldest son and the second daughter died young. Guomindang killed the second son, a communist, in 1927. Cai Chang would later become one of the most important female leaders in the CCP. She and Deng Yingchao were perhaps the best educated of the older communist women. Cai Chang was also one of the thirty veteran communist women who completed the Long March. Luo, "Caimu Ge

Jianhao" (Mother Cai, Ge Jianhao) in Hu, ed., *Zhonggong dangshi renwu zhuan*, 6: 48–54.

6. In spring 1914, Ge Jianhao, together with her son, her eldest daughter, and her granddaughter, went to school in Changsha. Cai Hesen went to First Normal to study; daughter Cai Qingxi went to a girl's school; and granddaughter Liu Ang went to a kindergarten. It became a common saying that three generations went to school together in Changsha. Because of her age, the girls' teacher's school first rejected Ge. After suing the school, the judge ordered the school to break the rule and admit her. Wang Qingshui, "Ge Jianhao" in Congshu Bianweihui, ed., *Shifan qunying guangyao zhonghua* (Honorable Heroes from Normal Schools in China) (Xian: Shanxi renmin jiaoyu chubanshe, 1992), 1: 44.

7. Luo, "Caimu Ge Jianhao" in Hu, ed., *Zhonggong dangshi renwu zhuan*, 6: 50.

8. Ibid.

9. Ibid., 49.

10. Xiang Jingyu (1895–1928), a Tu minority of Hunan, became Cai Hesen's wife in 1920 and had two children. She was the first head of the Women's Bureau of the CCP, and the first female member of the CCP Central Committee. Xiang came from a well-to-do family and began to study at a private tutorial school at about age 6. In 1913, she was admitted by the Provincial Girls' First Normal School, which was regarded as the "Cradle of Female Revolutionaries." In 1914, she transferred to Zhounan Girl's School. Xiang was an active member of the *Xinmin xuehui* and helped organize women in the work–study program in France. She left for France in December 1919 and became a staunch Marxist in 1920. She joined the CCP and held important positions. In 1925, she went to study at Sun Yat-sen University in the Soviet Union. During the same period, her marriage with Cai developed problems, and they permanently separated in 1926. At the end of that year, she returned to China and organized factory labor. She was arrested and executed by Guomindang on May 1, 1928, at the age of 32. Gu Ci, "Xiang Jingyu" in Hu, ed., *Zhonggong dangshi renwu zhuan*, 6: 58–90.

11. Luo, "Caimu Ge Jianhao" in Hu, ed., *Zhonggong dangshi renwu zhuan*, 6: 52.

12. Ibid., 56.

13. Xibei shifanxueyuan zhengzhixi, ed. *Zhongguo gongchandang yinglie xiaozhuan* (The Biographical Sketch of the Chinese Communist Martyrs) (Lanzhou: Gansu renmin chubanshe, 1980), 183.

14. Ibid.

15. Luo, "Cai Hesen" in Hu, ed., *Zhonggong dangshi renwu zhuan*, 6: 2–3.

16. Ibid., 3.

17. Liu Ang (Cai's niece), "Mian huai Cai Hesen tongzhi" (In memory of comrade Cai Hesen). *Zhongguo renmin yongyuan jizhe ta: Ji nian Cai Hesen danchen 110 zhou nian* (Chinese people always remember him: In commemoration

of Cai Hesen's 110 birthday), Zhonggong Hunan shengwei xuanchuanbu (Chinese Communist Party, Hunan Branch, Department of Publicity) ed. (Changsha: Hunan renmin chubanshe, 2005), 262; Xiao San, "Huainian Cai Hesen tongzhi" (In memory of comrade Cai Hesen). *Zhongguo renmin yongyuan jizhe ta*, 194–95.

18. Emi Siao, *Mao Tse-tung, His Childhood and Youth* (Bombay: People's Publishing House Ltd., 1953), 52.

19. Liu Ang, "Mian huai Cai Hesen tongzh," 262.

20. Luo Zhanglong, "Huiyi Cai Hesen tongzhi" (Recalling Comrade Cai Hesen), *Zhongguo renmin yongyuan jizhe ta*, 214–15.

21. Liu Ang, "Mian huai Cai Hesen tongzhi," 262.

22. Ibid., 39.

23. Ibid., 262.

24. Luo Zhanglong, "Huiyi Cai Hesen tongzhi," 216.

25. Emi Siao, *Mao Tse-tung*, 40–41.

26. Ibid., 41.

27. Ibid.

28. Li Yichun, "Huiyi Hesen tongzhi" (Recalling Comrade Hesen). *Zhongguo renmin yongyuan jizhe ta*, 253.

29. Emi Siao, *Mao Tse-tung*, 44; Xiao San, "Huainian Cai Hesen tongzhi;" Liu Ang, "Mian huai Cai Hesen tongzhi."

30. Ibid., 44.

31. Ibid.

32. Zhang Shizhao, "Yang Huaizhong bie zhuan" (The supplementary biography of Yang Changji). (The original article was not published; it can be found in Wang Xingguo, ed., *Yang Changji wenji* (The collected works of Yang Changji) (Changsha: Hunan Educational Press, 1983), 388–89.

33. Li Ming (Li Lisan), "Jinian Cai Hesen tongzhi" (In memory of Comrade Cai Hesen) Hua Yingshen, ed., *Zhongguo gongchandang lieshi zhuan* (The Biography of the Chinese Communist Martyrs) (Hong Kong: Xinminzhu, 1949), 56.

34. For more information on Cai's activities in Hunan, see Cai Hesen jinian guan, ed., *Cai Hesen zhuan* (Biography of Cai Hesen) (Changsha: Hunan renmin chubanshe, 1980); Howard Boorman, *Biographical Dictionary of Republican China* (New York: Columbia University Press, 1971), 4: 284.

35. The blueprint for their New Village, a utopian society, resembled the Welsh social reformer Robert Owen's [1771–1858] idea of utopian socialism in which he advocated the abolition of classes. They got this idea from the Japanese writer, Mushanokoji Saneatsu (1885–1976). For more information on this, see Mao Zedong, *Mao Zedong zaoqi wengao 1912 .6–1920. 11* (Early Writings of Mao Zedong 1912. 6–1920. 11) (Changsha: Hunan chubanshe, 1990), 449 and footnote 2 in Notes to Introduction.

36. The school of Mohism was founded by Mozi (470–390 BC) in the Spring and Autumn Period of Eastern Zhou. Mozi advocated judging ideas

and objects through the human senses, by their utility and their antiquity. He denounced offensive warfare, extravagant funerals, and music, and tried to replace Chinese family and clan structure with the concept of *jian-ai* (impartial caring/universal love), stressing the care for all people equally. In this, he argued directly against Confucians who had emphasized that it was natural and correct for people to care about different people in different degrees.

37. Xie Binghuai, "Cai Hesen shi minzhu zhuyizhe ma?—xinmin xuehui chengli qianhou Cai Hesen sixiang qianxi" (Was Cai Hesen a democrat?—A brief examination of Cai Hesen's thought before and after the founding of the "Xinmin xuehui"), *Hunan dangshi luncong* (On the History of the Communist Party of Hunan Branch) (Changsha: Hunan renmin chubanshe, 1986), 177.

38. Luo Wenhua, "Mao Zedong zaonian 'xinmin' sixiang yanjiu" (The study of Mao Zedong's 'new citizens' thought in his early years) in *Zhonggong Hunan dangshi luncong* (On the History of the Communist Party of Hunan Branch), Zhonggong Hunan shengwei dangshi ziliao zhengji yanjiu weiyuanhui bian (The Editorial Committee of the historical documents of the Hunan Provincial Communist Party) (Changsha: Hunan renmin chubanshe, 1986), 111–23; Li Rui, "Xuexi Xinmin xuehui xianbei de gemin jingshen," (Learn the revolutionary spirit of the predecessors of the Xinmin xuehui), Zhonggong Hunan shengwei dangshi, 19; Stuart Schram, *Mao Tse-tung* (New York: Simon and Schuster, 1966), 40–42.

39. This phrase was quoted by Xie, "Cai Hesen shi minzhu zhuyizhe ma?" 176.

40. Ibid.

41. Tang Duo, "Huiyi wode liangshi yiyou—Cai Hesen tongzhi" (Recalling my good teacher and helpful friend—comrade Cai Hesen), *Zhongguo renmin yongyuan jizhe ta*, 231–32.

42. Ibid., 22.

43. Shen Yijia, "Wo suo zhidao de zaoqi zhi Cai Hesen" (what I know about the early years of Cai Hesen). *Zhongguo renmin yongyuan jizhe ta*, 245–46.

44. Ibid., 246.

45. For more information on Yang's admiration of Tan, see Yang's diary of March 1915 in Wang Xingguo, *Yang Changji de shengping ji sixiang* (Life and Thought of Yang Changji), 48.

46. Wang Xingguo, "Yang Changji and the xinmin xuehui" *Zhonggong Hunan shengwei dangshi*, 25.

47. Averill, "Cultural Politics," 11.

48. In 1915, he wrote the *jinbainian lai de guochi shigang* (The historical compendium of national humiliation in the past one hundred years), an essay that provoked strong repercussions among First Normal students and teachers.

49. Averill, "Cultural Politics," 11.

50. Ibid.

51. Liu Ang, "Mian huai Cai Hesen tongzhi," 263–64.

52. Zhang Kundi, Diary of Zhang Kundi (Zhang Kundi riji) (Changsha: Hunan Provincial Museum, [B]).

53. Cai Chang earned eight yuan per month. Cai's older sister Cai Qingxi sometimes also provided subsidies for the family. Ibid., 5.

54. Siao Yu, Mao Zedong and I were Beggars, 46.

55. On June 5, 1931, he was arrested in Hong Kong by British colonialists and extradited to the KMT in Guangzhou. There, he died a martyr's death at the age of 36, after refusing to renounce his beliefs in the midst of torture. He had been spread-eagled on a wall, with his hands and feet nailed into the wall, and beaten to death, his breast torn by bayonet wounds. Cai Chang, "Huiyi Xinmin xuehui de huodong" (Reflections of the activities of the New Citizen Association) in Xinmin xuehui ziliao (Documents Collection and Memories of the New Citizens' Study Society), ed. by Zhongguo geming bowuguan and Hunan sheng bowuguan (The Editorial Committee of the Archives of Chinese Revolution and Hunan Provincial Archives) (Beijing: Renmin chubanshe, 1980), 574; Renwu zhuan, 6: 45–46.

56. Siao Yu, Mao Zedong and I were Beggars, 46–47.

57. Diary of Zhang Kundi (Zhang Kundi riji), August 23, 1917 (Changsha: Hunan Provincial Museum, [B]).

58. Ibid.

59. Ibid.

60. Averill, "Cultural Politics," 18.

61. Averill, "The transition from Urban to Rural," 87–88.

62. Luo, "Cai Hesen," Renwu zhuan, 6: 6–7.

63. Averill, "The transition from Urban to Rural," 90–91.

64. Averill, "Cultural Politics," 25.

65.Luo Zhanglong, "Huiyi Cai Hesen tongzhi" (Recalling Comrade Cai Hesen), Zhongguo renmin yongyuan jizhe ta, 214–15.

66. Siao-Yu, Mao Tse-Tung and I Were Beggars, 61.

67. For more information on Cai Hesen's involvement with the work–study program in France, see Cai Hesen jinian guan, ed., Cai Hesen zhuan; Boorman, Biographical Dictionary of Republican China, 4: 284.

68. Cai Linbin letter to Mao Zedong, July 24, 1918, in Xinmin xuehui wenxian huibian, 1: 15–16.

69. Cai Hesen letter to Mao Zedong, August 21, 1918, in Xinmin xuehui wenxian huibian, 1: 17.

70. Luo, "Cai Hesen" Renwu zhuan, 6: 11.

71. Tang Duo, "Huiyi wode liangshi yiyou—Cai Hesen" (In memory of my good teacher and helpful friend—Cai Hesen), in Huiyi Cai Hesen tongzhi (In Memory of Comrade Cai Hesen) (Beijing: Renmin chubanshe, 1980), 100.

72. Cai Linbin (Cai Hesen) letter to Chen Shaoxiu, Xiao Zizhang (Xiao San), Xiao Zisheng, and Mao Zedong, August 27, 1918, in Xinmin xuehui hui-yuan tongxin lu, 1: 10.

73. Cai Chang, "Huiyi Xinmin xuehui huiyuan de huodong" in *Xinmin xuehui ziliao* (Documents Collection and Memories of the New Citizens' Study Society), Hunan Provincial Archive, 1920, 570.

74. Li Weihan, "Huiyi Xinmin xuehui" in *Xinmin xuehui ziliao* (Documents Collection and Memories of the New Citizens' Study Society), 472–73.

75. Sia, *Mao Tse-tung and I Were Beggars*, 45.

76. Liu Ang, "Huiyi jingai de Xiang Jingyu tongzhi" (Reminiscence of the beloved comrade Xiang Jingyu), in *Jinian Xiang Jingyu tongzhi yingyong jiuyi wushi zhounian* (In Memory of comrade Xiang Jingyu on the fiftieth anniversary of her martyrdom) (Beijing: Renmin chubanshe, 1978), 8–9. The English translation can be found in Marilyn A. Levine, *The Founding Generation: Chinese Communists in Europe during the Twenties*, 53–54.

77. Cai Chang, "Huiyi Xinmin xuehui huiyuan de huodong" in (Documents Collection and Memories of the New Citizens' Study Society), 570; Song Feifu, *Xinmin xuehui* (New Citizens' Study Society), 21.

78. Cai Linbin (Cai Hesen) letter to Mao Zedong, May 28, 1920, in *Xinmin xuehui huiyuan tongxin lu*, 3: 82.

79. Ibid., 81.

80. Ibid.

81. Song, *Xinmin xuehui* (New Citizens' Study Society), 22.

82. Mao Zedong took over the leadership of those New Citizens' Study Society members who remained in Hunan.

83. Cai Hesen, *Cai Hesen wenji* (Beijing: Renmin chubanshe, 1980), 33–48.

84. Ibid., 78.

85. Conred Erandt, "The French Returned Elite in the Chinese Communist Party," in *Symposium on Economic and Social Problems of the Far East*, ed. E. F. Szczpanik (Hong Kong: Hong Kong University Press, 1962), 230–31.

86. Erandt argues that the failure of the anarchist leaders to provide the work–study students in France with the means of survival caused them to become disaffected with anarchism and consequently to embrace Marxism. Erandt's statement might or might not be true of the work–study students in France who had converted from anarchism to Marxism.

87. Cai, *Cai Hesen wenji*, 33–48.

88. Ibid., 65.

89. Cai Linbin (Cai Hesen) letter to Mao Zedong, August 13, 1920, in *Xinmin xuehui huiyuan tongxin lu*, 3: 86–87.

90. Ibid., 86.

91. Cai, *Cai Hesen wenji*, 74.

92. For more information, see *Cai Hesen wenji*; Cai's letters to other members.

93. Li Weihan, "Huiyi Xinmin xuehui," 493.

94. These articles and letters are in *Cai Hesen wenji* and also in *Xinmin xuehui ziliao* and *Xinmin xuehui wenxian huibian*.

95. The "*Gongxue shijie she*," originally called the "Qingong jianxue lijin she," was formed by Li Weihan, Luo Xuezan, Zhang Kundi, and Li Fuchun in February 1920 in France.

96. The thirteen members who attended the Montargis Meeting were Cai Hesen, Xiang Jingyu, Chen Shaoxiu, Xiao Zizhang (Xiao San), Zhang Kundi, Luo Xuezan, Cai Chang, Li Weihan, Xiong Guangchu, Xiong Jiguang, Xiong Shubin, Ouyang Ze, and Xiao Zisheng, who were working with the French–Chinese Educational Association. For more information, see Li Weihan, "Huiyi Xinmin xuehui" in *Xinmin xuehui ziliao*, 477.

97. Xiao Xudong (Xiao Zisheng) letter to Mao Zedong. This is a long letter, in which Xiao gives a report of the Montargis Meeting, and his views of the participants' opinions. Xiao started writing it in July but finished it in early August 1920. The letter can be found in *Xinmin xuehui huiyuan tongxin lu*, 3: 93.

98. Ibid.

99. Ibid.

100. Li, "Huiyi Xinmin xuehui," 477.

101. The Third International refers to the Comintern, which was an organization of the Communist Party of the Soviet Union and international communist organizations. It was formed by Lenin in 1919 and was disbanded in 1943.

102. The Second International was an organization of the Social Democratic Party and the Socialistic Labor Unions, which was formed in 1889. In its early stage, the organization was influenced by Engels and adopted Marxism as its principle. In its later period, revisionists ruled the organization. The organization disbanded in 1914.

103. Li, "Huiyi Xinmin xuehui," 479.

104. The three favorite female students of Yang Changji were Xiang Jingyu, Tao Siyong, and Ren Peidao.

105. Xiang Jingyu, *Xiang Jingyu wenji* (Collected Works of Xiang Jingyu) (Changsha: Hunan renmin chubanshe, 1980), 64.

106. Luo, "Cai Hesen" in Hu, ed., *Zhonggong dangshi renwu zhuan*, 6: 15. However, Cai Chang recalled "Zhao Shiyan, Zhou Enlai, Wang Ruofei, Chen Yannian, Liu Bojian, and Nie Rongzhen founded the Socialist Youth League (S. Y.), which was later renamed the Chinese Youth (party) (C. Y.). C. Y. became the European branch of the CCP after the Shanghai branch of CCP approved it. C. Y. was established either at the end of 1921 or spring 1922. Cai Hesen was sent back to China because of his political activities in October 1921. Therefore, Cai was not one of the founders of the branch." Cai Chang, "Huiyi Xinmin xuehui huiyuan liufa qijian de huodong," 573.

107. Cai presented his ideas on the establishment of the CCP in his two long letters to Mao on August 13, 1920 and September 16, 1920 and one long letter to Chen Duxiu on February 11, 1921. All three letters are in *Cai Hesen wenji*, 22–38 & 51–56.

108. Yang Ximan, "Xinmin xuehui yu Zhongguo gongchandang de jianli," in *Hunan dangshi luncong*, 66–67.

109. Cai Hesen played a very important role in introducing Marxism to China and was an early, but not the first, Marxist theoretician in China. Li Dazhao had already published a series of articles on Marxism and Russian Revolution in *New Youth* and other journals before Cai left for France in 1920.

110. Cai Linbin (Cai Hesen) letter to Mao Zedong, August 13, 1920, in *Xinmin xuehui huiyuan tongxin lu*, 3: 85–90.

111. Cai Hesen's letter to Chen Duxiu on Februry 11, 1921, in *Cai Hesen wenji*, 51–56.

112. Cai Linbin (Cai Hesen) letter to Mao Zedong, August 13, 1920, in *Xinmin xuehui huiyuan tongxin lu*, 3: 87.

113. Ibid., 86.

114. Ibid.

115. Cai, *Cai Hesen wen ji*, 71.

116. Ibid., 51.

117. Ibid., 87.

118. Ibid.

119. Cai Linbin (Cai Hesen) letter to Mao Zedong, August 13, 1920, in *Xinmin xuehui huiyuan tongxin lu*, 3: 87.

120. Yang, "Xinmin xuehui yu Zhongguo gongchandang de jianli," 67.

121. Xia Yuanshen, "Lun Xinmin xuehui xiangwai fazhan yu guonei yanjiu bingzhong de yiyi" in *Hunan dangshi luncong*, 133–34.

122. Luo, "Cai Hesen" in Hu, ed., *Zhonggong dangshi renwu zhuan*, 6: 17.

123. Cai Linbin (Cai Hesen) letter to Mao Zedong, September 16, 1920, in *Xinmin xuehui huiyuan tongxin lu*, 3: 107–116.

124. Ibid.

125. Ibid., 114–15.

126. Cai, *Cai Hesen wen ji*, 78.

127. Mao Zedong letter to Cai Hesen, January 21, 1921, in *Xinmin xuehui huiyuan tongxin lu*, 3: 116.

128. Robert A. Scalapino, "The Evolution of a Young Revolutionary— Mao Zedong in 1919–1921," *Journal of Asian Studies* 1 (November 1982): 56.

129. Two examples of his leadership were the Twenty-eighth Movement of February 1921 and the Lyons Incident of 1921. Boorman's *Biographical Dictionary of Republican China* has the date of the "Twenty-eighth Incident" incorrectly listed as 8 February 1921. According to *Zhonggong dangshi renwu zhuan* (Biographies of Chinese Communists), and written memories of Li Weihan and Cai Chang, the "Twenty-eighth Incident" broke out on 28 February 1921. It later developed into the Twenty-eighth Movement, which was named because of the date of the demonstration. Led by Cai Hesen, about four hundred students gathered in front of the Chinese consulate on rue Babylon in Paris on Februry 28, 1921, to petition the Chinese consulate for "the right to live, the right

to study" (*shengcun quan, qiuxue quan*), asking 400 francs each month for four years. Police dispersed the crowd in a violent clash. Although unsuccessful, the Twenty-eighth Incident showed that some students were willing to take direct action. Li, "Huiyi Xinmin xuehui," 20–22; also see Cai, "Huiyi Xinmin xuehui huiyuan de huodong," 571–72.

The Lyons Incident was the most important struggle of the worker-students in France. Some Sino-French Educational Association leaders originally promised the newly established Sino-French Institute at Lyons University for the worker-students in France. However, they learned that Wu Zhihui was bringing more students from China to become the first students at the institute and refused to accept them. The new institute at Lyons University represented the last hope for the worker-students in France, because sources for loans and government support had totally dried up. Starving and despairing, a vanguard of 125 students, led by Cai Hesen and Zhao Shiyan, occupied a dormitory at Lyons University on September 21, 1921, to make their demands known. However, the students were arrested and within one month were deported back to China. Li, "Huiyi Xinmin xuehui," 22–23; also see Cai, "Huiyi Xinmin xuehui huiyuan de huodong," 572–73.

130. Li, "Huiyi Xinmin xuehui," 22. Also see Luo, "Cai Hesen," in Hu, ed., *Zhonggong dangshi renwu zhuan*, 6: 19.

131. According to Zhonggong dangshi, *Zhonggong dangshi renwuzhuan* (Biographies of Chinese Communists), the journal's name was *Xiangdao*, which was published weekly. Boorman, *Biographical Dictionary of Republican China*, has the journal's name incorrectly as *Xiangdao zhoubao*.

132. Luo, "Cai Hesen," in Hu, ed., *Zhonggong dangshi renwu zhuan*, 6: 22.

133. Ibid., 28–33.

134. Cai, "Huiyi Xinmin xuehui de huodong," 574; *Zhonggong dangshi renwu zhuan*, 6: 45–46.

135. When Mao discussed the founding of the association in *Xinmin xuehui huiwu baogao* number 1, he wrote: "Another reason [that contributed to the founding of the association] was that most of the members were students of Mr. Yang Huanzhong. The students were influenced by Yang's teaching, and became committed to the betterment or improvement of each individual, strengthening his moral and spiritual fiber and improving his education as their philosophy. Of the twenty-one founding members . . . twenty were students of Yang Changji from First Normal. . . . The New Citizens' Study Society envisioned a renewal of Chinese society through reeducation of its citizens: many of its members later designed the new institutions and policies of the People's Republic." Mao Zedong, "Xinmin xuehui huiwu baogao" (Report of the affairs of the New Citizenss' Study Society) (1920), in *Xinmin xuehui zilia*, no. 1: 2.

136. Snow, *Red Star over China*, 130.

Glossary

Aiwan ting 愛晚亭
Anhua 安化
Anhui 安徽
Bancang 板倉
ban zhuren 班主任
Baoding 保定
Baohuang hui 保皇會
baojia 保甲
Baoweiju 保衛局
Ben 本
Ben xiao gu jiaoshou Yang Huaizhong xiansheng shiji 本校故教授楊懷中先生事跡
Cai Chang 蔡暢
Cai Guangxiang 蔡廣祥辣醬店
Cai Hesen (Cailin Bin) 蔡和森 (蔡林彬)
Cai Yuanpei (Jiemin) 蔡元培 (孑民)
Changde 常德
Changsha 長沙
Changsha ribao 長沙日報
chedi gaizao sixiang 徹底改造思想
Chen Baozhen 陳寶箴
Chen Chang (Chen Zhangfu) 陳昌(陳章甫)
Chen Duxiu 陳獨秀
Chen Shaoxiu 陳紹休
Chen Shunong 陳書農
Cheng 誠
chengfen zhiyu qianshan gaiguo 懲忿窒欲，遷善改過
Cheng Hao 程灝
Chengnan shuyuan 城南書院
Cheng Yi 程頤
Chuyi xiaoxue 楚怡小學

Chuanshan xueshe 船山學社
Ci 詞
Cixi 慈禧
cun tianli, mie renyu 存天理滅人欲
Dagong bao 大公報
Dahua zhai riji 達化齋日記
Datongshu 大同書
daxueling 大學令
Da xuetang 大學堂
Dao 道
Daoguang 道光
deyu 德育
Dongshan 東山
Dongxiang 東鄉
Dongting hu 洞庭湖
Daohai lieshi Yang jun Shouren shilue 蹈海烈士楊君守仁事略
Dushu lu 讀書彔
Duan Fang 端方
Duanzhu shuowen 段注說文
Du Tongjian Lun 讀通鑒論
Duiyu jiaoyu fangzhen zhi yijian 對于教育方針之意見
Ershi si shi 二十四史
Fan Yuanlian 范源濂
Fang Weixia (Zhuya) 方維夏(竹雅)
Feile 非樂
Fenghuang 鳳凰
Fu 賦
funü zhijia 婦女之家
fuwu sheng 服務生
Ge Jianhao 葛健豪
Gewu 格物
Gongche shangshu 公車上書
Gongfu 功夫
Gonghedang 共和黨
Gongxue shijie she 工學世界社
Gongyan Zhazi 公言雜誌
Gongyang 公羊
guannian shijie 觀念世界
Guangxi 廣西
Guoshi guan 國史館

guowen 國文
Guomindang 國民黨
gushi 古詩
Gu Yanwu 顧炎武
Guang Shangtong 廣尚同
Hankou 漢口
Han Wenju 韓文舉
Han Yu 韓愈
He Changgong 何長工
He Guo 賀果
He Shuheng 何叔衡
Hong Xiuquan 洪秀全
Hou Wailu 侯外廬
Hu Anguo 胡安國
Hu Hong 胡宏
Huaining 懷寧
Huang Shutao 黃澍濤
Huang Xing 黃興
Huang Zongxi 黃宗義
Huang Zunxian 黃遵憲
Hubei 湖北
huiyilu 回憶錄
Hunan dangshi dashi nianbiao 湖南黨史大事年表
Hunan diyi shifan xiaoshi 湖南第一師範 校史
Hunan gaodeng shifan 湖南高等師範
Hunan gongbao 湖南公報
Hunan gongli diyi shifan xuexiao 湖南公立第一師範學校
Hunan quansheng shifan xuetang 湖南全省師範學堂
Hunan Jiaoyu zazhi 湖南教育雜誌
Hunan renmin gemingshi 湖南人民革命史
Hunan shengli diyi shifan xuexiao 湖南省立第一師範學校
Hunan shifan guan 湖南師範館
Hunan youdeng shifan 湖南优等師範
Hunan Youji Normal College 湖南优級師範學堂
Huxiang wenhua 湖湘文化
jiran bu dong 寂然不動
Jia yi bing ding 甲乙丙丁
Jiayin zazhi 甲寅雜誌
jianyi shifan xuetang 簡易師範學堂
Jiang Biao 江標

Jiangnan zhizaoju 江南製造局
Jiangtang lu 講堂彔
Jiang Weiqiao 蔣維喬
Jiang Zhuru 蔣竹如
Jiao Dafeng 焦達峰
Jiaotang 教堂
Jiaoyang xuesheng zhi yaozhi 教養學生之要旨
Jiaoyu yu zhengzhi 教育與政治
Jiaoyu shang dang zhuyi zhi dian 教育上當注意之點
Jiaoyu xue jiangyi 教育學講義
jiaoyu zongzhi 教育宗旨
Jiaoyu zongzhiling 教育宗旨令
jie biaobingguan yishi 皆彪炳冠一時
jinshi 進士
jin yang shiyuan 金洋十元
jing 靜
jing 敬
Jinghu nanlu anchashi 荊湖南路按察使
jingshi 經世
jingshi zhi dalüe 經世之大略
Jingshi daxue tang 京師大學堂
Jingshi wenbian 經世文編
jingshi zhiyong 經世致用
jingzuo fa 靜坐法
Jiuge qiangu 九哥千古
ju jing 居敬
juren 舉人
Juan 卷
Junshi heyi 君師合一
Qu Zongduo 瞿宗鐸
Kang Youwei 康有為
Kong Zhaoshou 孔昭綬
Kongzi pingyi 孔子平議
Kuai Guangdian 蒯光典
Li 理
Li 裏
Li Dazhao 李大釗
ligong sheng 例貢生
Li Fuchun 李富春
Li Hongzhang 李鴻章

Lijiao 禮教
Li Jinxi (Shaoxi) 黎錦熙 (劭西)
Li Lisan 李立三
Li Rui 李銳
Li Shizeng 李石曾
Lishi yuyuan 李氏芋園
Li Weige 李維格
Li Weihan 李維漢
Li Xiaodan 李肖聃
Lixue 理學
Li Yuandu 李元度
li ze feng chang 麗澤風長
Li Zehou 李澤厚
Lizhi 立志
Liang Qichao 梁啟超
Liao Mingjin (Hutang) 廖名縉 (笏堂)
Liu Ang 劉昂
Liu Caijiu 劉采九
Liu Diwei 劉棣蔚
liufa qingong jianxue 留法勤工儉學
Liu Renxi 劉人熙
Liuyang 瀏陽
Lu Jiuyuan (Lu Xiangshan) 陸九淵 (陸象山)
Lun Hunan zunzhi sheli shangwuju yi xian
zhenxing nonggong zhixue 論湖南遵旨設立商務局宜先振興農工之學
Lunlixue yuanli 倫理學原理
Lunyu 論語
Lunyu leichao 論語類鈔
Luo Xuezan 羅學瓚
Luo Zhanglong 羅章龍
Makesi zhuyi yu zhongguo wuchan jieji 馬克思主義與中國無產階級
Mao Zedong (Mao Runzhi) 毛澤東 (毛潤之)
Mao Zedong zaoqi wengao 毛澤東早期文稿
meigan zhi jiaoyu 美感之教育
Min bao 民報
minquan 民權
Minsheng zazhi 民聲雜誌
minzhi 民知
minzhu 民主
Mingde zhongxue 明德中學

Mojia 墨家
Mozi 墨子
mu 畝
Nan xuehui 南學會
Nanxuan fuzi ci 南軒夫子祠
Neihua daode 內化道德
Ningxiang 寧鄉
Qiangxue bao 強學報
Qiangxue hui 強學會
Qingong jianxue lijin hui 勤工儉學勵進會
Qiushi shuyuan 求實書院
Quanxue pian 勸學篇
Ou Jujia 歐矩甲
Ouyang Zhonggu 歐陽中鵠
Putang 蒲塘
Putongke 普通科
Pi Xirui 皮錫瑞
qi 氣
qu zhu da lu, hui fu Zhong hua 驅逐韃虜 恢復中華
Qunxue yiyan 群學肄言
Ren 仁
renge bu wanquan 人格不完全
Ren ren 仁人
Renxue 仁學
Renzi. guichou xuezhi 壬子. 癸丑學制
Riji 日記
Shanxing 繕性
Shaonian shijie 少年世界
Shaonian Zhongguo xuehui 少年中國學會
shenxin bingyong 身心並用
Shen Yijia 沈宜甲
shengren zhi ben 聖人之本
shengyuan 生員
Shi Cuntong 施存统
shifan benke 師範本科
Shifan guan 師範館
shifan jiaoyu ling 師範教育令
shifan xuexiao guicheng 師範學校規程
shijie guan jiaoyu 世界觀教育
shiti shijie 實體世界

Shiwu bao 時務報
Shiwu xuetang 時務學堂
Shumo 述墨
Shuyuan 書院
Shuangfeng 雙峰
Siao San (Xiao Zizhang) 蕭三 (蕭子暲)
Siao Yu (Xiao Zisheng, Xiao Xudong) 蕭瑜(蕭子升, 蕭旭東)
Suchengke 速成科
Suchengshifan ke 速成師範科
Suigan lu 隨感彔
Sun Zhongshan 孫中山
Taiji Tushuo 太極圖說
Taiping 太平
taixue sheng 太學生
Tan Sitong 譚嗣同
Tan Yankai 譚延闓
Tanzhou 潭州
Tang Caichang 唐才常
Tang Xiangming 湯薌銘
Tao Xingzhi 陶行知
ti 體
tiyu 體育
Tiyu zhi yanjiu 體育之研究
Tian 天
Tian Han 田漢
Tongmeng hui 同盟會
Tongwen guan 同文館
Tongshu 通書
Waifan daode 外範道德
wanshi moguiyu yi 萬事莫貴于義
Wang Da 王達
Wang Fengchang 王風昌
Wang Fuzhi (Wang Chuanshan) 王夫之 (王船山)
Wang Jifan 王季範
Wang Xianqian 王先謙
Wang Yangming 王陽明
Wei Yuan 魏源
Wenhuaren 文化人
Wuchang 武昌
Wu Dacheng 吳大澄

wuxing zhi ben baixing zhi yuan 五行之本 百行之源
Wu Yuzhang 吳玉章
Wu Zhihui 吳稚輝
wusi sixiang 五四思想
wusi yundong 五四運動
wusi aiguo yundong 五四愛國運動
Xiyang lunlixue shi 西洋倫理學史
xianzhi xianjue 先知先覺
Xiang bao 湘報
Xiangdao 向導周報
Xiang jiang 湘江
Xiang Jingyu (Jiuer) 向警予 (九兒)
Xiang jun 湘軍
Xiangshang tongmeng 向上同盟
Xiangtan 湘潭
Xiangxiang 湘鄉
Xiangxue 湘學
Xiangyin 湘陰
xianshi xingfu 現世幸福
Xiangxue bao 湘學報
xiao 孝
Xiaolian tang 孝廉堂
Xiao xuetang 小學堂
xiaoxue xiaoling 小學校令
xiaoxun 校訓
Xie Binghuai 謝炳懷
Xinmin 新民
Xinmin xuehui 新民學會
Xinmin xuehui huiwu baogao 新民學會會務報告
Xinmin xuehui wenxian huibian 新民學會文獻匯編
Xin Qingnian 新青年
Xinzheng 新政
Xinzhili 心之力
xingli chuhai 興利 除害
xing tianxia zhi li, chu tianxia zhi hai 興天下之利, 除天下之害
xingshen rike 省身日課
xiucai 秀才
Xiong Kunfu (Guangchu) 熊焜甫 (光楚)
Xiong Xiling 熊希齡
Xiushen 修身

Xiuye xuexiao 修業學校

xixian guohua zhidi, lanzhi shengting, qizi rushi, ze xiangzhong zidi zhenglai

jiangxue zhiqu ye 昔賢過化之地，蘭芷升庭，杞梓入室,則又湘中子弟爭來講學之區也

Xu Renzhu 徐仁鑄

Xu Teli (Xu Maoxun) 徐特立 (徐懋恂)

Xuejian 學監

xuejian zhuren 學監主任

Xuetang 學堂

Xueyou hui 學友會

Xuewuchu 學務處

xuexiao xitong 學校系統

Xuezijian 學子監

xun gexiaosheng ling 訓各校生令

xunli quyu 循理 去欲

Yan Fu 嚴復

Yang 陽

Yang Changji (Yang Huaizhong Yang Bisheng) 楊昌濟 (楊懷中)

Yang Changji wenji 楊昌濟文集

Yang Kaihui 楊開慧

Yang Shaohua 楊韶華

Yang Yulin (Yang Shouren) 楊毓麟 (楊守仁)

Yao Shun Yu Tang, hu bao chai lang 堯舜禹湯 虎豹豺狼

Ye Dehui 葉德輝

Ye Juemai 葉覺邁

yi 義

Yi Baisha (Kun) 易白沙 (坤)

yi chengwei jieshu wei chengwei shaji 已成為劫數 未成為殺機

yixia zhibian 夷夏之辨

yin 陰

yixiang sheng 邑庠生

Yiyang 益陽

Yongfeng lajiang 永峰辣醬

Yongfeng xian 永峰縣

Yoshida Seichi 吉田靜致

youxin 遊心

Youxue yibian 游學譯編

youzu xinshi 尤足信實

Yu gailiang shehui zhi yijian 余改良社會之意見

Yu guiguo hou duiyu jiaoyu zhi ganxiang 余歸國後對于教育之感想
Yuke 預科
Yu Liansan 俞廉三
Lu Yuanding 陸元鼎
Yuan 元
Yuanjiang 沅江
Yuan Shikai 袁世凱
Yuan Zhongqian 袁仲謙
Yuelu shan 嶽麓山
Yuezhou 嶽州
Zeng Guofan 曾國藩
Zeng Peilin 曾沛霖
Zhang Gan 張幹
Zhang Guoji 張國基
Zhang du 張毒
Zhang Jingyao 張敬堯
Zhang Jingshun 張敬舜
Zhang Jingyu 張敬禹
Zhang Jingtang 張敬湯
Zhang Kundi 張昆弟
Zhang Kundi riji 張昆弟日記
Zhang Shi 張栻
Zhang Shizhao 章士釗
Zhang Taiyan 章太炎
Zhang Zhidong 張之洞
Zhao Erxun 趙爾巽
Zhexue 哲學
Zhexue shang gezhong lilun zhi lueshu 哲學上各種理論之略述
Zhexue yanjiu xiaozu 哲學研究小組
zhen 貞
zhengfeng yundong 整風運動
zhi cheng 至誠
zhi cheng dong wu 至誠動物
Zhichi 知恥
zhiji dati zhi gongli, buji xiaoti zhi lihai 只計大體之功利, 不計小體之利害
zhiye 職業
zhi yu 制欲
zhiyu 智育
Zhonglu shifan xuetang 中路師範學堂

Zhong xuetang 中學堂
Zhong xue xiaoling 中學校令
Zhongguo sixiang tongshi 中國思想通史
Zhongguo gongchandang lü ou zhibu 中國共產黨旅歐支部
zhongxing mingchen yidai ruzong 中興名臣一代儒宗
Zhou Dunyi 周敦頤
Zhounan nüzi xuexiao 周南女子學校
Zhounan nüzi liufa qingongjianxue xuehui 周南女子留法勤工儉學學會
Zhou Shizhao 周世釗
Zhu Xi 朱熹
zhuzhong shangwu jingshen ling 註重尚武精神令
Zhuzi wu guilun 諸子無鬼論
Juzi Zhou 桔子洲
zili 自立
Zizhi tongjian 資治通鑒
Zongfa 宗法
Zuo Zongtang 左宗堂

Selected Bibliography

Annals of Hunan First Normal School Committee, *Hunan shengli diyi shifan xuexiao xiaozhi* (Annals of Hunan Provincial First Normal School). Changsha: Hunan Provincial Archives, 59–5–37, 1918.

Averill, Stephen C. "The Transition from Urban to Rural in the Chinese Revolution," *The China Journal*, 48. Australia: Australia national university, 2002.

———. "The Cultural Politics of Local Education in Early Twentieth Century China," *Twentieth Century China*, 32, no. 2 (April 2007).

Baijuanban *Zhongguo quanshi* bianji gongzhuo weiyuanhui *Zhongguo quanshi* (The Complete History of China) (vol. 91, 94, and 98). Beijing: Renmin chubanshe, 1994.

Bailey, Paul J. *Reform the People: Changing Attitudes Towards Popular Education in Early Twentieth Century China*. Vancouver: University of British Columbia Press. 1990.

———. (Trans. with an introduction), *Strengthen the Country and Enrich the People: The Reform Writings of Ma Jianzhong (1845–1900)*, Surrey: Curzon Press Ltd., 1998. (Durham East Asia Series no. 2)

Bastid, Marianne. Trans. by Paul J. Bailey. *Educational Reform in Early Twentieth-Century China*. Ann Arbor: Center for Chinese Studies, University of Michigan, 1988.

Bianco, Lucien. *Origins of the Chinese Revolution, 1915–1949*. Stanford: Stanford University Press, 1971.

Bo Yibo. *Ruogan zhongda juece yu shijian de huigu* (Major policies and events revisited). 2 vols. Beijing: Zhonggong zhongyang dangxiao chupanshe, 1991.

Boorman, Howard L. *Biographical Dictionary of Republican China*. vol. 4. New York: Columbia University Press, 1971.

Cai Hesen. "Wo dang chansheng de beijing jiqi lishi shiming" (Background for the birth of our Party and our Party's historical mission) (original date not found). *Zhongguo Gongchandang diyi ci daibiao dahui dang'an ziliao zeng ding ben* (Expanded edition, Archival materials on the First Party Congress of the Chinese Communist Party), edited by Zhongyang dang'an guan (Central Party Archives). Beijing: Renmin chupanshe, 1984.

————. *Cai Hesen wenji* (Collections of Cai Hesen). Beijing: Renmin chupanshe, 1980.

Cai Renhou. "Nansong Hushi jiaxue yu Huxiang xuetong" (Hu's family study in Southern Song Dynasty and scholastic tradition in Hunan) in *Kongmeng xuebao* [Journal of "Confucius and Mencius Society" of the Republic of China], 21 (April 1971): 75–88.

Cai Yuanpei. "Yang Dusheng xiansheng daohai ji" (On committing suicide of Mr. Yang Dusheng by drowning himself into sea), Cai yuanpei xiansheng quanji [The complete works of Mr. Cai Yuanpei], ed. by Sun Changwei, Taiwan: The Commercial Press, 1968, vol. 2, 582–84.

Cai Yuanpei et al., "Fugao" (An obituary notice morning Mr. Yang Changji), in Beijing daxue rikan, no. 521, 22 January 1920; also *Dagong bao* (Hunan) 13 March 1920. Reprinted in *Yang Changji wenji* (The Collected Works of Yang Changji), Wang Xingguo, ed. Changsha: Hunan Educational Press, 1983. For English translation see Mao's Road to Power, by Schram, 1991, 1, 487–89.

Cao Dianqiu. "Yang Changji xiansheng zhuan" (Biography of Mr. Yang Changji) (The original article was not published, 1920). In *Yang Changji wenji* (The Collected Works of Yang Changji), ed. Wang Xingguo. Changsha: Hunan Educational Press, 1983.

Chan, Wing-tsit. Religious trends in modern china, New York: Columbia University Press, 1953.

————. *A source book in Chinese philosophy*. Princeton: Princeton University Press, 1973.

Chai, Winberg. *Essential Works of Chinese Communism*. New York: A National General Company, 1971.

Chan, Wing-Tsit. *A Source Book in Chinese Philosophy*. Princeton: Princeton University Press, 1963.

————. ed. *Chu Hsi and Neo-Confucianism*. Honolulu: University of Hawaii Press 1986.

Chang, Hao. Liang Ch'i-ch'ao and Intellectual Transition in China: 1890–1907. Cambridge: Harvard University Press, 1971.

————. *Chinese Intellectuals in Crisis, Search for Order and Meaning, 1890–1911.* Berkeley: University of California Press, 1989.

————. *Youan yishi yu minzhu chuantong* (The Democratic Tradition and the Consciousness of the Dark Side of Life). Taiwan: Lianjing chuban shiye gongsi, 1989.

————. "Xingxiang yu shizhi: zairen wusi sixiang" "Image and reality: a reexamination of the May Fourth thinking." In *Ziyou minzhu de sixiang yu wenhao* (The Liberal and Democratic Thinking and Culture). Taiwan: Zili wanbaoshe, 1990.

————. "The Intellectual Heritage of the Confucian Ideal of *Ching-shih*" in *Confucian Traditions in East Asian Modernity*. ed. Tu Wei-ming. Cambridge: Harvard University Press, 1996.

Changsha shi bowuguan (Changsha Archives). *Zhongguo gongchandang xiangqu zhixing weiyuanhui shiliao huibian* (Historical documents of the Chinese Communist Party Hunan Branch). Changsha: Hunan chupanshe, 1993.

Changsha Xian Zhi (Gazetteer of Changsha county), ed. Zhao Wenzai & Yi Wenji et La., 1817. Reprinted in Taibei: Chengwen chubanshe, 1976.

Chen, Joseph T. *The May Fourth Movement in Shanghai: The Making of a Social Movement in Modern China.* Leiden: E. J. Brill, 1971.

Chen Tanqiu. "Diyi ci daibiao dahui de huiyi" (Reflections of the First Party Congress) (Original date not found). In *Yida qianhou: Zhongguo diyi ci daibiao dahui qianhou ziliao xuanbian* (Before and after the First Party Congress: Selected edition of materials on the First Party Congress of the Chinese Communist party), edited by Zhongguo shehui kexueyuan xiandai shi yanjiu shi and Zhongguo geming bowu guan dangshi yanjiu shi. Beijing: Renmin chupanshe, 1980, vol. 2.

Chen Wangdao. "Huiyi dang chengli shiqi de yixie qingkuang" (Reflections of the founding days of the Party) (original date not found). In *Yida qianhou: Zhongguo diyi ci daibiao dahui qianhou ziliao xuanbian* (Before and after the First Party Congress: Selected edition of materials on the First Party Congress of the Chinese Communist party), edited by Zhongguo shehui kexueyuan xiandai shi yanjiu shi and Zhongguo geming bowu guandangshi yanjiu shi. Beijing: Renmin chubanshe, 1980, vol. 2.

Chen, Xiaomei. *Occidentalism: A Theory of Counter-discourse in Post-Mao China.* Lanham, MD: Rowman and Littlefield Publishers, Inc, 2002.

Chesneaux, Jean & etc. *China from the 1919 Revolution to Liberation.* New York: Pantheon Books, 1977.

China Social Sciences Institute Modern Chinese History Department. *Wu si aiguo yun-dong* (The May Fourth Patriotic Movement) vol. 1. Beijing: China Social Science Institute Press, 1979.

Chinese Academy of Historical Studies. ed. *Wuxu bianfa* (The Reform Movement of 1898), vols. 1–4. Shanghai: People's Publishing House, 1957.

Chiu Wei-chun, *Morality as politics: The restoration of Ch'eng-Chu NeoConfucianism in late imperial China* (PhD dissertation), The Ohio State University, 1992.

Chow, Tse-tsung. *The May Fourth Movement: Intellectual Revolution in Modern China.* Cambridge: Harvard University Press, 1960.

———. "The anti-Confucian movement in early republican China" *The Confucian Persuasion.* Stanford: Stanford University Press, 1960, 288–312.

Cohen, Paul, "The quest for liberalism in the Chinese past: Stepping stone to a cosmopolitan world or the last stand of Western parochialism?—A review of The Liberal Tradition in China" in *Philosophy East and West,* 35. 3 (July 1985): 305–10.

———. Cohen, Paul, and Goldman, Merle (ed.), *Ideas across culture: Essays on Chinese thought in honor of Benjamin I. Schwartz,* Cambridge: Harvard University Press, 1990.

Cong, Xiaoping. *Teachers' Schools and the Making of the Modern Chinese Nation-State, 1897–1937.* Vancouver: The University of British Columbia Press, 2007.

Congshu bianweihui. Shifan qunying guangyao zhonghua (Honorable Heroes from Normal Schools in China). Fan Yujie, ed. vol. 1. Xian: Shanxi renmin jiaoyu chubanshe, 1992.

———. *Shifan qunying guangyao Zhonghao* (Honorable Heroes from Normal Schools in China). Chen Bai-yu, ed. vol. 13. Xian: Shanxi renmin jiaoyu Chubanshe, 1994.

de Bary, Theodore. *The Liberal Tradition in China.* New York: Columbia University Press, 1983.

———. *The Message of the Mind in Neo-Confucianism,* New York & London: Columbia University Press, 1989.

———. *The Unfolding of Neo-Confucianism.* New York & London: Columbia University Press, 1975.

———. *Sources of Chinese Tradition.* New York: Columbia University Press, 1983. Denton, Kirk. *Modern Chinese Literary Thought.* Stanford: Stanford University Press, 1996.

Dirlik, Arif. *The Origin of Chinese Communism.* New York: Oxford University Press, 1989.

———. *Anarchism in the Chinese Revolution.* Berkeley: University of California Press, 1991.

———, and Ming Chan. *Schools into Fields and Factories: Anarchists, the Guomindang, and the National Labor University in Shanghai, 1927–1932.* Durham: Duke University Press. 1991.

Dow, Tsung-I. *Confucianism vs. Marxism: An Analytical Comparison of Confucian and Marxian Theories of Knowledge-Dialectical Materialism.* Lanham, MD: University Press of America, Inc., 1977.

Duicker, William. *Ts'ai Yuan-p'ei: Educator of Modern China.* University Park: Pennsylvania State University Press, 1977.

Elman, Benjamin A. and Woodside, Alexander, ed. *Education and Society in Late Imperial China 1600–1900.* Berkeley: University of California Press, 1994.

Esherick, Joseph W. *Reform and Revolution in China: The 1911 Revolution in Hunan and Hubei.* Berkeley: University of California Press, 1976.

Fairbank, John K. ed. *China's Response to the West.* Cambridge: Harvard University Press, 1954.

———. *China: Tradition and Transition.* Boston: Houghton Mifflin Company, 1989.

Fan Zhe. *Zhongguo gujin jiaoyujia* (Chinese Educators from Antiquity till Today). Shanghai: Shanghai jiaoyu chupanshe, 1982.

Feigon, Lee. *Chen Duxiu, Founder of the Chinese Communist Party.* Princeton: Princeton University Press, 1983.

Feng Youlan. *Zhongguo zhexue shi* (A History of Chinese Philosophy). Hong Kong: Taipingyang tushu gongsi, 1961.

Fogel, Joshua A. & Zarrow, Peter Gue (ed.), *Imaging the People: Chinese intellectuals and the concept of citizenship, 1890–1920*. New York & London: M.E. Sharpe, 1997.

Fu Jiaojin. *Hunan dili zhi* (Geographical Survey of Hunan). Changsha, 1933.

Furth, Charlotte. ed. *The Limits of Change: Essays on Conservative Alternatives in Republican China*. Cambridge: Harvard University Press, 1976.

———. "Intellectual change: from the reform movement to the May Fourth Movemnet, 1895–1920" *Cambridge History of China*, vol. 12, 1983.

Gao Jucun & etc. *Qingnian Mao Zedong* (Young Mao Zedong). Beijing: Zhonggong dangshi ziliao chubanshe, 1990.

Gao Pingshu, ed. *Cai Yuanpei quanji* (Collected works of Cai Yuanpei). Beijing: Zhonghua shuju chubanshe, 1988.

Goldman, Merle and Lee, Leo Ou–Fan. eds. *An Intellectual History of Modern China*. London: Cambridge University Press, 2002.

Grieder, Jerome. *Hu Shih and the Chinese Renaissance: Liberalism in the Chinese Revolution, 1917–1937*. Cambridge: Harvard University Press, 1970.

———. *Intellectuals and the State in Modern China: A Narrative History*. New York: Free Press London: Collier Macmillan, 1981.

Guo Zhiqi. "Huiyi Yang Changji xiansheng" (My recollections of Mr. Yang Changji), *Hunan wenshi ziliao xuanji* [The collection of Materials regarding Hunan's Culture and History] No. 11, Changsha: Hunan renmin chubanshe, 1979.

Hayhoe, Ruth and Bastid, Marianne, ed. *China's Education and the Industrialized World: Studies in Cultural Transfer*. Armonk, New York and London: M.E. Sharpe, 1987.

Hawkins, John N. *Mao Tse-tung and Education: His Thoughts and Teachings*. Hamden, CT: The Shoe String Press, Inc., 1974.

He Yikun. *Zeng Guofan pingzhuan* [A critical biography of Zeng Guofan]. Taibei: Zhengzhong shuju, 1964.

Ho, Kan-chih. *A History of the Modern Chinese Revolution*. Beijing: Foreign Languages Press, 1960.

Hofheinz, Roy Jr. *The Broken Wave: The Chinese Communist Peasant Movement, 1922–1928*. Cambridge: Harvard University Press, 1977.

Hoston, Germaine A. *The State, Identity, and the National Question in China and Japan*. Princeton: Princeton University Press, 1994.

Hou Wailu. *Zhongguo sixiang tongshi* (History of Chinese Philosophy) vol. 5. Beijing: Renmin chubanshe, 1956.

———. *Zhongguo sixiang tongshi* (History of Chinese Philosophy). Beijing: Foreign Languages Press, 1959.

———. *Zhongguo sixiang shigang* (An Outline of Chinese Intellectual History) vol. 1–2. Beijing: Zhongguo qingnian chubanshe, 1981.

Huang, Philip. *Liang Ch'i-ch'ao and Modern Chinese Liberalism*. Seattle: University of Washington Press, 1972.

Hunan diyi shifan xiaoshi bianxiezu (The Editing Committee of the History of Hunan First Normal School). *Hunan diyi shifan xiaoshi*—1903–1949 (The History of Hunan First Normal School—1903–1949). Shanghai: Shanghai Educational Press, 1983.

Hunan jinbainian dashi jishu [Chronological record of major events in Hunan during the last hundred years], comp. by Committee for the compilation of a Hunan provincial gazetteer, Changsha, 1959. Reprinted in Tokyo, 1966. (vol. 1 in a projected 12 volumes new-style provincial gazetteer).

Hunan lishi ziliao (The Historical Documents of Hunan), Hunan lishi ziliao bianjishi, ed. vol. 2. Changsha: Hunan renmin chubanshe, 1980.

Hunan sheng bowuguan lishibu (Hunan Provincial Museum, History Section). Xinmin xeihuiwenxian huibian (Documents Collection of the New Citizens' Study Society). Changsha: Hunan renmin chubanshe, 1980.

Hunan shengli diyi shifan xuexiao xiaozhi (Annals of Hunan Provincial First Normal School). Changsha: Hunan Provincial Archives: 59–5–37, 1918.

Hunan renmin chubanshe, ed. *Wusi yundong zai Hunan—huiyilu* (Reflections of the May Fourth Movement in Hunan). Changsha: Hunan renmin chubanshe, 1979.

Hunan shengzhi bianzuan weiyuanhui (Editorial Committee for the Hunan Provincial Gazetteer), ed. *Hunan Shengzhi: Hunan jinbainian dashijishu* (Hunan Provincial Annals: Chronological record of major events in Hunan during the past one hundred years), vol. 1. Changsha: Hunan renmin chubanshe, 1959.

Hunan sheng difangzhi bianzuan weiyuanhui (Editorial Committee for the Hunan Provincial Gazetteer), ed. *Hunan sheng zhi: Xinwen chuban zhi* (Hunan Provincial Gazette: History of press and publication) vol. 20. Changsha: Hunan chubanshe, 1991.

Ji Wenfu. "Wang Chuanshan de xueshu yuanyuan" (The intellectual source of Wang Fuzhi) in *Wang Chuanshan xueshu luncong* (Collected essays on scholarship and thought of Wang Fuzhi) Beijing: Sanlian shudian, 1978, 33–46.

———. "Chuanshan zhexue" (philosophy of Wang Fuzhi), part II "Lishi zhexue" (philosophy of history), in *Wang Chuanshan xueshu luncong* (Collected essay on scholarship and thought of Wang Fuzhi). Beijing: Sanlian shudian, 1978, 122–63.

Jiang Daoyou. "Xiangju wanli xinxi xiangtong" (Ten thousand miles apart, their hearts are linked together—about Mao Zedong and He Guo). In *Zianmen de lingxiu Mao Zedong* (Our Great Leader Mao Zedong). ed. Lin Mushen. Beijing: Jiefangjun chubanshe, 1992.

Jin Yu & Wang Xingguo. *Mao Zedong: zouxiang makesi zhuyi* (Mao Zedong: Towards Marxism). Hangzhou: Zhejiang renmin chubanshe, 1993.

Kant, Immanuel. *Critique of Pure Reason*, Trans. Norman Kemp Smith. New York: St. Martin's. 1929 [1965].

Kim, Bounghown, "A study of Chou Tun-i (1017–1073)'s thought (PhD dissertation), The University of Arizona, 1996.

Keenan, Barry C. *Imperial China's Last Classical Academies: Social Change in the Lower Ynagzi, 1864–1911*. Berkeley: Institute of East Asian Studies, University of California Press, 1994.

Knight, Nick, ed. "The Philosophical Thought of Mao Zedong: Studies from China" In *Chinese Studies in Philosophy*, Spring–Summer 1992, vol. 23, No. 3–4. New York: M. E. Sharpe Inc., 1992.

Ladany, Laszlo. *The Communist Party of China and Marxism, 1921–1985*. London: C. Hurst & Company Ltd., 1988.

Lao, Yan-shuan. "Junshi heyi yu Cheng-Zhu *zhengzhi sixiang*" (Ruler–teacher unity and Cheng-Zhu's political thoughts) in (Lao Zhenyi xiansheng jiuzhi rongqing lunwenji (*Collection of essays for the Celebration of Mr. Lao Zhenyi's Ninetieth Birthday*). Taipei: Lantai, 1997.

Lee, Leo Ou-fan. *The Romantic Generation of Modern Chinese Writers*. Cambridge: Harvard University Press, 1973.

Lee, Samuel C. *Ts'ai Ho-shen, Marxism and the First Communist-Kuomintang United Front*. MA thesis, University of Wisconsin-Madison, 1987.

Levenson, Joseph. *Confucian China and its Modern Fate*. Berkeley: University of California Press, 1965.

———. *Liang Ch'i-ch'ao and the Mind of Modern China*. Berkeley: University of California Press, 1967.

Levine, Marilyn A. *The Found Generation: Chinese Communists in Europe, 1919–1925* (PhD dissertation), University of Chicago, 1985.

———. *The Founding Generation: Chinese Communists in Europe, 1919–1925*. Seattle: University of Washington Press, 1993.

Lewis, Charlton M. *Prologue to the Chinese Revolution: The Transformation of Ideas and Institutions in Hunan Province, 1891–1907*. Cambridge: Harvard University Press, 1976.

Li, Dun J. ed. *The Road to Communism: China since 1912*. New York: Van Nostrand Reinhold Company, 1969.

Li Ming (Li Lisan). "Jinian Cai Hesen tongzhi" (In memory of Comrade Cai Hesen) in *Zhongguo gongchandang lieshi zhuan* (The biography of the Chinese Communist martyrs), ed. by Hua Yingshen. Hong Kong: Xinminzhu, 1949.

Li Peicheng. *Yang Changji jiaoyu sixiang jianlu* (Yang Changji's Educational Philosophy). Changsha: Hunan Educational Press, 1983.

Li Rui. *Mao Zedong tongzhi di chuqi geming huodong* (Early revolutionary activities of Comrade Mao Zedong). Beijing: Zhongguo qingnian chubanshe, 1957.

———. *Mao Zedong de zaonian yu wannian* (Mao Zedong's Early Age and Old Age). Guizhou: Guizhou renmin chubanshe, 1992.

―――. "Qingnian Mao Zedong de sixiang fanxiang" (The ideological trend of young Mao Zedong), *Lishi yanjiu*, [Historical research], 1 (1979): 33–51.

―――. *Mao Zedong zao nian dushu shenghuo.* (The early reading life of Mao Zedong]. Liaoning: Renmin chubanshe, 1992.

―――. *Sanshisui yiqian de Mao Zedong* (Mao Zedong before Thirty Years Old). Guangzhou: Guangdong renmin chubanshe, 1994.

Li, Weihan. *Li Weihan xianji* (Collected Works of Li Weihan). Beijing: Renmin chubanshe, 1987.

―――. "Huiyi Xinmin xuehui" (Recall of New Citizens' Study Society). *Xinmin xuehui ziliao* (Documents Collection and Memories of the New Citizens' Study Society). Changsha: Hunan Provincial Archive, 1920.

―――. *Huiyi yu Yanjiu* (Written Memories and Studies). Beijing: Zhonggong dangshi ziliao chubanshe, 1986.

Li Xiaodan, "Benxiao gu jiaoshou Yang Huaizhong xiansheng shiji" (Memories of late Mr. Yang Huaizhong of our school) in Beijing daxue rikan, 1920, 1, 28 (Beijing University Daily, January 28, 1920).

―――."Yang Huaizhong xiansheng yishi" (Anecdotes of Mr. Yang Huaizhong), first published in Hunan jiaoyu zazhi [Journal of Hunan education], 1: 5 (1920).

―――. Xiangxue lüe [An outline of history of Hunan scholarship], Changsha: Yuelu shushe, 1985. (This book was first published by Hunan University in 1946).

Li Xisuo. "Xinhai geming qian de liuri xuesheng yundong" (The Chinese student movement in Japan before the 1911 Revolution), *Jinian Xinhai geming qishi zhounian xueshu taolunhui lunwenji* [Collection of essays presented at the symposium for celebration of the seventieth anniversary of the 1911 Revolution]. Beijing: Zhonghua shuju, 1983, vol. 1, 606–47.

―――. *Jindai liuxuesheng yu zhongwai wenhua* [Overseas students and cultural exchange between China and other countries in the modern history]. Tianjin: Renmin chubanshe, 1992.

Li Yichun, "Huiyi Hesen tongzhi" (Recalling Comrade Hesen). *Zhongguo renmin yongyuan jizhe ta: Ji nian Cai Hesen danchen 110 zhou nian* (Chinese people always remember him: In commemoration of Cai Hesen's 110 birthday). Zhonggong Hunan shengwei xuanchuanbu (Chinese Communist Party, Hunan Branch, Department of Publicity) ed. Changsha: Hunan renmin chubanshe, 2005.

Li Yongli. *Zhongxi wenhua yu Mao Zedong zaoqi sixiang* (Western and Chinese Culture with Mao Zedong thought). Chengdu: Sichuan University Press, 1989.

Li Zehou. "Qingnian Mao Zedong" (The young Mao Zedong) in his *Zhongguo xiandai sixiangshi* [Essays on contemporary Chinese thoughts]. Beijing: Dongfan chubanshe, 1987, 122–42.

———. *Dangdai sichao yu zhongguo zhihui* (Modern Trends of Thought and Chinese Wisdom). Taipei: Fengyun Shidai chuban gongsi, 1989.

Li Zehou and Schwarcz, Vera. "Six Generations of Modern Chinese Intellectuals" *Chinese Studies in History.* Armonk NY: M. E. Sharpe Inc., 17.2 (Winter 1983/84): 42–56.

Lin Nengshi. *Qingji Hunan de xinzheng yundong, 1895–1898* [The political Reform movement in Hunan during the late Ch'ing period]. Taibei: Guoli Taiwan daxue wenxueyuan, 1972. (History and Chinese Literature Series o. 38 Taipei. Taiwan University).

Lin, Yu-sheng. *The Crisis of Chinese Consciousness: Radical Antitraditionalism in the May Fourth Era.* Madison: University of Wisconsin Press, 1979.

Liu Ang. "mian huai Cai Hesen tongzhi" (In memory of comrade Cai Hesen). *Zhongguo renmin yongyuan jizhe ta* (Chinese people always remember him). Zhonggong Hunan shengwei xuanchuanbu (Chinese Communist Party, Hunan Branch, Department of Publicity) ed. Changsha: Hunan renmin chubanshe, 2005.

Liu, Liyan. *Yixue boshi Hume zhai Zhongguo (Edward H. Hume M.D. in China).* Hong Kong: Hong Kong Yinhe chupanshe, 2000.

———. *Reflections across the Yellow Sea: Essays of Chinese and Japanese Studies.* Hong Kong: Milky Way Press, 2001.

Liu Renrong & Wang Changzhu. *Zhongguo gemingshi: shijian yu renwu* (The Revolutionary History of China: Events and people). 2 volumes. Changsha: Hunan Daxue chubanshe, 1986.

Liu Shuxian. *Zhexei sikao manbu* (Philosophical questions to ponder). Taipei: Sanmin shuju gufen youxian gongsi, 1995.

Liu Siqi. ed. *Mao Zedong yu wenhuaren* (Mao Zedong and Intellectuals). Beijing: Zhongguo shudian chuban, 1993.

Lu Haijiang. "Qingnian jiaoyou zhongtu yangbiao" (Friends from youth parted later: about Mao Zedong and Xiao Zi-sheng). In *Zianmen de lingxiu Mao Zedong* (Our Great Leader Mao Zedang). ed. Lin Mushen. Beijing: Jiefangjun chubanshe, 1992.

Luo Ergang, *Xiangjun xinzhi* (A new treatise on the Hunan Army). Changsha: Shangwu chubanshe, 1939.

Luo Wenhua, "Mao Zedong zaonian 'xinmin' sixiang yanjiu" (The study of Mao Zedong's 'new citizens' thought in his early years) in *Zhonggong Hunan dangshi luncong* (On the history of the Communist Party of Hunan Branch), Zhonggong Hunan shengwei dangshi ziliao zhengji yanjiu weiyuanhui bian (ed. The Editorial Committee of the historical documents of the Hunan Provincial Communist Party). Changsha: Hunan renmin chubanshe, 1986.

Luo Zhanglong, "Huiyi Cai Hesen tongzhi" (Recalling Comrade Cai Hesen). *Zhongguo renmin yongyuan jizhe ta* (Chinese people always remember him). Zhonggong Hunan shengwei xuanchuanbu (Chinese Communist Party,

Hunan Branch, Department of Publicity) ed. Changsha: Hunan renmin chubanshe, 2005.

Ma Yuqing. *Mao Zedong de chengzhang daolu* (The Way Mao Zedong Grew). Xian: Shanxi renmin chubanshe, 1986.

Mao Lirui. *Zhongguo jiaoyu tongshi* (The History of Chinese Education) vol. 4 & 5. Jinan: Shandong jiaoyu chubanshe, 1987.

Mao Zedong. Zhonggong zhongyang wenxian yanjiushi, Zhonggong Hunanshengwei Mao Zedong zaoqi wengao bianjizu bian, ed. *Mao Zedong zaoqi wengao 1912.6—1920.11* (Early Writings of Mao Zedong 1912.6—1920.11). Changsha: Hunan chubanshe, 1990.

———. *The Chinese Revolution and the Chinese Communist Party.* Peking: Foreign Languages Press, 1967.

McDonald, Angus W. Jr. *The Urban Origins of Rural Revolution: Elites and the Masses in Hunan Province, China 1911–1927.* Berkeley: University of California Press, 1978.

McElroy, Sarah C. *Transforming China through Education: Yan Xiu, Zhang Bolin, and the Effort to Build a New School System, 1901–1927* (PhD dissertation), New Haven: Yale University, 1996.

McMahon, Daniel. "The Yuelu Academy and Hunan's Nineteenth-Century Turn Toward Statecraft" in *Late Imperial China,* vol. 26, no.1. Baltimore: The Johns Hopkins University Press, 2005.

McMorran, Ian, "Wang Fu-chih and the Neo-Confucian tradition," *The unfolding of the Neo-Confucianism.* New York & London: Columbia University Press, 1975.

Meisner, Maurice. *Li Ta-chao and the Origins of Chinese Marxism.* Cambridge: Harvard University Press, 1967.

———. *Mao Zedong: A Political and Intellectual Portrait.* Cambridge, UK: Polity Press, 2007.

Meng Xiangdi & etc. ed. *Mao Zedong jiaoyu sixiang tianyuan* (Study of Mao Zedong's Educational Thought). Changsha: Hunan Educational Press, 1993.

Metzger, Thomas. Escape from Predicament: Neo-Confucianism and China's Evolving Political Culture. New York: Columbia University Press, 1977.

Moseley, George. *China since 1911.* New York: Harper & Row, Publishers, 1968.

Paulsen, Friedrich. *Lunlixue yuanli* (The principles of ethics), trans. Cai Yuanpei. Reprinted. Zhonggong zhongyang wenxian yanjiushi (The Department of Research on Party literature, central Committee of the Chinese Communist Party). Beijing: zhongyang wenxian yanjiushi, 1990 [1909].

Peng Dacheng. *Huxiang wenhao yu Mao Zedong* (Huxiang Culture and Mao Zedong). Changsha: Hunan Press, 1991.

Peng Ming. *Wusi yundong shi* (A history of the May Fourth Movement). Revised ed. Beijing: Remin chubanshe, 1998.

Peterson, Glen, Hayhoe, Ruth and Lu, Yongling, ed., *Education Culture, and Identity in Twentieth Century China*. Michigan: The University of Michigan Press, 2001.

Polizzotto, Dean A. *Young Chinese Revolutionaries in France: How They Contributed to the Success of the Chinese Communist Revolution* (PhD dissertation), 1996.

Qian Jibo. *Jinbainian Hunan xuefeng* [The intellectual trends and scholarship of Hunan in the last hundred years]. Changsha: Yuelu shushe, 1985.

Ren Jianshu. *Chen Duxiu dazhuan* (*Chen Duxiu's Biography*). Shanghai: Shanghai renmin chupanshe, 1999.

Salisbury, Harrison. *Changzhen xinji* (The Long March: An Untold Story). ed. and trans. by Xinhuashe cankaoziliao bianjibu (Department of reference material editing, Xinhua News Agency). Beijing: Xinhuashe cankaoziliao bianjishi, 1990.

Scalapino, Robert A. "Prelude to Marxism: The Chinese Student Movement in Japan, 1900–1910," in *Approaches to Modern Chinese History*, ed. by Albert Feuerwerker, Berleley & Los Angles: University of California Press, 1967.

———. "The Evolution of a Young Revolutionary: Mao Zedong in 1919–1920," in *Journal of Asian Studies*, 42. 1 (Nov. 1982): 29–61.

Siao, Emi. *Mao Tse-tung, His Childhood and Youth*. Bombay: People's Publishing House Ltd., 1953.

Siao, Yu. *Mao Tse-tung and I were Beggars*. London: Hutchinson & Co. Ltd., 1961.

———. *Wo he Mao Zedong de yiduan quzhe jingli* (The Story of Mao Zedong and me together). Beijing: Kunlun chubanshe, 1989.

———. *Mao Tse-tung qingnian shidai* (The Young Mao Zedong). Hong Kong: Mingba chubanshe, 1977.

Schirokauer, Conrad. "Chu His and Hu Hung," in Wing-tsit Chan, ed., *Chu Hsi and Neo-Confucianism*. Honolulu: University of Hawaii Press 1986.

Schram, Stuart. "A review article: Mao Tse-tung as Marxist dialectician" in *China Quarterly*, 29 (January–March, 1967): 155–65.

———. *The Political Thought of Mao Tse-tung*. Harmondsworth: Penguin Books, 1969.

———. ed. *Mao's Road to Power: Revolutionary Writings 1912–1949: The Rise and Fall of the Chinese Soviet Republic 1931–1934* (Mao's Road to Power: Revolutionary Writings, 1912–1949). Armonk NY: M. E. Sharpe, 1997.

———. "Mao Studies: Retrospect and Prospect" in *China Quarterly*, 97 (March 1984): 95–125.

———. *Mao Tse-tung*. New York: Simon and Schuster, 1966.

———. *The Thought of Mao Tse-tung*. Cambridge: Cambridge University Press, 1989.

Schwarcz, Vera. *The Chinese Enlightenment: Intellectuals and the Legacy of the May Fourth Movement of 1919*. Berkeley: University of California Press, 1986.

Schwartz, Benjamin I. *In Search of Wealth and Power: Yen Fu and the West.* Cambridge: Harvard University Press, 1964.

———. *Chinese Communism and the Rise of Mao.* Cambridge: Harvard University Press, 1964.

———. *Reflections on the May Fourth Movement.* ed. Cambridge: Harvard University Press, 1973.

———. *A Documentary History of Chinese Communism.* New York: Atheneum, 1952.

———. *The World of Thought of Ancient China.* Cambridge: Harvard University Press,1985.

Shao Yanmiao. *Xinhai yilai renwu nianli lu* (Who's Who from the Republican Period to Present). Nanjing: Jiangsu renmin chubanshe, 1993.

Shen Guanqun. *Cong yapian zhanzheng dao wusi yundong shiqi de jiaoyu* (Chinese Education from the Opium War to the May Fourth Movement Period). Beijing: Education & Science Press, 1984.

Shen Yijia. "Wo suo zhidao de zaoqi zhi Cai Hesen" (What I know about the early years of Cai Hesen). *Zhongguo renmin yongyuan jizhe ta* (Chinese people always remember him). Zhonggong Hunan shengwei xuanchuanbu (Chinese Communist Party, HunanBranch, Department of Publicity) ed. Changsha: Hunan renmin chubanshe, 2005.

Shi Xiaoming. "An Outlook of the Work–Study Program for Chinese College Students from the Perspective of Times." *Canadian Social Science,* 5. 4, 47–53, 2009.

Short, Philip. *Mao: A Life.* New York: Holt Paperbacks, 2001.

Shu Jincheng. "Wang Fuzhi lun `cheng`" (Wang Fuzhi's interpresteion of cheng), *Zhongguo zhexuefanchouji* [Essays on pivotal categories of Chinese philosophy]. Beijing: Renmin, 1985, 371–84.

Shu Xincheng. *Jindai Zhongguo liuxue shi* [A history of Chinese students abroad in modern times]. Shanghai, Zhonghua, 1929.

Skinner, G. William. ed. *Modern Chinese Society: An Analytical Bibliography,* vol. 1, Publications in Western Languages, 1644–1972. Stanford: Stanford University Press, 1973.

Snow, Edgar. *Red Star over China.* New York: Random House, 1938.

———. *Inside Red China.* New York: Doubleday, Doran & Company, Inc., 1939.

Song Feifu. *Xinmin xuehui* (New Citizens' Study Society). Changsha: Hunan renmin chubanshe,1980.

Spence, Jonathan D. *The Gate of Heavenly Peace: The Chinese and Their Revolution 1895–1980.* New York: Penguin Group, 1982.

———. *The Search for Modern China.* New York: W W Norton & Co Inc, 1999.

———. *Mao Zedong.* New York: Penguin Group, 2006.

Sun Hailin. ed. *Hunan diyi shifan mingren pu* (Who's Who from Hunan First Normal School). Changsha: Hunan First Normal School, 2003.

———. "Yihu xunchang de guanhuan he aihu" (Extraordinary care and love). In *Xu Te-li yenjiu* (Xu Te-li Study) No. 31, 1996.

Tang Duo. "Huiyi wode liangshi yiyou—Cai Hesen tongzhi" (Recalling my good teacher and helpful friend—comrade Cai Hesen). *Zhongguo renmin yongyuan jizhe ta* (Chinese people always remember him). Zhonggong Hunan shengwei xuanchuanbu (Chinese Communist Party, Hunan Branch, Department of Publicity) ed. Changsha: Hunan renmin chubanshe, 2005.

Tang, Zongli. *Maoism and Chinese Culture.* New York: Nova Science Publishers, Inc., 1996.

Tao Xingzhi. *Tao Xingzhi Quanji* (Complete Works of Tao Xingzhi) vol. 1. Chengdu: Sichuan Education Press, 1991.

———. *Jiaoxuezuo heyi taolunji* (Collected Essays on the Unity of Teaching, Learning and Doing). Shanghai: Shanghai ertong shuju, 1932.

Tao Yuchuan. *Zhongguo jiaoyushi bijiao yanjiu* (Comparative Study of Chinese Educational History) vol. 2 & 3. Jinan: Shandong jiaoyu chubanshe, 1988.

Teng Ssu-yu. "Wang Fu-chilies views on history and historical Writing" *Journal of Asian Studies,* 28. 1 (1968): 111–23.

———. "Tseng Kuo-fan" Reading *in Modern Chinese* history. New York: Oxford University Press, 1971.

The History Department of Taiwan University, ed. *Qingji Hunan de xinzheng yundong, 1895–1898* (Hunan's Reform Movement in the Qing Dynasty, 1895–1898). Taiwan: TaiwanUniversity Press, 1973.

Tillman, Hoyt Cleveland. *Confucian Discourse and Chu His's ascendancy.* Honolulu: University of Hawaii Press, 1992.

Trotsky, Leon. *Problems of the Chinese Revolution.* New York: Paragon Book Reprint Corp., 1966.

Tu, Wei-ming. Humanity and self-cultivation: essays in *Confucian thought.* Berkeley: Asian Humanities Press, 1979.

———. *Confucian thought: selfhood as creative transformation.* New York: State University of New York Press, 1985.

Uhalley, Stephen Jr. *A History of the Chinese Communist Party.* Stanford: Hoover Institution Press, 1988.

van de Ven, Hans J. *From Friend to Comrade—The Founding of the Chinese Communist Party, 1920–1927.* Berkeley: University of California Press, 1991.

Wakeman, Frederic. *History and Will: Philosophical Perspectives of Mao Tse-Tung's Thought.* Berkeley: University of California Press, 1973.

Wang Fuzhi. Chuanshan quanji (The Complete Works of Wang Fuzhi). Taibei: Dayuan wenhua fuwushe, 1965.

Wang Shubai. *Mao Zedong sixiang de zhongguo jiyin* (Chinese Gene in Mao Zedong's Thought). Hong Kong: Shangwu chubanshe, 1990.

Wang Xingguo. *Yang Changji de shengping ji sixiang* (Life and Thought of Yang Changji). Changsha: Hunan renmin chubanshe, 1981.

———. (ed.) *Yang Changji wenji* (The collected works of Yang Changji). Changsha: Hunan Educational Press, 1983.

———. "Yang Changji yu xinmin xuehui" (Yang Changji and the xinmin xuehui) in *Zhonggong Hunan shengwei dangshi ziliaozhengji yanjiu weiyuanhui bian, ed., Hunan dangshi luncong* (On the history of the Hunan Branch of the Communist Party). Changsha: Hunan renmin chubanshe, 23–31, 1986.

———. *Mao Zedong: zouxiang makesi zhuyi* (Mao Zedong: Towards Marxism). Hangzhou: Zhejiang renmin chubanshe, 1993.

———. *Qingnian Mao Zedong de sixiang guiji* (The Development Pattern of Young Mao Zedong's Thought). Changsha: Hunan Press, 1993.

Wei Zhengtong. "Chuantong Zhongguo lixiang renge de fenxi chonggu jiazhi quxiang de yanjiu" (An analysis of the conception of the ideal personality in the Chinese tradition: an inquiry into the value orientation of honouring the antiquities), *Rujia yu xiandai Zhongguo* [Confucianism and Modern China]. Shanghai: Renmin chubanshe, 1990.

———. *Rujia yu xiandai Zhongguo* [Confucianism and Modern China]. Shanghai: Renmin chubanshe, 1990.

Weber, Max. *The Religion of China: Confucianism and Taoism*. New York: Free Press, 1964.

Wen Lu. "Xuexi qinfen tibo jianqiang" (Hard work and strong physique—Zhang Guoji recall Mao Zedong at Hunan First Normal School). In *Zianmen de lingxiu Mao Zedong* (Our Great Leader Mao Zedong). ed. Lin Mushen. Beijing: Jiefangjun chubanshe, 1992.

Wen shi ziliao xuanji (Historical Events and Documents Collection), vol. 8, 9, 19, 28, and 38. Beijing: Zhongguo wenshi chubanshe, 2000.

Wen Xuande. ed. *Lishi fengbei* (Historical Monument). Changsha: Hunan Normal University Press, 1993.

Weston, Timothy B. *Beijing University and Chinese Political Culture, 1898–1920* (PhD dissertation), University of California, Berkeley, 1995.

Wright, Mary. *The Last Stand of Chinese Conservatism: The T'ung-chih Restoration, 1862–1874*. Stanford: Stanford University Press, 1962.

Wu Xiuquan. *Li Lisan zhuan* (Biography of Li Lisan). Haerbin: Heilongjiang renmin chubanshe, 1989.

Xiao Gongquan. *Zhongguo zhengzhi sixiangshi* (History of Chinese Political Thought). Taibei: Lianjing, 1982.

Xiangbao (1898) [Hunan Daily] (facsimile). Beijing: Zhanghua shuju, 1965.

Xiangxue xinbao (1897–1898) [New Journal of the Hunanese Studies, 1897–8] (facsimile). Taiwan: Hualian chubanshe, 1966, 4 vols.

Xibei shifanxueyuan zhengzhixi, ed. *Zhongguo gongchandang yinglie xiaozhuan* (The Biographical Sketch of the Chinese Communist martyrs). Lanzhou: Gansu renmin chubanshe, 1980.

Xie Binghuai, "Cai Hesen shi minzhu zhuyizhe ma?—xinmin xuehui chengli qianhou Cai Hesen sixiang qianxi" (Was Cai Hesen a democrat?—A brief examination of Cai Hesen's thought before and after the founding of the "Xinmin xuehui") in Zhonggong Hunan shengwei dangshi ziliaozhengji yanjiu weiyuanhuibian, ed., *Hunan dangshi luncong* (On the history of the Communist Party of Hunan Branch). Changsha: Hunan renmin chubanshe, 1986.

Xie Juezai. *Xie Juezai riji* (Diaries of Xie Juezai), 2 volumes. Beijing: Renmin chubanshe, 1984.

Xinmin xuehui ziliao (Documents Collection and Memories of the New Citizens' Study Society). Changsha: Hunan Provincial Archive, 1920.

Xiong Mingan. *Zhongguo gaodeng jiaoyushi* (History of Chinese Higher Education). Congqing: Congqing chubanshe, 1983.

Xiu Juan. ed. *Mao Zedong yu qinjuan* (Mao Zedong and his Relatives). Beijing: Zhongguo renmin daxue chubanshe, 1993.

Yan Ru. "Chundu de xuezhe—Li Jinxi" (The studious scholar—Li Jinxi). Shifan qunying guangyao zhonghua (Honorable Heroes from Normal Schools in China). Ma Xingfu, ed. vol. 2. Xian: Shanxi renmin jiaoyu chubanshe, 1992.

Yang Changji. "Lun Hunan zunzi sheli shangwuju yi xiam zhenxing nonggong zhi xue" (On how Hunan should take precedence in the promotion of studies of agriculture and industry over the establishment of a Commercial Bureau under the imperial edict). *Xiang Bao* (Hunan News), no. 153, 1898. Reprinted in *Yang Changji wenji* (The Collected Works of Yang Changji), Wang Xingguo, ed. Changsha: Hunan Educational Press, 1983.

———. *Dahua zhai riji* (Diaries of Dahua Studio) (1898). *Youxue yibian* (*Study Abroad and Translations*). Tokyo, vol. 8, May 1903. Reprinted in *Yang Changji wenji*, 1983.

———. "Yu guiguo hou duiyu jiaoyu zhi suogan" (My thoughts on education after returning to China). *Hunan jiaoyu zazhi* (Journal of Hunan Education), 2.17, November 1913. Reprinted in *Yang Changji wenji*, 1983.

———. "Jiaoyu yu zhengzhi" (Education and Politics). *Hunan Jiaoyu zazhi* (Journal of Hunan Education), 2. 16, October 1913. Reprinted in *Yang Changji wenji*, 1983.

———. "Jiaoyu shang dang zhuyi zhi dian" (Some points in the educational realm that need our attention). *Hunan Jiaoyu zazhi*, 2. 16, November 1913. Reprinted in *Yang Changji wenji*, 1983.

———. *Luyu leichao* (Category and commentary on Analects). Changsha: Changsha hongwei tushushe, 1914. Reprinted in *Yang Changji wenji*, 1983.

———. "Quanxue pian" (On encouraging learning). *Gongyan Zhazhi* (Public Opinion), Changsha, 1: 1, October 1914. Reprinted in *Yang Changji wenji*, 1983.

———. "Jiaoyu xue jiangyi" (Lecture notes on education). (mimeograph) 1914, n.p. Published in *Yang Changji wenji*, 1983.

———. "Yu gailiang shehui zhi yijian" (My suggestions on reforming social customs). *Gongyan Zhazhi* (Public Opinion), Changsha, 1: 2, November 1914. Reprinted in *Yang Changji wenji*, 1983.

———. "Daohai lieshi Yang jun Shouren shilue" (A brief biography of martyr Yang Shouren). *Jiayin zazhi* (The Tiger), 1: 4, November 1914. Reprinted in *Yang Changji wenji*, 1983.

———. "Zhexue shang gezhong lilun zhi lueshu" (A brief review of different philosophical theories). *Minsheng zazhi* (People's voice), Changsha (Nov.) vol. 2: 1, 2, & 3, 1916. Reprinted in *Yang Changji wenji*, 1983.

———. trans. *Xiyang lulixue shi* (A History of Western Ethics). Beijing: Beijing daxue chubanbu, vol. 1, Nov. 1918 and vol. 2, 1919.

———. *Dahua zhai riji* (Diaries of Dahua Studio). Changsha: Hunan renmin chubanshe, 1978 [1919].

———. *Yang Changji wenji* (The Collected Works of Yang Changji), Wang Xingguo, ed. Changsha: Hunan Educational Press, 1983.

Yang Nianqun. *Ruxue diyuhua de jindai xingtai: sanda zhishiqunti hudong de bijiao yanjiu* (The Modern Forms of Regional Confucianism: A Comparative Study of the Interactions among Three Intellectual Groups). Beijing: Sanlian shudian, 1997.

Yang Qing. *He Shuheng*. Shijiazhang: Hebei renmin chubanshe, 1997.

Yang Yulin. *Xin Hunan* [New Hunan]. Tokyo, 1903. It is reprinted in *Xinhai geming qian shinianjian shilun xuanji* [Selected essays on current events from the decade before the 1911 Revolution], edited by Zhang Nan and Wang Renzhi (Beijing: 1962) vol. 2, 612–48.

Yao Weidou & Huang Zhen. *Wusi qunying* (A Group of Heroes in the May Fourth Period). Shijiazhuang: Hebei renmin chubanshe, 1981.

Yeh, Wen-hsin. *Provincial Passages—Culture, Space, and the Origins of Chinese Communism*. Berkeley: University of California Press, 1996.

Zarrow, Peter. *Anarchism and Chinese Political Culture*. New York: Columbia University Press, 1990.

Zhang Kundi. *Zhang Kundi riji* (Diary of Zhang Kundi, 1917). Changsha: Hunan Provincial Museum, [B].

Zhang, Ming. *A Journey between East and West: Yang Changji (1871–1920) and his Thought*. (PhD dissertation), University of Edinburgh, 2002.

Zhang Pengyuan. *Zhongguo xiandaihua de quyu yanjiu—Hunan Sheng* [Modernization in China,1860–1916: A regional study of social, political and economic change in Hunan province]. Taibei: Institute of Modem History, Academica Sinica, 1983.

Zhang Shizhao, "Yang Huaizhong bie zhuan" (The supplementary biography of Yang Changji) (The original article was not published, 1920). In *Yang Changji wenji* (The Collected Works of Yang Changji), ed. Wang Xingguo. Changsha: Hunan Educational Press, 1983.

Zhonggong dangshi renwu yanjiuhui bian. *Zhonggong dangshi renwuzhuan* (Biographies of Chinese Communists). Xian: Shanxi renmin chubanshe, 1982.

Zhonggong Hunan dangshiwei. *Hunan dangshi dashi nianbiao* (The Important Events Chart of Hunan Communist Branch). Changsha: Hunan renmin chubanshe, 1986.

————. *Hunan renmin gemingshi* (The Revolutionary History of Hunan People). Changsha: Hunan renmin chubanshe, 1991.

Zhonggong Hunan shengwei dangshi ziliaozhengji yanjiu weiyuanhuibian. *Hunan dangshi luncong* (On the history of the Communist Party of Hunan Branch). Changsha: Hunan renmin chubanshe, 1986.

Zhonggong zhongyang wenxian yanjiu shi (The Department of Research on Party Literature, Central Committee of Communist Party of China) (ed.), *Mao Zedong nianpu, 1893–1949* [Mao Zedong's chronology, 1893–1949]. Beijing: Renmin chupanshe & Zhongyang wenxian chubanshe, 1993.

————. *Zhongguo gongchandang de qishinian.* (The History of the Chinese Communist Party in the Past Seventy Years). Beijing: Zhonggong dangshi chubanshe, 1991.

Zhongguo geming bowuguan. *Xinmin xuehui ziliao* (Documents Collection and Memories of the New Citizens' Study Society). Beijing: Renmin chubanshe, 1980.

Zhongguo renmin zhengzhi xieshang huiyi, Hunan sheng weiyuanhui wenshi weiyuan huibian. Hunan jin 150 nian shishi rizhi, 1840–1990 (The Daily Records of Hunan's Historical Events in the Latest 150 Years, 1840–1990). Beijing: Zhongguo wenshi chubanshe, 1993.

Zhongguo shehui kexueyuan jindaishi yanjiusuo, ed. *Wusi yundong huiyilu* (Reflections of the May Fourth Movement). Beijing: Zhongguo shehui kexueyuan chubanshe, 1979.

Zhou Shizhao. *Wo men de shibiao* (Our Teacher and Model). Beijing: Beijing chubanshe, 1958.

————. *Maozhuxi qingnian shiqi de gushi* (Stories of Chairman Mao when he was in his Youth). Beijing: Zhongguo shaonian ertong chubanshe, 1977.

————. "Xiangjiang de nukong," in *Xinmin xuehui ziliao*. Beijing: Renmin chubanshe, 1980.

Zhou Yanyu. "Gongshi jiaoyu qingyi shendu" (Together worked in the educational field, profound friendship developed—friendship between Mao Zedong and Zhou Shizhao), in *Zianmen de lingxiu Mao Zedong* (Our Great Leader Mao Zedang). ed., Lin Mushen. Beijing: Jiefangjun chubanshe, 1992.

————. *Mao Zedong yu Zhou Shizhao* (Mao Zedong and Zhou Shizhao). Changchun: Jilin renmin chubanshe, 1993.

Zhu Deshang, "Guimao riji" (Diaries in the Guimao Year of 1903) in Hunan lishi ziliao (The Historical Documents of Hunan), vol. 1, 1979.

Zhu Hanmin, *Huxiang xuepai yuanliu* (The Origin of Huxiang School). Changsha: Hunan Education Press, 1992.

————. *Zhu Hanmin Huxiang xuepai yu Yuelu shuyuan* [The scholarship of Huxiang school and the Yuelu Academy]. Beijing: jiaoyu kexue chubanshe, 1991.

Index